The Gods of Televangelism

THE HAMPTON PRESS COMMUNICATION SERIES

Critical Studies in Communication
Leslie T. Good, supervisory editor

The Gods of Televangelism: The Crisis of Meaning and the Appeal of Religious Television
Janice Peck

Forthcoming

Voices of Difference: Studies in Critical Philosophy and Mass Communication
Thomas McCoy

The City as Discourse: The Origins of American City Planning
Katharine Tehranian

The Gods of Televangelism

Janice Peck
University of Minnesota

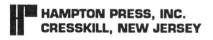

HAMPTON PRESS, INC.
CRESSKILL, NEW JERSEY

Printed in the United States of America

Cover photos: AP/Wide World Photos, Inc.

Library of Congress Cataloging-in-Publication Data

Peck, Janice.
   The gods of televangelism: the crisis of meaning and the appeal of religious television / Janice Peck.
        p. cm .— (The Hampton Press communication series)
   Includes bibliographical references and indexes.
   ISBN 1-881303-65-9. (cloth). — ISBN 1-881303-66-7 (paper)
   1. Television in religion—United States. 2. Evangelistic work-
-United States—History—20th century. 3. 700 Club (Television program). 4. Jimmy Swaggart telecast. 5. Robertson, Pat.
6. Swaggart, Jimmy. 7. Communication—Religious aspects-
-Christianity. 8. United States—Church history—20th century.
I. Title. II. Series.
BV656.3.P43 1992
269'.26'0973—dc20   92-32476
                                                                                          CIP

Hampton Press, Inc.
23 Broadway
Cresskill, NJ 07626

Table of Contents

Preface

This study of evangelical television, in its conception, aims, method, and theoretical and practical concerns, is situated within the field of cultural studies.[1] Cultural studies resists neat categorization, as Grossberg points out: It "refuses to construct itself as a finished or singular theoretical position" and "refuses to define its own theoretical adequacy in academic or narrowly epistemological terms." Cultural studies can be defined, however, by (a) its interdisciplinary character, which is "built on the recognition that much of what one requires to understand cultural practices and relations is not, in any obvious sense, cultural"; (b) its willingness to use whatever means and resources necessary to understand and explain cultural practices, products, and their intersection; and (c) its chosen terrain of study—"describing and intervening in the ways 'texts' and 'discourses' (i.e., cultural practices) are produced within, inserted into, and operate in the everyday life of human beings and social formations, so as to reproduce, struggle against and perhaps transform the existing structures of power."[2]

Beyond the primary goal of this book—to understand the meanings of evangelical television, its sociohistorical moorings, and its contemporary structure of appeal—a secondary aim is to create a bridge between rhetorical and sociological approaches to communication research without residing entirely in either camp. It has taken what is usable from both research traditions, but it neither originates in nor subscribes to their disciplinary boundaries. Implicit in this study, then, is a critique of the disciplinary limitations of sociology and rhetoric which, in my view, arise from a lack of attention to the historical dimensions of communication and cultural forms.

Rhetorical criticism has traditionally focused on how speakers shape their communication to elicit agreement from listeners, on the character of their communicative relationship, and on the strategies and forms of persuasion embedded in specific types of discourse. As a field of study and a social practice, rhetoric predates typographic and electronic media. As Eagleton points out, rhetoric was Europe's "received form of critical analysis all the way from ancient society to the eighteenth century."[3] Grounded in public oratory, the rhetorical tradition has tended to treat communication as an interpersonal, immediate event between speakers and audiences, even when the object under study has been removed from its spoken context and turned into a printed text, or removed from its historical context and turned into an artifact. While one of rhetorical criticism's strengths is its conception of communication as a living practice involving "forms of power and performance,"[4] its methods and analytical categories often lack historical sensitivity. Aristotelian constructs, for example, may be taken as timeless and universal, equally applicable to the epistles of Paul as to television sitcoms. Missing is a sense that rhetorical forms themselves are the products of history, symbolic solutions to problems that history has posed.

Equally problematic is a lack of adequate conceptualization of the distinct character of specific communication media, their relationship to the legitimation of particular social orders, and the forms of social relations they encourage and discourage. Despite a significant body of work on the history of communication technologies and their relationship to the social circumstances that called them forth and set them into place, rhetorical criticism has not yet incorporated that knowledge in a systematic way.[5] Rhetorical scholars only relatively recently have begun to attend closely to the influence of media technologies and institutions upon rhetorical situations and attendant forms of expression. Such attention is necessary because rhetorical analysis cannot be adequately applied to mediated communication without a solid understanding of the role of cultural industries, the capacities and limitations of particular media technologies, and the specificity of the audience/text relationship peculiar to modern mediated communication.

When the printing press, and later, the electronic media, altered the spatial and temporal relationships between speakers and listeners, the process of communication was dramatically extended and amplified, making it also more distant and impersonal.[6] The anonymity and standardization of these new media of communication paralleled new forms of association that were emerging in the urban centers of newly industrialized societies. The concept of "mass communication" developed in conjunction with that of "mass society," and the sociological approach to the study of media grew up alongside these distinctly modern objects of study.[7] The American sociological tradition of communication research has historically operated within a functionalist paradigm; it examines the identifiable functions that mass media play in modern society and asks how we can best account for those functions and their social and individual effects. Because of its positivist roots and its view of communication and audiences as mass phenomena, media sociology has generally favored quantitative research methods—experiments, surveys, and content analyses. Further, because this approach sees communication as a process of transmission between centralized sources of production (media industries) and large, but dispersed, points of reception (audiences, consumers), it has chiefly been interested in determining the relative effectiveness of that transmitting process. Although media sociology acknowledges that different receivers may make different uses of mediated messages, the meaning of any given message is typically regarded as static and transparent. The overriding research problem therefore becomes the precise measurement of messages, effects, and uses for purposes of prediction.[8]

As the process of communication is depersonalized and abstracted as functions and effects, however, what gets lost is a sense of human intention within that process, and of media technologies and texts themselves as responses to perceived social needs—that is, as intentional solutions to particular historical problems.[9] The sociological approach has tended to neglect questions about the specific character of expressive forms, how they come to have meaning for particular creators and receivers, the process of meaning construction in general, the material conditions under which communication is produced and received, and the relations of power by which some are accorded the right to speak and others are designated as listeners. Anthropologist William Roseberry described an approach to the study of culture that might serve as a corrective to these oversights. He proposes a historical approach that connects the political, economic and symbolic dimensions of culture, thereby situating "public symbols and cultural meanings . . . in social fields characterized by differential access to political and economic power."[10] Eagleton echoes this position:

> Discourses, sign systems and signifying practices of all kinds, from film and television to fiction and the languages of natural science, produce effects, shape forms of consciousness and unconsciousness, which are closely related to the maintenance or transformation of our existing systems of power.[11]

Thus, he argues, rhetorical analysis should be guided by attention to the connection between discourses and power, and to "the linguistic structures and material situations" that determine the context of communication and the relationships between specific speakers and listeners.[12]

Carey distinguished American and European approaches to the study of communication by suggesting that they circulate around different metaphors or models. The former, he says, employs a "transportation" metaphor and sees communication as "a process of transmitting messages at a distance for the purpose of control." The latter adopts a "ritual" metaphor and views communication as "a process through which a shared culture is created, modified and transformed."[13] The sociological and rhetorical traditions of communication research might be similarly distinguished: Media sociology has emphasized the transportation model, while rhetorical criticism leans toward the ritual paradigm. As a result of their historical origins (rhetoric has roots in ancient Europe, media sociology developed in the 20th century United States), these two research traditions have also been separated by philosophical and disciplinary boundaries. Rhetoric has been aligned with the humanities and is considered the domain of speech departments; the sociology of media identifies with the social sciences and is located in departments of mass commmunication and journalism.

These divisions have been steadily eroding in the last decade or so, as evidenced in departmental mergers, the creation of new programs in communication studies, the development of new courses, an increase in cross-disciplinary research, a greater sharing of concepts, methods, and objects of study, and a growing number of scholars who traverse these traditionally distinct spheres. My study of religious television is a conscious attempt to hasten the erosion of those boundaries. In part, this synthesis reflects my own hybrid background. I was originally trained as a journalist and left that profession for graduate studies, first in a traditional mass communication department and later in an interdisciplinary program that approached communication from a critical, cultural perspective. It was during my doctoral work that I encountered rhetorical criticism through the writings of Kenneth Burke—a discovery that contributed to my current residence in a speech communication program.

More important, though, it reflects my belief that communication is by its very nature interdisciplinary because it is an activity intimately connected to every sphere of human existence. So this is more than a proposal for greater fluidity between two communication research traditions; it is an argument for their transformation, and for viewing communication as a field of study rather than as a discipline with a received tradition of theoretical paradigms, appropriate research objects, and techniques of analysis. It seems to me that intellectual work does not begin by arming ourselves with a set of concepts and techniques in search of an appropriate object, but by asking questions that matter most to us and seeking whatever means necessary to answer them. The true measure of our endeavor is not whether we have arrived at an uncontestable conclusion, but whether the questions we have generated are vital enough to merit such sustained attention. Put simply: Are these questions worth asking, to whom do they matter, and why?

The questions that guide this study are: What is the structure of appeal of evangelical television programming? How and why does that appeal become effective (persuasive) for particular viewers (or communities)? Finally, how is the appeal of these programs, and of evangelical Protestantism generally, connected to American history and culture? Evangelical television is obviously "about" communication and religion; it is also about, and no less importantly, politics, culture, ethics, philosophy, history, psychology, economics, and more. Any attempt to shed light on the appeal of televised religion requires acknowledging the interrelationship of all these elements and weaving them together into a meaningful whole. The best word for such an approach is *dialectical*. Dialectical method is necessarily interdisciplinary and open-ended. It sees intellectual work as an ongoing process of discovery with no preordained conclusions, and it assumes that both the inquiring subject and the object of inquiry will be transformed by the process of investigation.

I stress the open-ended nature of this approach because it was through the process of trying to answer my questions that I arrived at my method. It is important here to distinguish between "methods," as a set of techniques honed over time and institutionalized within a given discipline, and "method," as a dynamic relationship between the questioner and the question, between the knower and the knowledge being sought. Wander's and Jenkins's discussion of the work of the critic helps clarify this relationship. Criticism, they argue, is a "coming to terms with an object in light of one's values."[14] The critic's values come into play in choosing an object (or problem) to attend to, in trying to understand both the object and what makes it compelling, and in deciding what to say about it. The product of this encounter is criticism, and its task is to express what the critic sees as the truth about that meeting. Thus, "the critic selects an object to carry the truth [s]he considers worth talking about."[15] For this to become more than idle talk or idiosyncratic monologue it must enter into dialogue with others. As Wander and Jenkins say, "The purpose of writing criticism is to share a world of meaning with other human beings." That is, when we write criticism, we are inviting others to enter into the relationship we have cultivated with our object of inquiry, and to share our belief that what we have asked, and what we have discovered, do matter. As the authors conclude: "Criticism, at its best, is informed talk about matters of importance."[16]

If intellectual work is about asking questions that make a difference, rather than asking only those questions we already know how to answer, then our inquiries are bound to continually transform our objects of study, the tools we use to apprehend them, and our understanding of ourselves and of the world in which we live. Implicit in this study, then, is an argument about method in cultural analysis. The integration of ideas, techniques, and research from rhetorical criticism, media sociology, religious studies, history, cultural anthropology, and philosophy reflects neither a desire to be intellectually fashionable nor a failure to master the methodological inventory of my designated discipline. Rather, it is an attempt to "use all there is to use," in Burke's words, in the quest to develop satisfying answers to my guiding questions.[17] Thus, this examination of religious television is interdisciplinary because what I was studying demanded it be so. So, while I draw on Burke's ideas about communication as social action, this is not a Burkeian analysis of televised religion. It is equally indebted to work by scholars of religion and religious history, philosophy, and cultural criticism. I chose evangelical television as the vessel for the truth I consider worth talking about precisely because of its complex relationship to so many strands of contemporary experience; I believe it has much to tell us about our history, our culture, and ourselves.

The interdisciplinary approach, the focus on the creation of meaning, and the critical interpretive stance place this study within a cultural studies perspective. But it is cultural studies' compability with historical analysis that made it the most appropriate, perhaps the only possible, perspective for this work. As I argue throughout the book, evangelical programming makes sense only when situated in history. I would make the same argument about the study of any cultural form, and herein lies my criticism of the weaknesses of much of the work within both rhetorical and sociological approaches to media. This study aims to demonstrate the ways in which cultural forms are historically produced, transformed, and given their persuasive power. For this reason, it contains an implicit suggestion that both rhetorical criticism and media sociology are in need of greater sensitivity to the historical dimensions of communication and media. My hope here is to encourage and contribute to a greater dialogue among students of rhetoric ("speech"), students of media ("communication"), and those in other fields who believe that expressive forms and communicative relationships are matters of importance. Because what we talk about is so obviously related, I believe we have a great deal to say to each other. I hope this study, in both its theoretical and empirical elements, contributes to that conversation.

Carey also urged such an interdisciplinary approach to the study of communication. Much American media research, he says, has too long neglected sustained consideration of cultural forms (such as religious television, for example). He cites the need to explore "the relation of these forms to social order, the historical transformation of these forms, their entrance into a subjective world of meaning and significance, the interrelations among them, and their role in creating a general culture."[18] I can think of no better way to describe the goal of my study of evangelical television. It is up to the reader to determine if I have met Carey's challenge.

This project began as a doctoral dissertation in the late 1980s that sought to understand the relationships among the dramatic reconfiguration of the U.S. sociopolitical landscape, the resurgence of the Christian Right, and the meteoric rise of televangelism and the sources of its appeal. While many of the ideas presented here first found expression in that original work, others are the result of subsequent evolutions in my thinking about religious television and society. In particular, my arguments about the historical basis for the creation and appeal of cultural forms, and about the necessary relationship of transformations in the socioeconomic order to changes in religious beliefs and practices, have been substantially refined and made more central in the present work.

I began this research when Jimmy Swaggart was the top-rated televangelist in the U.S., and most of the analysis of his preaching is based on telecasts done during the height of his popularity. I continued to follow the program after the 1988 scandal and his dismissal from the Assemblies of God and noticed that he became both more self-critical and more cautious in his critiques of others. However, the core themes of his telecast remained the same—individual salvation, rejection of "the world" and the arduous task of being a "Bible-believing Christian," the importance of his telecast to the "Great Commission," and the absolute dichotomy of Christianity and apostasy. Indeed, Swaggart had no choice but to adhere to these themes because they form the very basis of his separatist theology. Following the second scandal in October, 1991, Swaggart left the crusade circuit. His telecast is now reruns of earlier crusades and televised services from his home church in Baton Rouge. Many stations have dropped the program, which is now aired predominantly on smaller cable systems in the United States. The ministry has continued to expand its foreign broadcast efforts, however. Because my analysis is based on the program during Swaggart's peak, in some ways it is a "historical" study, but I believe the appeal of his preaching and theology is not "history," in the sense of being in the past and done with. The book spells out in detail why I believe Swaggart's theology, as a response to contemporary society, is still very much alive because the historical conditions and problems that produced both his preaching, and the theology behind it, remain with us.

NOTES TO PREFACE

1. The development, guiding concepts, methods, typical objects of study, and goals of cultural studies are discussed in Stuart Hall, "Cultural Studies: Two Paradigms," *Media, Culture and Society* 2: (1980), pp. 57-72; Richard Johnson, "What is Cultural Studies Anyway?" *Social Text* 16: (1986), pp. 38-80; Lawrence Grossberg, "The Circulation of Cultural Studies," *Critical Studies in Mass Communication* 6: (December 1989), pp. 413-420; and John Fiske, "British Cultural Studies and Television," in Robert C. Allen, ed., *Channels of Discourse* (Chapel Hill and London: University of North Carolina Press, 1987), pp. 254-289.

2. Lawrence Grossberg, "The Circulation of Cultural Studies," pp. 414-415.

3. Terry Eagleton, *Literary Theory* (Minneapolis: University of Minnesota Press, 1983), p. 205.

4. Ibid.

5. Among those scholars of communication who have addressed the relationship between social structure and media of communication are Harold A. Innis, *The Bias of Communication*, 7th ed. (Toronto: University of Toronto Press, 1982) and *Empire and Communications* (Oxford: Clarendon, 1950); Marshall McLuhan, *The Gutenberg Galaxy* (Toronto: University of Toronto Press, 1962); James Carey, "Canadian Communication Theory: Extensions and Interpretations of Harold Innis," in G. J. Robinson and D. F. Theall, eds., *Studies in Canadian Communications* (Montreal: McGill University Press, 1975), pp. 27-59, and "Culture, Geography, and Communication: The Work of Harold Innis in an American Context," in W. Melody, L. Salter, and P. Heyer, eds., *Culture, Communication, and Dependency: The Tradition of H. A. Innis* (Norwood, NJ: Ablex, 1981), pp. 73-91; and David Crowley and Paul Heyer, *Communication and History: Technology, Culture, Society* (New York: Longman, 1991).

6. David Harvey relates this to the general "space-time compression" that has accompanied capitalist expansion and technological development. The pressures of this compression are experienced more radically in some periods than in others. *The Condition of Postmodernity* (London: Basil Blackwell, 1990).

7. Tony Bennett, "Theories of Media, Theories of Society," in Michael Gurevitch et al. (eds.), *Culture, Society and the Media* (London: Methuen, 1982), pp. 30-55.

8. This is the "uses and gratifications" school in mass communication research; see Jay Blumler and Elihu Katz, *The Uses of Mass Communication* (Beverly Hills: Sage, 1974). For a critique of this theo-

retical perspective, see David Morley, *The Nationwide Audience: Structure and Decoding* (London: British Film Institute, 1980).

9. For a further discussion of this point see Raymond Williams, *Television: Technology and Cultural Form* (New York: Schocken Books, 1975), and Brian Winston, "How Are Media Born?" in John Downing, Ali Mohammadi, and Annabelle Sreberny-Mohammadi, eds., *Questioning the Media* (Newbury Park, CA: Sage, 1990), pp. 55-72.

10. William Roseberry, *Anthropologies and Histories: Essays in Culture, History, and Political Economy* (New Brunswick, NJ, and London: Rutgers University Press, 1989), pp. 36-37.

11. Eagleton, *Literary Theory*, p. 210.

12. Ibid., p. 206.

13. James W. Carey, "Mass Communication Research and Cultural Studies: An American View," in James Curran, Michael Gurevitch, and Janet Woollacott, eds., *Mass Communication and Society* (Beverly Hills, CA: Sage, 1979), p. 412.

14. Philip Wander and Stephen Jenkins, "Rhetoric, Society, and the Critical Response," *Quarterly Journal of Speech* 58 (December 1972), p. 441.

15. Ibid., 449.

16. Ibid., 450.

17. Quoted in Walter Davis, *The Act of Interpretation* (Chicago: University of Chicago Press, 1978), p. 6.

18. Carey, "Mass Communication Research," pp. 413-414.

Acknowledgments

Many people have been instrumental in making this book possible. My original doctoral committee members, Martin Laba and William Leiss of Simon Fraser University and Roger Simpson of the University of Washington, contributed their time, ideas and encouragement. My external examiner, Charles Anderson, University of British Columbia, gave me valuable insights into some of the biblical foundations of Swaggart's preaching style and sermon materials. Portions of this manuscript have also benefitted from thoughtful readings by Quentin Schultze (Calvin College) and George Lipsitz (University of California-San Diego), whose knowledge about media, religion, and American culture enriched my thinking about televised religion. Several people, including my sister Susan (Sullivan) Peck, shared with me their own experiences as evangelicals and greatly aided my ability to imagine myself as a member of the communities addressed by Swaggart and Robertson.

I'm also grateful to my colleagues in the department of Speech-Communication at the University of Minnesota for their encouragement and responses to my work, and for their generosity in providing me time and financial support to revise this manuscript. The revision process was made much more pleasant thanks to the unfailing support of my editors, Leslie Good and Brenda Dervin, and the excellent suggestions of my anonymous reviewers.

Finally, I want to thank Bill Riordan, who believed in this project, and in my ability to carry it through, from the beginning. He is present in this book in more ways than he can know.

1

Evangelicalism, Evangelical Television, and the Crisis of Meaning

I don't have any technique. The only thing I'm trying to do is lead you to Jesus and he'll handle it. (Jimmy Swaggart)[1]

Our concept is to present our program in as simple and as direct a style as appropriate...However, to maintain standards in our industry and to be effective in the marketplace, a degree of entertainment and showmanship is necessary. Communication by mass media is not the same as the direct personal contact between pulpit and pew. (Pat Robertson)[2]

By the late 1980s, Jimmy Swaggart and Pat Robertson were two of the most prominent figures in religious television. Both were among the top-10 rated TV ministers, and Swaggart regularly occupied the number one spot. Each Sunday, for 60 minutes, some 8 million people became part of Swaggart's congregation. Bound together by electromagnetic waves and flickering images, they congregated across geographical and demographic distances to watch him strut across a fern-covered stage, raise the Bible heavenward, and intone: "You need a redeemer." Another 4.5 million Americans woke up and started their weekdays with Robertson's "700 Club." Amid the bustle of morning routines they tuned in to "God's television" to learn from Robertson and a host of celebrities and experts how to live, love, and prosper in a Christian way.[3]

The regular audience for the "electronic church" in 1985 was estimated at 13 to 15 million, although religious broadcasters regularly cited much higher numbers.[4] Because the vast majority of this programming is produced by evangelical Protestants, most of it reflects that belief system. In 1986, one regional and three national TV networks were devoted to spreading the evangelical message (PTL, Robertson's Christian Broadcasting Network, Trinity Broadcasting System, and the Southern Baptist Convention's ACTS satellite network). Some 200 religious television stations were operating across the country by the mid-1980s, and the annual income of the TV pulpit in 1987 was estimated at $2 billion.[5]

Much has happened in the world of religious television since then. Jim and Tammy Bakker's PTL network collapsed amid revelations of financial fraud and sexual scandal. Oral Roberts suffered national ridicule over his claim that God would "call him home" if viewers failed to pay $8 million ransom. Swaggart's broadcasting empire shrank dramatically after he confessed on national TV to unspecified sins with a prostitute.[6] Robertson's bid for the Republican presidential nomination failed miserably; his Christian Broadcasting Network has been under investigation by the Internal Revenue Service, and the "700 Club" has lost a third of its broadcast audience.[7] It might appear, then, that "pray TV's" apex has come and gone, a fleeting facet of the Reagan phenomenon that will in time seem as anachronistic as the "great communicator" himself.

But while evangelical television has certainly suffered severe setbacks, I believe it is a much more hardy institution than some critics suggest. As historian David Harrell noted, religious television might be "wounded," but it is certainly not dead.[8] Swaggart remains on the air, although the program now consists of re-runs of past crusades and taped services from his Baton Rouge church, and his international ministry is actively expanding in the former Soviet Union and Africa. Robertson has made cast, set, and programming changes to the "700 Club" to recapture disaffected viewers and woo new ones. And, after two years of declining audiences, donations, and program slots, the downward slip of the "electronic church" seems to have stabilized.[9] The resilience of televised religion is not solely dependent on the habits of its stars, however. Its appeal and its future are deeply grounded in the history of American Protestantism, in the memories and aspirations of the one in five Americans who profess evangelical beliefs, and in the culturally central role of television itself.[10]

Religion and television are two of the most firmly embedded institutions and social practices in American culture. According to a

1979 Gallup poll, some 94% of U.S. adults said they believe in God—the highest incidence of belief of all Western nations.[11] Faithfulness to television is even more pervasive. More households in this country have television sets than boast indoor plumbing; the family set is turned on an average of seven hours daily, 97% of Americans view some programming every day, and by the time they graduate, most children will have spent more hours watching TV than attending school. Some writers have even suggested that Americans' relationship with television borders on a form of religion itself.[12]

But such generalizations do not explain why the marriage of TV and religion takes the specific forms that it does, nor why evangelical Protestantism seems particularly disposed to televised expression. The contemporary union of television and religion in "televangelism"[13] reflects Protestantism's historical affinity for the use of mass media. It was the first belief system to exploit the communicative capacity of the printing press and later to embrace radio and television with equal enthusiasm. Evangelical Protestants have been the most fervent users of mass media because of their commitment to proselytism and conversion. In the process they have also become highly skilled at adapting the gospel to the latest medium. Evangelicalism's affinity for television, Schultze suggests, resides in its emphasis on dramatic, emotional expressions of belief that make it highly compatible with the entertainment logic of TV, and in its general attitude toward technology.[14] Evangelicals' relationship with mass communication is grounded in Western culture's historical belief that progress is synonymous with technological development—an attitude that was "transformed by pragmatic and optimistic Americans into a popular faith in technology itself."[15] Schultze argues that evangelical television represents a "confluence of contemporary evangelicalism and American technological optimism."[16] The resulting "mythos of the electronic church," he notes, revolves around "the simple but attractive belief that communication technologies are potent forces that will transform evil into good."[17] Further, the tendency toward rationalization characteristic of capitalism as first described by Weber has also shaped the development of TV ministries. The equation of viewers reached with souls saved is firmly institutionalized in religious broadcasters' programming, fund-raising, and investment strategies. This quantitative approach to salvation is, in turn, reinforced by the TV ministries' pervasive faith in the power of modern communication technologies.

Once again, though, we have generalizations that fail to account for the variety and the appeal of the programming associated with evangelical television. What are the sources of this diversity? To whom do the programs appeal? How is that appeal constructed in the form and substance of the shows? To answer such questions we need to ask others. In particular, we need to investigate the belief system that informs the messages of evangelical programming and the experiences and values of those who produce and those who accept those messages. Thus, an analysis of the programs must be grounded in the history of the evangelical belief system, because it is only through such a dual excavation that the appeal of the programs becomes clear.

I first encountered evangelical television as an accidental viewer, and my reaction was typical of urban academics outside that belief system: incredulity, cynicism, and amusement. At the same time, I was intrigued by the programs and by the beliefs that bound together the preachers and their audiences. My previous conception of the "electronic church" as a generic brand of religious hucksterism was undermined by the diversity of the programming and the theologies espoused therein. I soon realized that my cynicism and preconceptions were serious impediments to understanding what these shows, and these theologies, meant to the people who proclaimed and watched them.

Carey suggested that a cultural analyst who wishes to truly comprehend her or his object of study must approach it much like a literary critic tackles a text. She or he must "grasp hold of the meanings people build into their words and behavior and . . . make these meanings, these claims about life and experience, explicit and articulate."[18] My decision to take evangelicalism's claims about life and experience seriously meant taking evangelical television very seriously indeed. It meant entering into the worldview of the programs deeply enough to grasp the meaning they held for their creators and audiences. How is that meaning constructed, communicated, and appropriated? Why is this particular version of Christianity attractive to a significant number of people—enough people, in fact, to support a multimillion dollar broadcasting industry? How does this religious perspective conceive of the nature of society and the individual's place in it? What makes it appealing: that is, what is the structure of its appeal? These questions guided me as I began exploring the history of evangelicalism and its forms and means of expression. It is my aim in this study to shed some light on the ways in which evangelical programming creates a particular set of meanings or interpretations of the world, and how and why it appeals to people to take up those meanings as a guide for their beliefs and actions.

Analysts and practitioners of television evangelism have coined a variety of terms for this form of religious communication: the "electric church," "prime-time preaching," the "TV pulpit, "pray TV," and "televangelism." I find the last to be the most suitable, vivid term for my study as it treats evangelical programming as persuasive communication and as a cultural form. Televangelism connotes the modern adaptation of a key cultural form of 19th-century evangelicalism: the religious revival designed to win converts and save souls. Televangelism combines some of the elements of revivalism with the formats and constraints of the television medium; it is thus simultaneously a fusion of an older cultural form (the revival) with a new means of communication (television), and a transformation of that form imposed by the imperatives of the televisual medium. Television created a new type of social relationship between speaker and listener that necessarily affects the methods of evangelism and the character of the evangelical belief system expressed there.

I chose to focus on two distinct forms of religious programming: the weekly revival/religious service typified by "The Jimmy Swaggart Telecast," and the talk show/news magazine program pioneered by Pat Robertson's "700 Club," because they represent what I see as contrasting poles of the spectrum of evangelical programming. Swaggart's crusades closely adhere to the 19th-century revival form, albeit influenced by television's distinct economic and aesthetic demands. Robertson's relaxed, chatty, weekday show is constructed within a format that has been wholly determined by the television medium with religious content inserted. Put simply, Swaggart's program represents television adapted for religion, while the "700 Club" constitutes religion adapted to TV.[19] This distinction is evident in the ways Swaggart and Robertson define themselves and their goals: Swaggart is a "country preacher" or evangelist, Robertson is a "religious broadcaster." The kinds of programming that follow from these divergent identities are markedly different, as I argue in the program analysis.

This study attempts to answer questions about the appeal of evangelical television by looking deeply into these two programs while simultaneously looking broadly at the history that has made them possible. It is an argument that the appeal of these shows is grounded in the different, indeed conflicting, responses within modern American evangelicalism to the processes and results of historical change. Further, it is an argument that the appeal of these programs is embedded in their forms, which are the symbolic embodiment of those historical responses. On a broader theoretical level, then, this study is an investigation of the historical appeal of cultural form.

EVANGELICALISM AND EVANGELICAL TELEVISION

In 1984, the Annenberg School of Communications and the Gallup Organization released the results of one of the largest quantitative studies of religious television to date. Initiated at the behest of religious broadcasters, the study grew out of a 1980 seminar (titled "Consultation on the Electronic Church") sponsored by the National Council of Churches, National Religious Broadcasters, and the U.S. Catholic Conference. The results of that research, titled *Religion and Television*, were released in 1984.[20] The $175,000 project, directed by George Gerbner, was paid for by 39 religious organizations (Robertson's Christian Broadcasting Network, for example, gave $27,000; Jerry Falwell donated $20,000). The study was divided into the following categories: demographic analysis, content analysis, uses and gratifications, and audience effects. Put simply, the study asked who watches, what does the programming say, what do people do with these programs, and how are they affected. Despite the time involved (2 years), the amount of data gathered (Gallup interviewed more than 2,000 people), and the size of the report (two volumes of analysis and tables), the findings were predictable and undramatic. The report noted, for example, that "viewers of the programs are by and large also the believers, the churchgoers, the contributors,"[21] and that the "religious television mainstream tends to run conservative and restrictive rather than permissive."[22]

In a critique of that study, Schultze pointed out the limitations of such quantitative research:

> In trying to say something about everyone, it says nothing about anyone in particular. Modern statistical analysis is founded to a large extent on an atomistic view of society and assumes that the 'masses' of people should be studied only quantitatively as respondents to surveys and questionnaires, or as participants in experiments.[23]

While information (from this and other quantitative studies) about audience composition and general program themes is useful, these data alone are insufficient for understanding the complex relationship between the creation and reception of religious programming as it occurs in a concrete social context. Schultze charged that the Annenberg study "gives no insight into the styles of media evangelism, the nuances of popular religion, or the visual appeal of televised services and entertainment."[24] It is precisely such questions that concern me. Rather than trying to divine knowledge about specific programs from data about religious television in general, my work takes the opposite route. By conducting a detailed analysis of two specific shows, I hope to offer a greater understanding of televised religion as a historically constructed cultural form and as a site for the creation of social meanings.

A 1979 Gallup poll found that one in five adults in the United States identified him- or herself as evangelical Christian.[25] The election of Jimmy Carter, a self-proclaimed "born again" Christian, and of Ronald Reagan, who vowed in his campaign to outlaw abortion and put God back in the schools, appeared to signal the birth of a new conservative religious force in American politics and social life. Indeed, Gallup declared that the results of a survey commissioned by *Christianity Today* magazine made the 1980s "the decade of the evangelicals."[26] The "New Christian Right" gained national attention during Reagan's first campaign. The 1980 "Washington for Jesus" rally drew 500,000 people, most of whom identified Reagan as their candidate. The president-to-be was the keynote speaker at the eastern division of the National Religious Broadcasters convention that year, and Jerry Falwell claimed that his Moral Majority, founded in January 1979, was a key factor in Reagan's victory. The mass media rushed to locate and identify this new "social trend"; newspapers and popular magazines ran numerous articles proclaiming the emergence of a new "Fundamentalist phenomenon" and a "New Christian Right."[27] Given the media's power to make an issue part of the public agenda, such reports not only informed people about the "rise" of an evangelical "movement," but also helped create that movement in the public imagination.[28]

These initial accounts and subsequent scholarly articles and books on the Christian Right, the evangelical movement, and the "electronic church" that takes their message to the airwaves have attempted to explain the resurgence of orthodox Protestantism and the growth of television ministries by referring to statistics on conservative church growth, shifts in public opinion, trends in the television industry, or new methods of political organizing. Many of these studies have treated the New Christian Right as an "effect" and set about to identify its "causes." What was often missing, particularly from secular analyses, was a willingness to enter into the worldview of conservative evangelicalism and to take its interpretations and values seriously. Evangelicalism is more than a political lobby or social movement—it is a way of life, of understanding oneself and the world. Followers accept the explanations and rationales of this belief system because they are meaningful—they locate the believer in a system of meaning. This meaning must continually be created, reproduced, and disseminated if conservative evangelicalism is to be a living belief system. Such is one of the roles of evangelical television programming. Entering into and understanding this system of meaning, and its representation and reproduction through TV evangelism, are the reason for and heart of my study.

Conservative evangelicalism is not a new phenomenon. It is a well-established, if now minority, tradition in American religious life. While the mainstream news media discovered its existence relatively recently, evangelical Protestantism is no newcomer to the mass media. This religious perspective constitutes the great majority of current religious programming on television and radio. Conservative evangelicals have achieved this dominance over religious broadcasting in the last three decades at the expense of mainline denominational programming.[29] Some 92% of religious programs are "paid-time" programming purchased from stations; most paid-time programs are evangelical or fundamentalist in theology.[30] This domination over religious television also serves to reinforce the public perception that evangelical Protestantism is a primary form of worship and belief in the United States. Mainstream media coverage of prominent television ministries has contributed to this perception by reporting grossly inflated audience figures based on claims of the TV preachers themselves.[31] As Horsfield pointed out in *Religious Television*, its dominance over religious programming and uncritical secular media attention have given this minority Christian perspective "an exaggerated influence over the development of American culture and institutions, and possibly over the nature of American and even global religious life."[32] Social movements are simultaneously material entities and symbolic constructions. Because television is one of the key sites of symbolic production in our society, its coverage of conservative evangelicals and its use by religious broadcasters are important means of constituting evangelicalism as a movement. While television preachers have inflated their audience sizes and the scope of their influence, this religious perspective and its representation in the "electronic church" have indeed become important social forces in the United States.

Evangelicalism is a general term encompassing a broad spectrum of religious practices, from strict fundamentalist to charismatic, and denominations, from large formal organizations such as the Southern Baptist Convention to small, localized, and unaffiliated churches. Evangelicalism was the dominant form of Protestant Christianity in 19th-century America. It has, since then, become a minority tendency in U.S. religious life, despite the fact that it is the primary form of worship portrayed on television and radio. Evangelical Christianity can be roughly defined as a pietistic, perfectionist, supernaturalist, and millennialist religious tradition. It views Scripture as the literal word of God, asserts the divinity of Christ, believes that a conversion experience is essential to individual salvation, conceives of Christ and Satan as personal beings, and considers testimony or evangelism as an imperative Christian activity.[33]

Although evangelicalism is an umbrella term that includes Fundamentalists, mainline evangelicals, Pentecostals, and other splinter groups of charismatic Christians, for the purpose of simplification I will use the terms *evangelical* and *evangelicalism* to denote a general religious tendency in America, which is a constellation of the beliefs and practices cited above, and which is also the force behind the majority of contemporary religious programming. It should be noted that I am focusing on the conservative wing of evangelicalism. Wacker points out that the "resurgence" of this religious perspective applies primarily to its conservative elements—what he terms the "Evangelical Right" and what others have called the "New Christian Right." The moderate and liberal wings of evangelicalism have experienced much less spectacular growth in the 20th century.[34]

It is important at the outset not to exaggerate the social and political influence of conservative evangelicalism and its television ministries. As some critics have pointed out, the secular news media succumbed to this temptation in the late 1970s and early 1980s, thereby becoming tools of the New Christian Right and of ambitious TV preachers.[35] This tendency to overestimate the power of the Christian Right is most pronounced in one study that refers to conservative evangelicalism and its religious programming as a dangerous and effective variant of "total propaganda."[36] At the same time, we cannot dismiss the increase in evangelical activism as a harmless or temporary shift in the political wind; a belief system that claims one-fifth of the adult population is a sizeable minority. Conservative Christians have become increasingly involved in local and national political issues, including fights to control public school curricula, opposition to statutes guaranteeing equal rights for women, homosexuals, and other minorities, campaigns to outlaw abortion that in some cases have led to bombing clinics, the creation of lobbying organizations at state and federal levels, and successful campaigns to replace liberal political representatives with right-wing Christian candidates. Older organizations such as the Moral Majority (now the Liberty Foundation), the Religious Roundtable (a coalition of right-wing political and religious leaders, including Pat Robertson), and Christian Voice (a southern California organization founded by Paul Weyrich in 1976 that issues "report cards" rating congress people on their adherence to "biblical" precepts) paved the way for the Christian Coalition, a tax-exempt national organization that aims to mobilize conservative "pro-family" voters in the 1992 election. Headed by Robertson, the Christian Coalition has more than 175,000 dues-paying members and chapters in 45 states.[37] He told attendees at a Christian Coalition conference that "We want to see a working majority of the Republican Party in the hands of pro-family Christians by 1996 or sooner."[38] Robertson also made a bid in May 1992 to buy United Press International for $6 million. If the deal goes through, the international news agency would be owned by the U.S. Media Company, a for-profit subsidiary of CBN. Although Robertson has said he will not interfere with UPI's editorial policy or content, his message to "700 Club" viewers was more ambiguous. According to a transcript of the show reported by People for the American Way, Robertson said he believes "it's important to have an alternative voice for news," and that UPI's worldwide operations "give us a chance to have some very, very significant news around the world."[39] Such efforts indicate that many conservative evangelicals, including Robertson, desire a social and political influence that exceeds their status as a minority religious presence.[40]

RELIGIOUS REVITALIZATION AND THE HISTORICAL CRISIS OF MEANING

Because I am arguing that the appeal of contemporary evangelical programming resides in its form, which has itself been historically created, it is necessary to provide a broader theoretical context for understanding the relationship of historical change to religious movements and the forms through which they communicate. But because this book is an analysis of the appeal of cultural form, rather than a study of the history of religious movements, this detour into a theory of historical change is necessarily sketchy and somewhat tentative. Further, the test of my argument that the appeal of cultural forms both embodies and reveals historical practices and relationships will require further research by cultural critics and historians. What follows, then, is a tentative framework for understanding the relationship between historical change and religious revitalization. Evangelical television has recently undergone a legitimacy crisis that it appears to have survived, although not without scars. I argue here that the dramatic growth of TV ministries and the "resurgence" of fundamentalist or neoevangelical Protestantism in the last 20 years are themselves products of, and responses to, cultural crisis. Indeed, it is possible to understand the history of Protestant revivalism in the United States as a story of recurring legitimation crises to which religious revival was a particular response. But what is the nature of these crises and these responses to them?

    Thomas, in a study of 19th-century revivalism, challenges the typical crisis explanation that has been widely used to account for the emergence of religious movements.[41] He criticizes this "crisis-theoretic perspective" for its reduction of such movements to individuals' anxiety reaction in the face of rapid change. Thomas proposes instead that while a religious movement *is* a response to changing social conditions, it is not merely a matter of instinctive, individual resistance to change, but is the effort of a collectivity to "articulate a new moral order" and "to have its version of that order dominate the moral-political universe."[42] Thomas argues that for a social institution (such as a religious belief system) to maintain its legitimacy, it must correspond, in a convincing way, to the larger cultural order. He uses the term isomorphism to describe this structural consistency across levels of culture. During periods of significant social transition, this isomorphic fit between an institution and its environment may decrease, leading to a delegitimation of the institution in question. The institution may deal with this legitimacy problem by simply embracing and adapting to the emerging order. If the required changes are extensive enough, however, a movement develops to negotiate the transition by combining essential elements of the old institution with some elements of the newly emerging order.

Thomas suggests that extensive social transitions usually elicit a number of movements, each espousing different solutions to the legitimacy problem. These groups seek legitimation for their projects by grounding their proposals in the emerging cultural order. Further, it is not unusual for at least one group to respond to the change by refusing it, both by trying to temper the demands of the new order and by protecting the institution from those demands.[43] Because the legitimacy of an institution does rest on its degree of fit with the larger society, however,

> a new movement, even one at odds with those in power ... will be most successful in mobilizing populations or subgroups precisely where its claims make the most sense—where they are most isomorphic with the organization of everyday life and the corresponding cultural order.[44]

Thomas's argument is compelling because it offers a way of understanding the recurrence of religious revivalism in American history. Historians of the 18th century have suggested that the First Great Awakening in the 1730s was related to changing socioeconomic conditions. The expansion of the market, increased immigration, growing class antagonisms, and the emergence of poverty in the colonies created a disjuncture between the older religious ethos and the new conditions of social life. Religious revival was a way of articulating and negotiating these changes and contradictions.[45] One of the features of this nascent religiosity, as expressed in religious revival, was an increased emphasis on individual responsibility for salvation that corresponded to the individualistic ethos of the expanding market economy. Thomas's study of 19th-century revivalism also connects changes in the socioeconomic order to the emergence of a new religious sensibility manifested in the Second Great Awakening and continuing in successive waves of revivalism throughout the century. His argument parallels that of scholars of the earlier revival period; changes in the socioeconomic order and the continued penetration of market structures into everyday life and consciousness provoked a reformulation of religious belief.

The 19th century brought an expansion of the internal market and the transition from a mercantilist to capitalist economic order. The formation of capitalism produced extensive changes in social relations exemplified in the demise of artisan labor and the rise of the capitalist wage relationship.[46] During this period the state also became more centralized, extending and concentrating its power and control over national monetary policy, taxation, and foreign policy. In keeping with the demands of this changing cultural social order, revivalism progressively incorporated the values of individualism and nationalism into the evangelical belief system. That is, religious revival movements transformed older belief structures and practices to make them more compatible with the new cultural order:

> The penetration of local communities by rationalizing processes dramatically changed social life. Identities and actions were reoriented to impersonal national structures of market and state and to a rationalized ontology of autonomous individuals, rational calculation, mechanical nature, and abstract God. As these changes took place, people began using the underlying ontology to rethink and reshape particular institutions. Movements emerged to build new institutions and new ways of doing things.[47]

The ongoing accommodation between revivalist Protestantism and the social conditions of an industrializing society proceeded in a relatively stable fashion for much of the 19th century. By the late 1800s, however, the acceleration of change in social and economic conditions threatened to fracture the fit between religious ethos and cultural order. Large-scale immigration of peoples from non-Protestant Europe and Asia and the explosive growth of urban centers entailed much greater contact with different beliefs, values, and practices that collided with the dominant Protestant ethos. The emergence of monopoly capitalism, the expansion of the market beyond national borders, and the subsequent explosion of productive capacity through assembly-line production and time management techniques launched American society into a full-fledged, rapid modernization phase.

It is important here to distinguish between modernization, as the transformation of socioeconomic practices, processes, and modes of organization and operation, and modernism, as the cultural manifestation and embodiment of that transformation. These should not be artificially separated nor set up in a causal relationship. That is, modernization did not simply "cause" modernism, nor is modernism a mere "reflection" of modernization. Rather, they are interdependent processes, related to each other in a mutually constitutive way. Both shape and reinforce each other; both are equally "productive" of social practices and consciousness. One of the ironies of conservatives' critique of cultural modernism, in fact, is their simultaneous embrace of societal modernization, as if it were possible to have one without the other. Habermas argues that this internal contradiction exposes the analytical weakness of the neoconservative critique of modernity: "Neoconservativism shifts onto cultural modernism the uncomfortable burdens of a more or less successful capitalist modernization of the economy and society" and thus "blurs the relationship between the welcomed process of societal modernization on the one hand, and the lamented cultural development on the other."[48]

This contradiction is evident in the theologies of both Robertson and Swaggart, albeit in different ways. Swaggart is able to argue for a separation from "the (modern) world" to an international audience through communication media technologies produced through modernization. Robertson's theology is thoroughly penetrated by the cultural values and ways of life made possible by modernization at the same time that he calls for a return to an abstractly conceived set of premodern values and beliefs. The program analysis explores these contradictory impulses in detail.

According to Thomas, the deep structural changes accompanying modernization undermined the older ethos and ontology that had been based on the "rational, self-determining, perfectable individual."[49] By the turn of the century, "increases in scale in industry and the greater importance of state action within the world system caused the cultural order to define an ineffectual individual. These changes began to erode the plausibility and legitimacy of revival religion."[50] It may be more accurate to say that this transformation required evangelical Protestantism to find ways to adapt its moral universe (both beliefs and practices) to more closely fit existing social conditions in order to ensure its survival. This period, not surprisingly, is marked by profound divisions within Protestantism that triggered the creation of new movements and factions such as Fundamentalism, Pentecostalism, premillennialism, liberalism, and the Social Gospel. All of these tendencies, says Thomas, emphasized in various ways "the inadequacy and limitations of the individual."[51]

Hunter has characterized the years between 1890 and 1919 as "the disestablishment of American Protestantism" which involved a dramatic reconfiguration of the place of religion in modern life.[52] Modern American evangelicalism emerged during these years and in this sense is a product of cultural crisis. This was not simply a matter of cumulative individual bouts of anomie, however; it was a crisis of meaning for particular religious communities who found that their cosmic frames of reference no longer accurately matched the changing world around them. Modern evangelicalism survived that transition much as Protestantism had weathered earlier crises of meaning— through the development of movements that negotitated new relationships between religious belief and the emerging cultural order. This is the historical legacy that has shaped contemporary conservative evangelicalism and the theologies espoused by television ministers. Thus, while televangelists appeal to viewers by proclaiming their ties to "that old-time religion," the theologies they profess, the values they embrace, and the forms through which they communicate are distinctly modern.[53]

A religious belief system, if it is to function as an adequate "frame of orientation and devotion," to quote Fromm,[54] must not only describe the world, but also recommend a plausible way of acting in it. When the belief system begins to fail in either respect, it faces a crisis of meaning. I suggest that the dramatic resurgence of conservative evangelical Protestantism in the last two decades is a response to just such a crisis. This most recent phase of religious revitalization, and the corresponding rise of a conservative Christian political movement, is a contemporary effort to articulate a new moral order to fit a rapidly changing cultural environment with the aim of achieving dominance in the moral-political universe. It is to the nature of that crisis that we now turn.

For most people the 1960s will be remembered as a decade of social upheaval giving birth to a variety of social movements. The seeds of the most recent resurgence of evangelical revivalism were sown in this period as old divisions between liberal and conservative Protestantism intensified around the Civil Rights and anti-war movements and the social changes that accompanied them. Subsequent pushes for equal rights by women and homosexuals, as well as Supreme Court decisions regarding abortion and school prayer, rising rates of divorce, teenage pregnancy, drug abuse, and the growth of the pornography industry were interpreted by orthodox Protestants as signs of general moral disintegration and, thus, as a threat to their moral universe. Their full-fledged arrival on the political scene, however, did not occur until the mid-1970s when the election of an evangelical president, Jimmy Carter, brought their religious perspective to the center of national attention.

If it is true that religious revival movements are responses to changes in the socioeconomic and cultural order, we need to understand exactly what kinds of changes were occurring in this period and how those changes are related to a variety of efforts to articulate a new moral order (e.g., the efforts of women, racial and ethnic minorities, and homosexuals may be similarly described). The modern migration of conservative evangelicalism from the margins to the center of public life has occurred largely in the last three decades. Have there been significant alterations in the socioeconomic order during this period that correspond to the growth of this religious movement?

Harvey makes a provocative argument that during the last 20 years there has been an important shift in the way capitalism operates, both in the United States and globally.[55] He suggests that the period of steady economic growth following World War II lasting until the early 1970s was based on a particular model of capitalist production that he calls "Fordism." The Fordist model, born in the early 20th century, was built on the complementary pillars of mass production and mass consumption that were made possible by new production techniques and methods of labor control and management (e.g., assembly lines, time management, increased division of labor, deskilling, etc.).[56] An essential component of this new economic order was access to cheap labor in the Third World made possible by expansionist foreign policies. Such labor was used to extract raw material and agricultural products for export to the United States where such products were manufactured and processed in American factories.

Fordism was also accompanied by a Keynesian model of state intervention in the economy that stabilized capitalism's tendency toward cyclical crisis. While such a system required workers to spend long hours at routinized jobs with negligible control over their labor or their products, the benefits of this arrangement were corporate recognition of labor unions, a steady growth in wages and benefits, and an increased number and variety of affordable consumer goods. Fordism was based on an implicit vision of how a modern capitalist society should operate; the logic of mass production and mass consumption implied "a new system of the reproduction of labour power, a new politics of labour control and management, a new aesthetics and psychology, in short, a new kind of rationalized, modernist, and populist democratic society."[57] Thus, Harvey says, postwar Fordism was not just a particular system of mass production, but "a total way of life." As both products and their consumption were standardized, there developed a new aesthetic and an intensified "commodification of culture."[58]

Such a system was not immune to internal contradictions—
the workforce that benefited most was mainly white, male and unionized; many people criticized the blandness of this standardized culture; and discontent arose among those at home and internationally
who were excluded from the fruits of Fordism. But for nearly four
decades, Harvey says, the Fordist system prevailed,

> and in the process did manage to keep a postwar boom intact that
> favoured unionized labour, and to some degree spread the 'bene-
> fits' of mass production and consumption even further afield.
> Material living standards rose for the mass of the population of
> the advanced capitalist countries, and a relatively stable environ-
> ment for corporate profits prevailed.[59]

This stability, already unraveling in the 1960s, was ultimately shat-
tered in the recession of 1973, triggering deep and relatively rapid
changes in the world economy and in the conditions of social life. The
resurgence of religious revival movements in this period is one of a
host of responses to the rupture between people's "mental maps" and
social reality.[60]

Harvey suggests that the transition from Fordism to what he
calls "flexible accumulation" resulted from the former's rigidity and
inability to adapt to changing technological, social, and political conditions. Fordism's failure is grounded in its inability to accommodate
either changing relationships between developed capitalist nations, or
changes in the relationship of the First and Third Worlds brought
about by the rise of numerous national independence movements in
the 1950s and 1960s. The Fordist model had been built on relations of
unequal development between the United States and Western Europe
and Japan, and between nations in the center and the periphery. This
international hierarchy has been undermined as Western Europe and
Japan recovered from World War II and achieved economic parity
with the U.S., and as Third World independence movements sought to
correct this inequality through the creation of their own projects of
national industrialization that had been denied them under their colo-
nial and neocolonial pasts.

Flexible accumulation emerged as a corrective to Fordism's
rigidity in responding to these changing world relationships as capitalism attempted to cope with inflation and recession while maintaining
profitability. This emergent socioeconomic system, Harvey says,
"rests on flexibility with respect to labour processes, labour markets,
products, and patterns of consumption." Flexible accumulation is
"characterized by the emergence of entirely new sectors of production, new ways of providing financial services, new markets, and,

above all, greatly intensified rates of commercial, technological, and organizational innovation."[61]

It is because of changes in the international economy that flexible accumulation has become a viable political-economic response to the crisis of Fordism. In the early 20th century, Third World labor was used primarily to procure raw materials for export to the developed nations where they were processed and manufactured with First World technology and labor. Today, workers in the Third World produce manufactured goods that are exported worldwide. Production of high technology equipment is still reserved for the developed capitalist centers, but multinational corporations now install that equipment in their Third World factories and use the cheap labor there to manufacture the finished products, hence, the transfer of jobs from the United States to Mexico, Brazil, the Philippines, and so on That is, flexible accumulation is possible only because there now exists an international labor market for capitalist production. The transition to flexible accumulation is felt in the United States in the decline of industry jobs and the unprecedented growth of the service sector, a vastly diminished role for unionized labor, more part-time employment with fewer benefits, the death of industrial towns and cities and migration of workforces to new areas of the country, shrinking real value of wages, confusion and anger about the United States' loss of absolute political and economic dominance in the world, and a general anxiety about the attainability of the "American Dream."

Accompanying such structural changes are significant transformations in cultural practices and social experience. Consumption has not only dramatically accelerated (providing an unprecedented increase in "lifestyle" options available to a mass market), but it has also shifted from material to "immaterial" goods and services, emphasizing once again the transitory nature of contemporary life. Harvey says that "the first major consequence" of this change in consumption patterns "has been to accentuate volatility and ephemerality of fashions, products, production techniques, labour processes, ideas and ideologies, values and established practices."[62] Instanteneity and disposability are emphasized not only in terms of products, but in "values, lifestyles, stable relationships, and attachments to things, buildings, places, people, and received ways of doing and being."[63] Managing and producing this volatility has become a vitally important part of contemporary political and economic life, hence the dramatic growth and influence of the "image production industry" (advertising, public relations, market research, political consultants, etc.). It is this emerging cultural order, and the socioeconomic conditions responsible for it, that Harvey describes as "the condition of postmodernity."

It may be no coincidence, then, that the most recent phase of evangelical revitalization has occurred precisely during this period of historical transition. The resurgence of religious revivalist movements might be understood as an attempt to respond to this transition by articulating new relationships between the older belief system and the values associated with this emerging "postmodern" order. Harvey notes that this "plunge into the maelstrom of ephemerality has provoked an explosion of opposed sentiments and tendencies." Dramatic changes in the conditions of social life necessarily elicit "questions of meaning and interpretation." Indeed, he says, "the greater the ephemerality, the more pressing the need to discover or manufacture some kind of eternal truth that might lie within."[64] Thus, the contemporary conservative evangelical movement may be seen as a striving to retain the legitimacy of its beliefs and values in the face of rapid, profound changes that have thrown all value systems into question. The rise of modernism in the late 19th and early 20th centuries was similarly accompanied by intense religious resistance against the loss of social moorings and spiritual authority. The splintering of Protestantism into liberal and conservative poles was the result of that crisis of meaning, just as the reinvigoration of internal tensions within conservative Protestantism flows from the most recent "sea-change in cultural and political-economic practices."[65]

The contemporary resurgence of conservative evangelicalism is, however, neither a monolithic force nor a univocal argument concerning the causes, consequences, or solutions to this "sea-change". As Thomas points out, large-scale social change usually engenders a number of movements, "each articulating their own version of the new order." Further, a given movement usually contains "competing factions and disputes related to the legitimacy problem." The ability to mobilize followers depends on the degree to which a faction's "claims, goals, methods, and rhetoric are isomorphic" with their experience and interpretation of the sociocultural conditions in which they find themselves.[66]

As I noted earlier, this book is not a study of religious movements, but an exploration of the symbolic terms through which two prominent evangelical broadcasters—Jimmy Swaggart and Pat Robertson—articulate the relationship between religious belief and the contemporary cultural order. Further, their characterizations of the present are simultaneously interpretations of the past and visions of the future. My analysis of these programs is an attempt to understand the nature of the different moral orders they propose and how those envisioned moral universes are connected to the history of evangelical Protestantism's responses to transformations in American culture.

Burke has described rhetoric as a "strategy for encompassing a situation."[67] I am treating these programs as representative symbolic strategies for encompassing the problems involved in maintaining a religious tradition amid a changing historical situation. Hunter argues that the forces and pressures of modernization act to delegitimize the structures and values of metaphysical belief systems.[68] Evangelicalism must cope with this threat of delegitimation by developing convincing explanations for its ongoing historical relevance. The rhetorical strategies adopted to this end may embrace the changes and modify the belief system to match them; reject the changes as illegitimate and assert the universal and eternal validity of the belief system; or try to straddle these two positions by accommodating some cultural changes and modifying some elements of the belief system. I argue in this study that liberal Protestantism has chosen the first option while conservative evangelicalism has taken the other two paths, and for this reason it is marked by deep internal divisions and contradictions. The programs I selected for analysis are symbolic representations of these competing responses to historical change within American evangelicalism. The "Jimmy Swaggart Telecast" represents the option of rejecting social change via a strategy of separation from the dominant cultural order; Pat Robertson's "700 Club" represents a modified accommodation to change in order to retain relevance within contemporary culture. These are generalizations, of course; there are signs of accommodation in Swaggart's program and theology, just as there are indications of resistance to change in Robertson's. But I believe the differences are great enough to warrant such a distinction.

Once more, then, we arrive at a set of questions: What are the specific historical conditions that provoked the crises of meaning to which the disestablishment of Protestantism and the resurgence of evangelical revivalism are responses? What differences characterize the strategies of separation and accommodation to these historical changes, and how are they manifested in evangelical television? What makes these divergent strategies appealing to different TV ministers and to their respective audiences, and how are both the crisis of meaning and possible solutions to it embedded in the messages and forms of the programs?

PERSPECTIVES ON THE ELECTRONIC CHURCH

One sign that the Christian Right and evangelical programming have acquired a heightened social presence is the increase in popular and scholarly analyses of these phenomena.[69] Such work takes a variety of approaches to the study of religious television. Horsfield's *Religious*

Television assesses the social impact of the dominance of evangelical perspectives in television and pulls together a number of empirical studies on religious broadcasting. His book is a comprehensive analysis of the characteristics of religious television (e.g., trends, audience size and composition, people's reasons for watching) and its relationship to the structure of commercial TV. Horsfield's discussion of the relation between religious television and American culture is particularly compelling: He argues that evangelical programming has acquiesced to the "normalizing" tendency of commercial TV by conforming to television's economic and formatting priorities. It has thereby "reinforced the power of television, with its limited views, to act as an adequate determination of the presentation of religious cultural thought.[70] Schultze concurs with this assessment. He suggests that the combination of traditional Protestantism and mass media has produced a pervasive popular religion that has become "the most characteristic form of religious expression in the United States."[71]

Fore's *Religion and Television* takes a more historical and philosophical view of the relationship between these two institutions.[72] Television, he claims, has usurped the role formerly reserved for the church. Fore decries this shift from what he calls a "religious center" to a "technological center;" he also argues that rather than challenging this displacement, the "electronic church" actually hastens it through an uncritical adoption of the commercial broadcasting system's practices and values. Schultze's *Televangelism and American Culture* makes a similar argument, suggesting that the electronic church "is probably the most characteristic and renumerative expression of American religion." His book examines the intimate relationship between broader American values and the particular character of televangelism which he calls "the nation's own religion."[73] These authors' critiques of evangelical programming, which are echoed by a number of theologians and religious scholars, point to evangelicalism's larger accommodation to the values of contemporary American culture.

Razelle Frankl's *Televangelism: The Marketing of Popular Religion* is a further argument that evangelicalism has undergone important transformations through its adoption of modern communication technologies. She examines the roots of evangelical television in 19th-century revivals and argues that televangelism is a "hybrid" of urban revivalism and television that has become a new social institution distinct from traditional forms of evangelical religious practice. She specifically examines the ways in which "television imperatives" have influenced the fundraising techniques of religious broadcasters.[74] Hadden's and Swann's *Prime Time Preachers* approaches the electronic church from a combined sociological and theological perspective.[75] They contend that evangelical programs appeal to certain individuals by playing on their loneliness and inability to cope with the complexity of modern life (it thus takes a "crisis-theoretic perspective"). Hadden and Swann emphasize the television ministries' ability to attract and build audience support through the use of computerized mailings and telephone banks. The authors conclude that because every modern social movement since the advent of television (I would say since the advent of the printing press) has been developed through the mass media, the Christian Right has the potential to become a powerful social force because it controls its own media and is also heavily represented on commercial television and radio.

Conway and Siegelman in *Holy Terror* assert this possibility from a more paranoid position. Televangelism, they contend, is the evangelical movement's "use of religion to legitimize a program of mass manipulation that is unparalleled in American media history."[76] These authors draw on cybernetics theory and propaganda studies, treating the evangelical movement as a cult that succeeds by brainwashing victims. While it is important to identify the elements of coercion in televised evangelism (particularly in its fundraising techniques), Conway and Siegelman overlook the fact that all communication (mediated or direct) attempts to manipulate (as in handle or guide) listeners' attitudes and perceptions. Further, by treating evangelicalism as a cult, these authors ignore its roots in an important American religious tradition.

Hoover refutes the idea that religious television viewers are merely manipulated dupes of crafty broadcasters.[77] His *Mass Media Religion* is a qualitative study of how selected "700 Club" members use and understand the program and incorporate it into their daily lives. Similar to Bourgault's ethnography of PTL viewers, Hoover focuses on "700 Club" members' own accounts of their relationship to the TV ministry.[78] His is one of the few studies of religious television that looks extensively into people's own interpretations of the programs rather than treating religious television viewers as statistical data. This interpretive, cultural approach enables Hoover to recognize that the relationship between program and viewer is a complex, interactive construction of significance, rather than a one-way injection of ideology. Further, his research shows that far from "causing" people to convert to conservative evangelicalism, watching TV ministries is merely one element in their general religious practice. For his research subjects, Hoover found, viewing evangelical television always came after their other religious involvements.

Hoover's findings are in direct conflict with the claims forwarded by Ben Armstrong, current president of the National Religious Broadcasters Association. Armstrong coined the term "electric church;" his book of that name extols the virtues of televised evange-

lism as a modern means of spreading the gospel.[79] Armstrong, like
most of the TV preachers, views television as an amplified, and therefore greatly extended mode of preaching. Horsfield points out that it is
common for evangelical broadcasters to hold a simplistic, "hypodermic model" view of television's effectiveness.[80] If the Bible directs
reborn Christians to spread their testimony, television simply makes
that task more far-reaching and efficient. Hunter argues that this quantitative approach to soul saving is related to the general tendency in
modern society toward rationalization; the number of viewers reached
equals the number of souls brought to God, and viewers are assured
that their donations are well spent because a given number of people
were reached and/or saved by a TV ministry in the past week.[81]

Not all evangelical broadcasters share this optimism about
televised evangelism's ability to win new converts. Bisset remarked in
Christianity Today that 85% of those who watch religious broadcasting
say they had already been "saved" before tuning in (Hoover's research
supports this claim). Bisset challenges the notion that television ministries are bringing new souls to Christ: "We are talking largely to ourselves while most of America (and the world) goes unevangelized in
the mass media." He also suggests that televangelism has failed in its
mission because it has adopted the competitiveness inherent in commercial television, thus fragmenting the "Christian market."[82]

A number of essays and articles on religious television and
the evangelical movement have also appeared in religious periodicals,
particularly in *Christianity Today* and *Christian Century*, published by
the National Association of Evangelicals and the mainline Protestant
National Council of Churches, respectively. Both magazines have
questioned television's effectiveness as a proselytyzing tool and its
ability to adequately represent the gospel message. *Christianity Today*
has generally been more laudatory of TV ministries, and more likely to
subscribe to technological optimism about the mass media's missionary capacity. *Christian Century* is more skeptical; it usually takes the
position that televised religion undermines both the Christian message and participation at local churches. These positions also reflect
the historical tension between conservative and liberal
Protestantism—a tension exacerbated by the fact that the orthodox
wing has been growing as the liberal wing declines. Arguments about
religious television's role in this uneven growth often seem to skirt
deeper theological issues behind this historical development.[83]

I noted earlier the shortcomings of treating religious television
as a unified entity and reducing specific programs to statistical variations within a generic institution. What gets lost in this process is an
understanding of the particular form of different programs, and thus
of their appeal and meaning for viewers. In 1988, Schultze said that

existing studies had "barely advanced our understanding of religious broadcasting" and that so far "its origins, significance, and dynamics are largely unknown." The remedy for such gaps in our knowledge, Schultze argued, is "careful cultural and historical analysis."[84] I agree that answering questions about the significance, or meaning, of tele-vangelism requires alternative ways of conceptualizing the relation-ships among religious belief, televised religion, and television viewers.[85] I try in this study to provide that conceptual framework by offering a way to think through those relationships from a historical perspective. The programs of Swaggart and Robertson make sense, both to believers and to those outside the belief system, only when they are situated within the intertwined histories of evangelical Protestantism and American culture. That is, their appeal and the meanings they offer viewers have developed in conjunction with con-servative Protestantism's dual responses to the process of moderniza-tion in the last century. The differences between the programs reflect different strategies for coping with that history. While both Swaggart's and Robertson' narratives are persuasive enough to attract sizeable audiences, the explanations they offer are not the same. In many ways, the theologies of these two men are incompatible; the stories they tell about the nature of the world, of God, and of humanity are in deep conflict with each other.

My goal has been to interpret those different stories to discov-er how and why they might appeal to particular groups of viewers. The route to such understanding, I believe, lies in conceiving the pro-grams as cultural forms whose meaning has been historically con-structed. The shows invite audiences to complete the stories—to make them meaningful—by appealing to viewers' collective memories of the past and their visions of the present and future. The "invitation" is the form of the programs themselves; as Burke says, form in com-munication is "the arousal and fulfillment of desires."[86] This study, then, is an inquiry into desire and into the ways it becomes embodied in cultural form. It approaches televangelism from a communications perspective, but one that seeks to synthesize ideas from a variety of traditions and fields, including rhetorical criticism, media sociology, theology, cultural anthropology and philosophy. The focus of this study is "meaning." It asks not only what televised evangelism means, culturally and politically, but also how it comes to have particular meanings. I am concerned with how conservative evangelicalism, as it is manifested in two television programs, creates a symbolic frame-work that describes and interprets the world. What is the character of those explanations? Through what techniques and strategies are they constructed, and to what end? How do they become effective through their appropriation by viewers, and what are the social implications of these particular interpretations of the world? That is, what kind of society evokes the desire for such forms of religiosity, and what does that desire tell us about our history, our society, and ourselves?

NOTES TO CHAPTER 1

1. KCPQ-TV, Channel 13, Tacoma, Washington, "The Jimmy Swaggart Telecast, " May 24, 1987.

2. Quoted in J. Thomas Bisset, "Religious Broadcasting: Assessing the State of the Art," *Christianity Today*, December 12, 1980, p. 31.

3. Robertson used this term on the "700 Club" according to Edwin Diamond, "God's Television," in Karl Love, ed., *Television and American Culture* (New York: W. Wilson, 1981), p. 80.

4. Estimates of the audience for religious television can be found in William Martin, "The Birth of a Media Myth," *Atlantic Monthly* 247 (June 1981): pp. 9-16; in George Gerbner et al. *Religion and Television, A Research Report by the Annenberg School of Communications, University of Pennsylvania and the Gallup Organization, Inc.*, Vol. I. (Philadelphia: Annenberg School of Communications, April 1984), p. 3. See also William Fore, "Religion and Television: Report on the Research," *Christian Century*, July 18-25, 1984, pp. 710-713, and Jeffrey Hadden, "The Great Audience Size Debate," *Religious Broadcasting*, (January, 1986), pp. 20-22.

5. This figure on income was widely quoted in the media and includes all religious programming. See "An Unholy War in the TV Pulpits," *U.S. News and World Report*, (April 6, 1987), p. 38; and Quentin Schultze, "The Mythos of the Electronic Church," *Critical Studies in Mass Communication* 4 (1987): p. 246.

6. It has been estimated that donations and viewers of Jimmy Swaggart Ministries declined by more than 50 percent after disclosure of the scandal. See Gustav Niebuhr, "TV Evangelists Rebound from Viewer Erosion," *Atlanta Journal*, May 1, 1989, p. 6; Peter Applebome, "Scandals Aside, TV Preachers Thrive," *New York Times*, October 8, 1989, p. A24; Randy Frame, "Surviving the Slump," *Christianity Today*, February 3, 1989, pp. 32-34.

7. April Witt, "Robertson Likely to Rejoin CBN," *Norfolk Virginian-Pilot*, May 11, 1988, pp. 10-11; Lamar Graham, "700 Club," *Norfolk Virginian-Pilot*, August 2, 1988, pp. 9-11; Marjorie Mayfield, "For CBN, The Worst May be Over," *Norfolk Virginian-Pilot*, March 5, 1989, pp. 7-8.

8. Peter Applebome, "Swaggart's Troubles Show Tension of Passion and Power in TV Evangelism," *New York Times*, February 28, 1988, p. A30.

9. See G. Niebuhr, "TV Evangelists Rebound" and Applebome, "Scandals Aside."

10. "The Christianity Today Gallup Poll: An Overview," *Christianity Today*, December 21, 1979, pp. 14.

11. "The Religious Personality of the Populace," *Christianity Today*, December 21, 1979, p. 15.

12. George Gerbner with Kathleen Connolly, "Television as New Religion," *New Catholic World*, March/April 1978, pp. 52-56; Gregor Goethals, *The TV Ritual: Worship at the Video Altar* (Boston: Beacon Press, 1981); Gregor Goethals, *The Electronic Golden Calf: Images, Religion and the Making of Meaning* (Cambridge, MA: Cowley Publications, 1990); William Fore, *Television and Religion: The Shaping of Faith, Values, and Culture* (Minneapolis: Augsburg, 1987); Virginia Stem Owens, *The Total Image: or, Selling Jesus in the Modern Age* (Grand Rapids, MI: W. B. Eerdman's, 1980).

13. This term comes from Razelle Frankl, *Televangelism: The Marketing of Popular Religion* (Carbondale: Southern Illinois University Press, 1978).

14. Quentin J. Schultze, "Balance or Bias" Must TV Distort the Gospel?", *Christianity Today*, March 18, 1988, pp. 29-30.

15. Quentin Schultze, "The Mythos of the Electronic Church," *Critical Studies in Mass Communication* 4 (1987): p. 247.

16. Ibid., p. 246.

17. Ibid., p. 258.

18. James W. Carey, " Mass Communication Research and Cultural Studies: An American View," in James Curran, Michael Gurevitch and Janet Woollacott, eds., *Mass Communication and Society* (Beverly Hills: Sage, 1979), P. 421.

19. Frankl, in *Televangelism: The Marketing of Popular Religion*, also places Swaggart and Robertson at opposite ends of the spectrum in terms of the degree to which their programs incorporate the various "imperatives" of the television medium and industry. See Chapter 9, "The Variety of Messages in the Electric Church."

20. Gerbner et al., *Religion and Television*.

21. Ibid., vol. I, p. 2.

22. Ibid., p. 12.

23. Quentin J. Schultze, "Vindicating the Electronic Church? An Assessment of the Annenberg-Gallup Study," *Critical Studies in Mass Communications* 2 (1985): p. 286.

24. Ibid., p. 285.

25. "The Christianity Today-Gallup Poll," p. 14.

26. "We Poll the Pollster," *Christianity Today*, December 21, 1979, p. 10; and "The Christianity Today-Gallup Poll: An Overview," *Christianity*

Today, December 21, 1979, pp. 12-19.

27. Examples of popular press coverage include: Kenneth L. Woodward, "Born Again!" *Newsweek*, October 25, 1976, pp. 68-78; "Back to that Oldtime Religion," *Time*, December 26, 1977, pp. 52-58; James Mann, " A Global Surge of Old-Time Religion," *U. S. News and World Report*, April 27, 1981, pp. 38-40; Frances FitzGerald, "A Disciplined, Charging Army," *New Yorker*, May 18, 1981, pp. 53-144; Dudley Clendinen, "Christian New Right's Rush to Power," *New York Times*, August 18, 1980, p. B7; Allan J. Maye, "A Tide of Born-Again Politics," *Newsweek*, September 15, 1980, pp. 28-36; Colin Nickerson, "Great Reawakening in New England—Fundamentalist Religion Grows," *Boston Globe*, July 26, 1981, p. 2; and Peter Ross Range, "Thunder from the Right," *New York Times Magazine*, February 8, 1981, pp. 23-54.

28. The "agenda-setting" theory of the news media, first proposed by Maxwell McCombs, has become widely accepted by U. S. media researchers. For the basic argument, see McCombs, "The Agenda-Setting Function of the Mass Media," *Public Opinion Quarterly* 36 (1972): 176-187.

29. Peter Horsfield, *Religious Television: The American Experience* (New York: Longman, 1984), p. 9.

30. The figure on income is widely quoted in the media, and includes all religious programming. See, for example, "An Unholy War in the TV Pulipts," *U.S. News and World Report*, April 6, 1987, p. 38; and Quentin Schultze, "The Mythos of the Electronic Church," *Critical Studies in Mass Communication* 4 (1987): p. 246.

31. Martin, "Birth of a Media Myth."

32. Horsfield, *Religious Television*, p. xiv.

33. George Marsden, a thoughtful and thorough historian of Fundamentalism, offers a definition of that branch of Evangelicalism, which also sheds light on the larger movement: "'Fundamentalism' refers to a twentieth-century movement closely tied to the revivalist tradition of mainstream evangelical Protestantism that militantly opposed modernist theology and culture change associated with it." Marsden, "Fundamentalism as an American Phenomenon, A Comparison with English Evangelicalism," *Church History* 46 (June 1977): p. 215.

34. Grant Wacker, "The Search for Norman Rockwell: Popular Evangelicalism in Contemporary America," in L. I. Sweet, ed., *The Evangelical Tradition in America* (Macon, GA: Mercer University Press, 1984), p. 295. For the diversity—social, cultural, and political—within evangelicalism, see also Richard Quebedeaux, *The Young Evangelicals* (New York: Harper & Row, 1974) and Robert D. Linder, "The Resurgence of Evangelical Concern," in D. F. Wells and J. D.

Woodbridge, eds., *The Evangelicals* (Nashville, TN: Abingdon, 1975), pp. 189-210. Black evangelicals are also, by and large, less conservative than their white counterparts, and are a small minority of the total evangelical population. See James D. Hunter, *American Evangelicalism: Conservative Religion and the Quandary of Modernity* (New Brunswick, NJ: Rutgers University Press, 1983), p. 50. For an overview of the Evangelical Right see Erling Jorstad, "The New Christian Right," *Theology Today* 38 (1981): pp. 193-200; Samuel S. Hill and Dennis E. Owen, *The New Religious Political Right in America* (Nashville, TN: Abingdon, 1982); and Robert C. Liebman and Robert Wuthnow, eds., *The New Christian Right: Mobilization and Legitimation* (Hawthorne, NY: Aldine, 1983).

35. See Martin, "Birth of a Media Myth." Martin was the first to systematically examine the media's and religious broadcasters' unrealistic claims about the size of the evangelical audience and the influence of the movement.

36. Flo Conway and Jim Siegelman, *Holy Terror: The Fundamentalist War on America's Freedoms in Religion, Politics and our Private Lives* (Garden City, NY: Doubleday, 1982), p. 276.

37. Joe Conason, "The Religious Right's Quiet Revival," *Nation*, April 27, 1992, pp. 541, 553.

38. Ibid., p. 556.

39. "TV Preacher Can Cancel U.P.I. Deal," *New York Times*, May 14, 1992, p. C24; "What's in the Offing After Robertson's Bid for UPI?" *Minneapolis Star-Tribune*, May 14, 1992, p. 4D.

40. The relationship between ultra-conservative political figures and organizations and leaders of the Christian Right was the subject of a study commissioned by the World Student Christian Federation in 1980. The research examined overlaps in membership and sources of funding for such organizations as Christian Voice, Campus Crusade for Christ, Christian Anti-Communism Crusade, various television ministries, and so on. Consider, for example, the Religious Roundtable, founded in September 1979; its 56 original members included representatives from CBN, Moral Majority, National Religious Broadcasters, National Association of Evangelicals, and other conservative Christian groups, as well as Phyllis Schafly, Richard Viguerie, and Paul Weyrich. The researchers argue that the union of Christian and political conservatives "is the result of the conscious recruiting efforts of leaders of the right wing" who "found in the Evangelical movement a potential constituency for their formerly unsellable economic program . . . Cloaked under the banner of anti-ERA, anti-gay rights, and now pro-morality and pro-God, the Right has found a new platform around which they may mobilize voters" (p. 76). Deborah Huntington and Ruth Kaplan, "Whose Gold is Behind the Altar? Corporate Ties to Evangelicals," *Contemporary*

Marxism 4 (Winter 1981-82): pp. 62-94. See also the special issue on the religious right in *Covert Action Information Bulletin* 27 (1987).

41. George Thomas, *Revivalism and Cultural Change: Christianity, National Building, and the Market in the Nineteenth Century United States* (Chicago: University of Chicago Press, 1989). The perspective he criticizes is represented in the work of William G. McLoughlin, Jr., *Modern Revivalism: Charles Grandison Finney to Billy Graham* (New York: Ronald Press, 1959) and *Revivals, Awakenings and Reform: An Essay in Religious and Social Change in America, 1607-1977* (Chicago: University of Chicago Press, 1978).

42. Thomas, *Revivalism and Cultural Change*, p. 2

43. Ibid., pp. 23-24

44. Ibid., p. 25

45. See Gary Nash, *The Urban Crucible: Social Change, Political Consciousness, and the Origins of the American Revolution* (Cambridge, MA: Harvard University Press, 1979) and Richard Bushman, *From Puritan to Yankee: Character and the Social Order in Connecticut, 1690-1765* (Cambridge, MA: Harvard University Press, 1967). Both authors connect socioeconomic changes to changes in religious belief and practice, though they do so from different political and theoretical perspectives.

46. For an empirical study of this transition from the perspective of a working class in formation, see Sean Wilentz, *Chants Democratic: New York City and the Rise of the American Working Class, 1788-1850* (New York: Oxford University Press, 1984).

47. Thomas, *Revivalism and Cultural Change*, p. 82.

48. Jurgen Habermas, "Modernity—An Incomplete Project," in Hal Foster, ed., *The Anti-Aesthetic: Essays on Postmodern Culture* (Port Townsend, WA: Bay Press, 1983), p. 7.

49. Thomas, *Revivalism and Cultural Change,* p. 82.

50. Ibid., p. 83.

51. Ibid.

52. Hunter, *American Evangelicalism*, p. 27.

53. Frank Lechner makes a similar argument about the modern cast to contemporary fundamentalism and also argues that sociocultural changes have been the major impetus behind religious revival movements in the U.S. He uses a Parsonian action theory framework to describe this historical relationship and concludes that while "revitalization episodes in American religious history had fundamentalist aspects [they] also entailed unintended modernizing consequences." "Fundamentalism and Sociocultural Revitalization in America: A Sociological Interpretation," *Sociological Analysis* 46 (1985): p. 243.

54. Erich Fromm, *Man for Himself* (Greenwich, CT: Fawcett, 1947), p. 56.

55. David Harvey, *The Condition of Postmodernity* (Oxford and Cambridge, MA: Basil Blackwell, 1989).

56. Harry Braverman documents this transformation of American labor in *Labor and Monopoly Capital: The Degradation of Work in the Twentieth Century* (New York: Monthly Review Press, 1974).

57. Harvey, *Condition of Postmodernity*, p. 126.

58. Ibid., p. 135.

59. Ibid., p. 140.

60. Ibid., p. 305.

61. Ibid., p. 147.

62, Ibid., p. 285.

63. Ibid., p. 286.

64. Ibid., p. 292.

65. Ibid., p. vii.

66. Thomas, *Revivalism and Cultural Change*, p. 28.

67. Kenneth Burke, *The Philosophy of Literary Form*, 2nd ed. (Baton Rouge, Louisiana State University Press, 1967), p. 1.

68. Hunter, *American Evangelicalism*.

69. For a comprehensive bibliography of books, articles, dissertations, and theses on religious broadcasting, see George H. Hill and Lenwood Davis, *Religious Broadcasting 1920-1983, A Selectively Annotated Bibliography* (New York: Garland, 1984).

70. Horsfield, *Religious Television*, pp. 157-58.

71. Schultze, "Evangelical Mass Media as a Securalizing Force," *Christian Century*, November 30, 1988, p. 1086.

72. William Fore, *Religion and Television: The Shaping of Faith, Values, and Culture* (Minneapolis, MN: Augsburg, 1987).

73. Quentin Schultze, *Televangelism and American Culture* (Grand Rapids, MI: Baker Book House, 1991), pp. 11-12.

74. Frankl, *Televangelism*; in pp. 128-142 she specifically discusses how the cost of programming and dependence on donations shape the form and substance of religious programs.

75. Jeffrey Hadden and Charles E. Swann, *Prime Time Preachers: The Rising Power of Televangelism* (Reading, MA: Addison-Wesley, 1981).

76. Conway and Siegelman, *Holy Terror*, p. 231.

77. Stuart Hoover, *Mass Media Religion: The Social Sources of the Electronic Church* (Newbury Park, CA: Sage, 1988).

78. Louise M. Bourgault, "The 'PTL Club' and Protestant Viewers: An Ethnographic Study," *Journal of Communication* 35 (Winter, 1985): pp. 132-148.

79. Ben Armstrong, *The Electronic Church* (Nashville, TN: Thomas Nelson Publishing, 1979).

80. Horsfield, *Religious Television*, pp. 29-30. Schultze makes this point as well in "The Mythos of the Electronic Church."

81. See Hunter, *American Evangelicalism*, p. 12, for a discussion of

rationalization.

82. Bisset, "Religious Broadcasting: Assessing the State of the Art," p. 30.

83. Bisset's "Religious Broadcasting" is a good example of the NAE position, and Fore's *Religion and Television* is representative of the NCC perspective.

84. Quentin Schultze, "Researching Televangelism," *Critical Studies in Mass Communication* 5 (1988): pp. 271, 274.

85. Hoover also cited a need for a "new type of research" in this study of the relationship between the "700 Club" and its viewers and in his attempt to understand "how [the show] is used and what meanings are engendered by its use," *Mass Media Religion*, p. 96.

86. Kenneth Burke, *Counter-Statement* (Berkeley: University of California Press, 1968), p. 124.

2

Evangelical Communication and the Historical Appeal of Form

RELIGION AS A SYMBOLIC SYSTEM: THE PROBLEM OF MEANING

Beginning from an understanding of human beings as "symbolizing, conceptualizing, meaning-seeking animals," Geertz proposes that "the imposition of meaning is the major end and primary condition of human existence."[1] That is, the act of attributing significance to the natural and social world, and to one's experience of it, is a condition of being human. The field in which this signifying activity takes place is human culture, comprising both material practices and expressive forms. Culture, says Geertz, is a "web of meanings" within which individuals "interpret their experience and guide their action."[2] The particular cultural forms through which a given people live and express their experience are historically determined, reflecting the material and mental tools available to them. What is universal about cultures is that they are formulated and expressed symbolically—symbols are the place where meanings are "stored." The study of culture, and of specific cultural forms such as religious television, necessarily involves the interpretation of symbols. As Geertz says, cultural analysis is an "interpretive science" concerned with "sorting out the structures of signification and determining their ground and import."[3] The cultural analyst's task is to identify the structures of signification specific to her or his culture and to tease out the meanings they hold for the human beings who both construct and live by them.

If the creation and imposition of meaning are fundamentally human endeavors, then questions about meaning necessarily have an ontological dimension. That is, to investigate meaning is to simultaneously raise questions about the nature and significance of being. Heschel makes this connection explicit:

> Human being is never sheer being; it is always involved in meaning. . . . The problem of being and the problem of meaning are coextensive. In regard to man, the first problem refers to what he is in terms of his own existence, human being as it is; the second refers to what man means in terms larger than himself, being in terms of meaning.[4]

Religion is explicitly concerned with both ontological and experiential dimensions of existence—with being and meaning. Religion provides a meaning for individual existence by grounding it in a larger, cosmic framework of significance. Many students of religion have suggested that religiosity originates in the human quest for personal and transcendental meaning. Weber, for example, argues that religion is the product of the human need "to understand the world as a meaningful cosmos and to take up a position toward it."[5] This quest, moreover, is a social activity. Wilson suggests that religion "establishes horizons for a culture, orienting the collectivity and the individuals who comprise it through time and across social space. Religion sets the forms in which thought takes place and condenses the values which guide behavior."[6] Berger says religion provides a "sacred and cosmic frame of reference," or a "sacred canopy," that legitimates and supports a given social order (thus the need for correspondence between a given religion and the cultural order it inhabits).[7] Fromm argues that human beings require such a "frame of orientation and devotion" to give their actions a purpose transcending their immediate lives.[8] While such frameworks need not be explicitly religious, they always refer to a meaning that lies beyond an individual's finite existence. Further, they offer guidelines for action that are grounded in ontology—in an explanation of what it is to be human. Frames of orientation and devotion, then, are directed at transcendent meaning; they seek a significance that supercedes and directs the individual's life. In Heschel's words: "What we are in search of is not meaning for me, an idea to satisfy my conscience, but rather a meaning transcending me, ultimate relevance of being."[9]

Religion provides this ultimate relevance, or frame of orientation and devotion, and does so through the construction of a system of sacred symbols that provide compelling answers to questions about being and meaning. Geertz defines religion as:

> 1) a system of symbols which acts to 2) establish powerful, per-
> suasive and long-lasting moods and motivations in men by 3) for-
> mulating conceptions of a general order of existence and 4) cloth-
> ing these conceptions with such an aura of factuality that 5) the
> moods and motivations seem uniquely realistic.[10]

Because sacred symbols "formulate general ideas of order,"[11] they
impose order on chaos by establishing a general meaning to social
reality that breathes life and significance into individual existence. It is
a symbolic means by which we make sense of the world and simultaneously make sense of our place in it. Religion, as a symbolic system,
is both a model of and a model for reality and everyday life. Religious
symbols both express and shape the world: "They shape it by inducing in the worshiper a certain distinctive set of dispositions which
lend a chronic character to the flow of his activity and the quality of
his experience."[12]

    For Geertz, religion is meaning-centered in another fundamen-
tal way. All religions, he says, address what he calls the "problem of
meaning" in human existence, that is, the question of order (significance, direction) versus chaos (meaninglessness, pointlessness). The
problem of meaning has to do with human limitations—intellectual,
physiological, and ethical (analytical capacities, powers of endurance,
and moral insight). The apparent inevitability of human bafflement,
suffering, and injustice or evil threaten to annihilate order—to make
life unfathomable. These human limitations constitute what Geertz
says are "radical challenges with which any religion . . . which hopes
to persist must attempt somehow to cope."[13]

    The problem of meaning, or the quest for principles of order,
is not confronted exclusively by religion. In our secularized modern
society, other symbolic systems are similarly endowed with the capacity to forge meaning out of chaos. Duncan, drawing on the work of
Burke, refers to order as the enactment of authority that takes some
kind of hierarchical form—order establishes a hierarchy of meanings
that derive their authority from an "ultimate appeal." Such "ultimates"
may be persons (parents, political figures, dieties) rules and codes
("law and order") the environment or nature (processes, structures,
natural laws) means (methods, instruments, magic) or perfect ends
(utopias, the Kingdom of God).[14] We can look at modern science as
such an orienting, symbolic framework, acting much like religion to
establish a sense of order that explains the complex processes of soci-

ety and personal existence. Conservative Christians' claim that "secular humanism" has become a contemporary alternative to religion (or a religion itself) is more comprehensible if we consider that humanist philosophy and social science also aim to construct a basis for order (a universal explanatory framework) that appeals to humanity as its ultimate term.

Duncan points out that a belief in any type of social legitimation process (e.g., science, philosophy, political ideology) functions in society in much the same way as does the supernatural in religion. That is, we legitimize (grant meaning to) hierarchies (conceptions of order) by grounding their "causes" in ultimate terms (nature, family, science, society, God, etc.). Like religion, then, science, philosophies, and political ideologies are strategies that create meaning in the face of potential meaninglessness; they provide a framework to explain and interpret the nature of the world and our place in it. From this perspective, evangelical Christianity can be understood as a particular set of solutions to the "problem of meaning"; it solves this problem by posing a specific frame of orientation and devotion that makes sense of society and existence, and it does so through the construction and invocation of a sacred symbolic system.

Geertz proposes that the interpretion of religion involves "first, an analysis of the system of meanings embodied in the symbols which make up the religion proper, and second, the relating of these systems to social-structural and psychological processes."[15] Applying this method to evangelicalism and its religious programming means examining the symbolic forms that constitute a particular conception of God and asking how this notion of divinity relates to believers' perceptions of social order, history, culture, and humanity's place within. The strict adherence to scriptural authority found in most forms of evangelicalism can be seen as involving a particular devotion to the primacy of the Word, which is the embodiment of supernatural (and therefore natural) authority. The Bible is thus a model of reality, and a model for individual existence within it. We can then begin to draw out connections between the system of meaning (the Bible as "Truth") and social and psychological processes (how this "Truth" is translated into believers' actions and values, e.g., witnessing, campaigning for social issues, developing alternative institutions, etc.).

Carey, who considers religion to be a cultural form similar to ideology, journalism, or everyday speech, suggests that an interpretive approach to culture asks: "What is the relationship between expressive forms . . . and social order?"[16] He characterizes this approach as a "ritual view" of communication, or communication as a "process through which a shared culture is created, modified, and transformed." Confronted with a particular expressive form, the cultural analyst must, like a literary critic, "figure out what it means, what interpretations it presents of life."[17] Like Geertz, Carey believes that cultural forms can be approached as "texts" that demand interpretation via understanding. In this sense, not only are religious TV programs texts, but so too is evangelicalism itself, which creates a "shared culture for its adherents." Carey's view of culture as ritual expression dovetails with Geertz' notion of "cultural performances"—rituals that symbolically fuse individual ethos (moods, motivations, attitudes) with the worldview contained in a given symbolic system.[18] It is within such "dramas," or ritualized forms, that the moods and motivations that sacred symbols induce in believers, and general conceptions about existence, meet and reinforce each other.[19]

Within evangelicalism, revivals, church services, Bible conferences, and prayer meetings have historically provided a dramatic, ritual context for affirming and propagating belief and for binding believers into a community. Sizer, in an analysis of gospel hymns in 19th-century revivals, argues that the hymns symbolized the basic beliefs and aspirations of revival participants.[20] The hymns' form, enacted within the context of the revival meeting, produced and reinforced a sense of belonging and identity among the faithful. The ritualized form of both the hymns and the revivals, based on a formula of prayer, exhortation and testimony, created an environment that upheld the tenets of evangelicalism and constructed a sacred space in which believers could enact their faith and create a shared culture. A number of religious programs serve this function today with their dramatic format of sacred music, exhortation, prayer, and testimony.[21]

The notion of community, and the ways in which it is created, maintained, threatened, and dissolved, has been treated extensively in cultural studies and cultural anthropology. Such work has examined the means by which cultural forms and practices contribute to the creation of a community and to the consciousness of its members; it has examined how symbolic frameworks (or discourses) provide unity and identity to social groups (or subcultures).[22] Sizer, for example, emphasizes the role of gospel hymns in the construction of a "community of intense feeling" that binds evangelicals to a common faith and, therefore, to a shared set of social practices.[23] Whitson contends that all religions grapple with the problem of meaning not in terms of the isolated individual, but in terms of a community as it exists in concrete social circumstances. He suggests that "every religion has come into existence at the point of crisis in the meaning of a community, and remains in existence as long as it continues to make possible the positive confrontation of succeeding crises."[24] This supports my argument that religious movements arise to negotiate such crises of meaning.

Evangelicalism, which was the dominant form of American

Protestant Christianity by mid-19th century, faced such a crisis in the late 1800s when Darwinian biology, German theology and "higher criticism" of the Bible began penetrating Protestant theology in the United States. This constellation of ideas became identified as modernism and constituted a dividing line between liberal and conservative factions. For conservative forces, modernism symbolized a threat to the very heart of Christianity, and as Protestant denominations split along ideological lines, new conservative tendencies such as Fundamentalism and Pentecostalism were born. This "second wing"[25] of Protestantism formulated its identity by rallying around a well-articulated set of religious symbols characterized by a literalist view of Scripture, a deeply supernaturalist theology, a premillennialist conception of history, and an antipathy toward liberal Protestantism and other "false" forms of Christianity (e.g., Catholicism, Mormonism, etc.).

The climax of this crisis period, the Scopes trial in 1925, damaged the reputation of the fundamentalist wing, but did not, as many of its critics predicted, spell conservative evangelicalism's demise. Fundamentalists, Pentecostals, and other conservative evangelicals spent the next three decades building alternative or "parallel" institutions and communication networks on the foundation of their original sacred symbols and religious rituals.[26] This sacred symbolic system has continued to provide a sense of community for a significant minority of Protestants for whom biblical inerrancy, supernaturalism, and premillennialism function as a coherent set of values and meanings.

Conservative evangelicalism, therefore, did not suddenly appear in the last decade. Rather, evangelicals once again became an active social movement in response to what they perceived as real threats to their community and world view (e.g., U.S. Supreme Court rulings on abortion and school prayer, the Equal Rights Amendment, demands for civil rights among homosexuals, escalating rates of divorce and teenage pregnancy, the growth of the pornography industry, etc.). While social movements are responses to changing social conditions, and in this sense are products of concrete material forces, Cathcart contends that they are also necessarily symbolic entities because a movement is "perceived, created, and responded to symbolically."[27]

A religious movement arises in response to significant alterations in social practices and conditions that threaten to delegitimize the values that have sustained its sacred canopy. It is socially recognized as a movement, however, only if it can elicit a "counterrhetoric." A movement is defined as such when it provokes "dialectical enjoinment in the moral arena."[28] Thus, to function as a social movement, conservative evangelicalism requires a counterterm or opposing symbol system in order to constitute itself. Today the term that accords unity to many conservative evangelicals is not modernism, but its contemporary equivalent: "secular humanism." By identifying a common symbolic enemy, evangelicals are able to create a shared culture constructed on an alternative moral order and symbolic system. Understanding the nature of conservative evangelicalism as a movement, therefore, requires analysis of its rhetoric in relationship to the cultural order and values it hopes to challenge.

My analysis of conservative evangelicalism attempts to outline the symbolic framework that constitutes its beliefs and guides its actions. The programs of Swaggart and Robertson, I propose, represent different symbolic responses to the "problem of meaning." This study looks at these programs as divergent models of reality for conservative evangelicals, and as conflicting models for viewers' actions within that reality. In later chapters I examine the substance of the programs' "ultimate terms" and the type of "order" that follows from them; the means by which Swaggart and Robertson, through the selection of certain symbols, constitute sacred versus profane space and create a particular kind of Christian community; and the structure of appeal of a televised revival and a Christian talk show as cultural performances. What I am after is an understanding of the relationship of believer and belief as they meet in a symbolic terrain. I am asking how televangelists, together with their audiences, "attain their faith as they portray it."[29] The route to this understanding, I believe, lies in being willing to seriously consider evangelicals' interpretations of the world—to enter their universe of meaning.

Through the selection and use of specific symbols, televangelists seek to invoke in their audience an agreement about what is significant and what is not. This study proposes that the interrelation of belief system, symbolic materials, speaker, and listener produces a particular set of meanings, and further, that these meanings are grounded in the history of American Protestantism. The aim of that production is the fusion of individual ethos and worldview. The language of Robertson and Swaggart is therefore motivated in pursuit of identification with their audiences, and to speak of motives is to raise the problem of persuasion.

RELIGIOUS COMMUNICATION AS RHETORIC: THE PROBLEM OF PERSUASION

Because religion provides an orienting symbolic framework that explains, interprets, and legitimizes a particular conception of the world and of personal existence, religious communication is necessarily persuasive. A religion "lives" because its interpretations of the world are considered meaningful by a group, a community, or a society, and it is perpetuated through time and across social space as long as its symbolic framework holds that explanatory power. In looking at conservative evangelicalism we must examine the structure, substance, and strategies of its symbolic appeal. This study, accordingly, treats televangelism as a form of persuasive communication. Every act of communication is situated in a particular view of the world and is, therefore, motivated by social and individual intentions. Evangelical persuasion is not static— an already accomplished fact— but a dynamic intention (implicit in all communication) that must be examined in relationship to the set of meanings that the belief system seeks to produce for religious broadcasters and audiences alike.

I am approaching persuasion from a rhetorical perspective— one that relies heavily on the ideas of Burke.[30] This approach does not treat persuasion as an isolated effect of communication as a technique, a function, or an individual's aim, but as an intrinsic aspect of all human communication. Like Geertz, Burke begins from an understanding of human beings as symbol-using, symbol-making, and symbol-misusing animals. In making "symbolicity" ontologically a priori, Burke proposes that human sociation is rooted in language, or in "symbolic action."[31] Language is not a reflection of reality for Burke, but helps to produce reality; it orders experience because it creates the forms that make it possible for us to communicate that experience to others and to ourselves. From this perspective, cultural analysis is always simultaneously symbolic analysis because it is through symbols that we act upon and within the world. We speak (via language and other symbol systems such as art, music, fashion, etc.) to give meaning to existence, to induce cooperation in others in a material field, and to create a certain type of order and locate ourselves within it. In Burke's view, communication is a motivated activity—it seeks to affect the actions of others. In this sense, all communication is rhetorical. As Burke says, rhetoric is "the use of language as a symbolic means of inducing cooperation in beings that by nature respond to symbols."[32]

Burke's "dramatistic" conception of society views human relations in terms of drama because people develop modes of social appeal as "actors."[33] While a speaker employs rhetoric to evoke the desired response in listeners, for the persuasion to be successful, the listeners must also be incorporated into the dramatic moment; they must unite with the speaker in a mood of "collaborative expectancy" if there is to be "communion."[34] Burke's dramatism is grounded in a conception of human sociation as the creation of order—or the enactment of authority that takes some kind of hierarchical form. Hierarchy implies social divisions (e.g., distinctions of class, gender, race, age, status, etc.). Such divisions inevitably produce tensions and potential threats to order that must be mitigated by communication across "difference" if a given order is to be maintained. These social separations are bridged by what Burke calls "courtship" or communication between "different kinds of beings."[35] In Burke's view, social order is not a static structure; it is a dynamic, historically variable tension between social cohesion and social division. Cohesion is achieved through communication that aims to create "consubstantiality" within and between different social groups.[36] Consubstantiality, or an acting together facilitated by symbols, occurs when individuals accept the terms that endow a particular hierarchy with the authority to uphold order. Individuals may feel themselves to be consubstantial with the society at large, or with particular segments of society, and the latter identification may be opposed to the former.

The degree to which a social group considers a given order to be "reasonable" is historically and socially contingent; in any particular period individuals and groups may take up attitudes of "acceptance," "doubt," or "rejection" toward the established hierarchy or parts thereof.[37] Burke argues that the study of rhetoric begins from the principle of social division because persuasion is concerned with the creation of consubstantiality; it therefore implies an initial separation. Such separations are, in fact, "the invitation to rhetoric."[38] I see televangelism as a form of rhetoric that seeks to create a particular consubstantiality—a sacred community characterized by a specific set of qualities and attitudes—and that does so by employing identifiable rhetorical forms and appeals.

Rhetoric's three aspects are identification, persuasion, and address. Persuasion is a "motive" in quest of identification between speaker and auditor—it is an invitation to accept a particular consubstantiality.[39] Sizer, using Burke, argues that 19th century gospel hymns were "arguments" for a particular interpretation of Christianity that appealed to listeners to identify with a specific social/religious community. Rhetoric, she suggests, "involves that aspect of the human condition whereby people express and recognize their mutual affinities, their belonging to the same group, to this group rather than that."[40] Thus, when a television evangelist says to his audience, "Since we're going to be spending eternity together in Heaven, why don't you all turn to your neighbors and love them up a little?" he is creating both an individual identification for each listener, and a consubstantiality of believers against unsaved others.[41] By starting from the principle of social division, Burkeian criticism looks for the ways in which particular consubstantiations are symbolically constructed. As Sizer says, this approach "seeks to make clear what the 'identifications' are, and how the 'belonging' is conceived."[42] Identifications are born in strife, according to Duncan; they arise from tensions within a particular social order and are potential challenges to (or doubts about) the legitimacy of that order.[43] Persuasion, then, presupposes difference or division because rhetoric is unnecessary between identical beings. If everyone were already "saved," television ministers would be superfluous.

The social nature of address is a key component of rhetoric because persuasion is pointless or impotent without an audience. The "paradox of all address," Duncan says, is that the hearer "alone can give us success."[44] The listener must be persuaded to enter into collaboration with a speaker's identifications. Both as speakers and as auditors, we are involved in symbolic activity: We speak to bring others into accord with our thinking, and as listeners we make others' words effective in the world. The television minister's words are impotent unless he can elicit identification with his audience. For example, when Jimmy Swaggart exclaims, "I know I'm plowing now and I'm hitting paydirt," he is both summoning the congregation's collaboration and reacting to the audience's response to his exhortations. He is assuming a consubstantiality in the making.[45]

Effective persuasion is that which resonates with a listener's "patterns of experience." These patterns, which vary between historical periods as well as between and within cultures and individuals, arise from our specific place in a social and cultural environment. They are the lenses through which every concrete experience of ourselves, others, and the world are refracted. In this sense, Burke says, patterns of experience are "creative;" we use these patterns to give meaning to our actions in the past and present and to make meaningful our intention to act in the future.[46] A speaker who wishes to affect our actions—to persuade us in a Burkeian sense—must take our patterns of experience into consideration in choosing the form of his or her appeal. As Burke argues, form in communication is "the arousing and fulfillment of desires.[47] A speaker has to "say the right thing" by employing a form that arouses our desires; this implies knowing what we consider desirable and fashioning a rhetoric that speaks to that desire and promises fulfillment.[48] This invocation of desire occurs in the realm of symbols. Burke says a symbol is most powerful and appealing when the speaker's and listener's patterns of experience closely coincide. A speaker's effectiveness depends on the ability to convert his or her patterns of experience into a symbolic form that corresponds to those of the audience—to initiate a merging of identifications or communion.

The conversion of experiential pattern into symbolic form operates ideologically—a speaker uses the beliefs and judgments of the audience (its ideology) to get an effect (to persuade). Persuasive communication manipulates (in the sense of handling) a listener's ideological assumptions, and does so by employing subject matter and forms that have been "charged" by auditors' previous experience.[49] For example, when Swaggart refers to San Francisco, his audience already brings to those words an ensemble of connotations penetrated with biblical symbolism. The "evilness" of that city, as a modern representation of Sodom and Gomorrah, is "fact" rather than interpretation, a corroboration of the literal truth of Scripture. Swaggart draws on the symbolic "charge" invested in the words San Francisco by his audience (e.g., their shared hostility to homosexuality). The city thus symbolizes the degeneracy of modern society; it is a "sign" of the imminence of the "last days" before the Second Coming. By employing this symbolic charge, Swaggart invokes the audience's collaboration by endowing events with a pattern of significance constructed from sacred symbols that correspond to his auditors' moods and motivations. To thus guide listeners' expectations, according to Burke, is to already have some conquest over them.[50]

Burke contends that the rhetoric of identification is also a key element of socialization. Social institutions (school, church, family, media, etc.) are persuasive insofar as they "educate" us to accept the given order as reasonable. We participate in this "education" (or become "indoctrinated") through the process of internal address—we complete the process of persuasion from within by addressing ourselves.[51] Burke holds that without this interior rhetoric, we would remain partially "outside" the dominant order. Thus, our support for the existing order necessarily depends on the degree to which our internal rhetoric corresponds to external forms of persuasion. Because identification is based on original social divisions, the degree of correspondence between internal and external rhetoric is variable. Every rhetorical situation poses a specific set of problems to a speaker. To be successful, he or she must say the right thing, but the right thing is contingent upon the context and audience. In Burke's view, this contingency inevitably produces a certain kind of "anguish in communication."[52] To attain the audience's collaboration, a speaker must consider the listeners' histories, their patterns of experience, and their symbolic frames of reference. Identification, or communion, occurs when a speaker employs a "voice from without that can speak in the language of the voice within."[53]

My aim in this study is to identify these two "voices" through a process of careful listening—to map out the relationship of belief, speaker, and listener in televised evangelical rhetoric. I suggested earlier that evangelicalism, as a symbolic system, offers a particular solution to the problem of meaning and simultaneously creates a framework of significance and a set of interpretive strategies (a "sacred canopy") for adherents. Burke says that rhetoric functions as a "strategy for encompassing a situation."[54] Sizer uses this notion to understand gospel hymns as "strategies" or "problem-solving tools." The hymns, she suggests, "represent strategies for solving general problems about the relations of human beings to each other and to the spiritual forces or beings of their universe."[55] Televangelism also serves this function. Robertson and Swaggart construct, out of symbolic materials, a particular type of sacred space, as well as specific conceptions of the creator, the ideal inhabitants of that space, and the kinds of enemies that threaten it. Televangelists and their audiences, therefore, must cooperatively create a universe of sacred meaning (a consubstantiality) if evangelical rhetoric is to become symbolic action.

My analysis of the symbolic universe of televangelism focuses on the nature of evangelicalism's conception of order and the place of the individual believer in that order; the identifications offered by Swaggart and Robertson (what are the ideal qualities of an evangelical Christian, what qualities constitute membership in the sacred community); the divisions that give that community its distinctive character (what qualities are ascribed to outsiders); the rhetorical style (methods, modes, and structures of appeal—in what terms is the "right thing" expressed); and the character of internal forms of persuasion (the institutions and social formations that support the message of these television ministers). In considering televangelism as a cultural form, I am interested in the choice of language (metaphors, themes), in the strategies and structure of the rhetoric, and in extraverbal forms of communication (music, visuals, gesture, setting, relations between speaker and auditors). It is on this symbolic edifice that a specific universe of sacred meaning is built. This symbolic system is persuasive to the extent that it provides believers with a frame of orientation and devotion that makes sense of the world and of their place in it.

I believe television evangelism operates much like the gospel hymns in Sizer's study. The hymns, she contends, "articulate a structure of the world and simultaneously create a community with its own specific identity and a technique of transcendence."[56] In other words, the rhetoric of conservative evangelicalism, whether found in gospel music or TV programs, provides a particular set of answers to the problems of being and meaning. To make those answers effective, television ministers are dependent on their audience. Communion can take place only when viewers accept the identifications offered by televangelists. Because the anguish of communication arises in the relationship between speakers and listeners, the possibility of communion resides in the degree to which the form of these programs resonate for both parties in the conversation.

RELIGIOUS TELEVISION AS CULTURAL FORM: THE PROBLEM OF HISTORY

To ask how cultural forms, such as TV evangelism, create a particular set of symbolic meanings is to address what Gitlin calls "the totality of [the] process of production, signification and consumption." He argues that the meaning of any cultural form is ultimately created in the process of its reception:

> The act of consuming appropriates and completes the work: it activates from among the work's range of possible meanings— those that are actually present in the work—those that will embody what the work means, to a given social group and to individuals within it.[57]

The question, then, is what meanings do these programs propose and how are they constructed in a way that will resonate for specific viewers? This brings us back to my original question concerning the structure of appeal of evangelical television. Where does this appeal reside, and how and why does it become effective for certain viewers? I believe that the appeal resides in the history of conservative evangelicalism which shapes the collective memories of believers and provides a basis for identification and belonging, and that it becomes effective through, and is embodied in, the form of the communication.

I noted earlier that Swaggart's crusade and Robertson's talk show represent opposite ends of the spectrum of evangelical television. Frankl argues that this polarity stems from the degree to which the programs have remained faithful to their cultural antecedent, 19th-century mass revivals. Swaggart's Sunday crusade, Frankl argues, is most faithful to that historical ancestor, while the "700 Club," a weekday talk show/news magazine, has strayed furthest from its revivalist roots. Of all evangelical programs she studied, Frankl says, the "700 Club" is the "most influenced by television."[58] She makes this argument in terms of the degree to which the programs have adapted themselves to the imperatives of commercial broadcasting (demands of format, ratings, flow, etc.).

I agree that Swaggart's crusade and Pat Robertson's talk show represent different poles of evangelical television; this polarity is grounded in orthodox Protestantism's two main responses to the historical process of socioeconomic modernization in the last century— those of separation and accommodation. Swaggart's and Robertson's uses of television and relations to revivalism reflect their separatist and accommodationist theologies. Further, the form of their programs embodies this polarity. The crusade is rooted in the 19th-century cultural form of urban revivalism; it has adapted television as a means to amplify and disseminate a more traditional, separatist form of evangelical Christianity. The talk show is grounded in the 20th-century cultural form of television itself; it has adapted theology to fit the demands of the medium and offers a more contemporary, accommodative version of conservative Christianity.[59] In short, Swaggart's program is televised religion while Robertson's show is religion-ized TV. This study attempts to show how I arrived at this distinction through my analysis of the programs' forms as responses to, and products of, the history of orthodox Protestantism.

Historical analysis is a continuous interweaving of past and present in which each moment progressively illuminates the other; neither moment is static because the process of investigation itself yields new insights about what has been and what is. Historical method is thus more an act of imagination than the application of a fixed set of techniques. Lipsitz identifies three general approaches to the historical study of mass communication: apparatus-centered criticism, socially based criticism, and textually oriented criticism.[60] These focus on the technological and economic structures of media the social context in which communication is created and received and the formal and substantial properties of cultural texts as they shape and reflect past and present society.

For most historians of communication, Lipsitz says, these approaches "overlap." In fact, overlap is not a strong enough term to describe the practical unity of these moments. While we may, as Lipsitz does, isolate apparatus, society, and text to draw theoretical distinctions, in practice they are inseparable. The structure of appeal of religious television issues simultaneously from the apparatus of television, the historical roots and contemporary manifestations of conservative evangelicalism, and the structure and substance of the programs (texts) themselves. The problem faced by cultural analysts/historians is to find a way to preserve that unity—to discover the glue that joins text, society and apparatus into a meaningful whole.

Andrew notes that the meaning of any particular cultural product results from "work"—both that done on the text in the activities of production and consumption, and that done by the text on its creators and receivers: "Everything results from a mechanics of work: the work of ideology, the work of a certain language designed to bring psyche and society into coincidence, and the work of technology enabling that language to operate."[61]

The structure of appeal of evangelical television may be conceived as the embodiment of such work and the programs as the site at which speakers and listeners come together to carry out this labor. Because the text is the bridge connecting speaker and listener, cultural analysis is also always the study of social relationships.

I suggest that form is the glue that unifies text, apparatus, and society; that the interpretation of form inevitably exposes the "work" done by speaker, text, and listener in the creation of meaning; and that the analysis of form necessarily locates us in history because cultural forms themselves are historically created and determined. Although this is an argument for the need to analyze the form of cultural texts, it is not a call for a return to formalist abstraction.[62] Johnson points out that formalism's shortcoming is not so much its tendency toward abstraction; in fact, he says, "we do end up with better, more explanatory histories, if we have comprehended, more abstractly, some of the forms and relations which constitute them."[63] Rather, problems arise when texts are lifted out of the historical conditions and relationships in which they are created and received.

The concept of form I am using resists this kind of ahistorical abstraction. Instead, it assumes a dynamic, creative relationship between speaker and listener, between text and reader, and between cultural form and history. The interpretation of form is a dialectical endeavor because it seeks to synthesize these relationships. This perspective insists, first, that form is neither the blueprint that dictates content nor the packaging selected for that content after the fact. Rather, as Davis says, "form *is* content."[64] Second, it holds that a cultural form cannot be separated from its history, from the work done by specific speakers and listeners to construct social meanings for that history, or from the work done by the text to bring those actors into a relationship in a concrete time and place. In this sense, the text is studied not as an end in itself, but as a means to understand "the subjective or cultural forms which it realizes and makes available."[65] The form of an utterance or text, then, is the vehicle for the flow of meaning; it embodies the speaker's intentions and the patterns of the auditors' experience, and it issues from the sociohistorical ground that permits speaker, text and listener to come together in the creation of meaning.

One of Burke's most valuable contributions to the study of communication is his insistence on the dynamic relation of form and content.[66] For Burke, form is not the outer shell of a message added on after we decide what we want to say, but is "a way of experiencing" intrinsic to our character as symbol-using beings.[67] The forms of art and other cultural products parallel and draw upon the "formal patterns which distinguish our experience." These patterns "apply in art, since they apply outside of art."[68] The appeal of any cultural text necessarily implicates the audience because cultural forms "have a prior existence in the experience of the person hearing or reading the work of art."[69] Thus, cultural forms "exercise formal potentialities of the reader. They enable the mind to follow processes amenable to it."[70] In this way, Burke says, "form is the appeal."[71]

It is important to note here that while symbolicity—the human capacity to construct and interpret symbolic forms—is a transhistorical condition of being human, the potential resonance of a particular communicative form is historically and culturally specific. Symbolic forms are created under concrete historical conditions and thus speak to those people who share that history. As Lipsitz says, a historical approach to the study of communication starts from the premise that "memory shapes individual and collective efforts to construct meaning, and they posit readers of cultural texts as historical beings who make meaning out of the present in dialogue with the past and in anticipation of the future."[72]

As I argue in the program analysis, Swaggart and Robertson (and their respective television flocks) have very different positions within the history of conservative evangelicalism. Both men appeal to viewers' collective memory in shaping their communication; those memories conflict, however, to the extent that Swaggart, Robertson and their respective audiences do not share identical pasts nor anticipate the same futures.

The appeal of a cultural form is, therefore, intrinsic to the quest for identification between speaker and listener. Communication is most powerful and appealing when the speaker's and listeners' patterns of experience closely coincide, and this coincidence includes a shared set of symbolic materials. For example, Swaggart uses the cultural form of folk preaching not because he discovered it guarantees the best TV ratings, but because his own experience and theology, his communicative motives, and the experiences and expectations of his audience demand this form. Folk preaching is the organizing principle that determines the function, structure, and purpose of Swaggart's communication. From this perspective, form is not just one part of an utterance or text, but is, in Davis' words,

> the synthesizing principle of structure which makes every component in the [text] a functional part of it. Form does not arise out of the mere combination of parts; it is, rather, that prior principle which, imposed on them, determines their relationship.[73]

I find this conception of form compelling because it was by analyzing the form of these two evangelical programs that I began to perceive relationships among the personae of Swaggart and Robertson, their choice of formats, their key themes, the structure and strategies of their appeals, their intended audiences, and their place in evangelical history and theology. My analytical approach resembles Geertz's "thick description."[74] The methods I use range from analyzing the modes of address, to describing camera placement, to exploring the function of metaphors in the texts, because all these elements, and more, contribute to the distinct forms of the two programs and, therefore, to their appeal.

Ultimately, the success of the appeals depends on viewers' willingness to accept the identifications offered—to enter into the conversation. Through this identification, viewers simultaneously create meanings for the programs and for themselves. Sartre contends that we invest the world around us with meaning through our dual roles as agents and objects of signification. We inhabit a universe of signs that have been designated as meaningful by past and present activity. While the past appears to be inert, already accomplished, and done with, in fact it is very much alive. Sartre reminds us that what appear to be

> objective significations, which seem to exist all alone and which are put upon particular men, are also created by men. And the men themselves, who put them on and present them to others, can appear as signified *only by making themselves signifying*.[75]

Thus, we are both signifying agents through our current actions and the signified objects of our individual and collective histories. In this way, our response to cultural forms is part of an ongoing dialogue between historical and contemporary experience. What this means for the analysis of religious television is that we must examine not only how the programs seek to establish meanings for the audience, and how viewers endow both the programs and their lives with meaning, but also how both processes are shaped by history. The creation of meaning is always a solution to the problems posed by a specific text in concrete historical circumstances. This study attempts to understand these two religous programs as responses to a particular historical problem—the collision of cultural modernization and traditional religious belief. It asks how these responses have become embedded in distinct, religious communicative forms, and why these forms resonate for different audiences. That is, I am seeking to interpret and reconstruct the dialogue between past and present by examining the meanings people make of the meanings they are given.

NOTES TO CHAPTER 2

1. Clifford Geertz, "Ethos, World-view and the Analysis of Sacred Symbols, " *Antioch Review* (December 1957): p. 436; Clifford Geertz, "Deep Play: Notes on the Balinese Cockfight," in C. Geertz, ed., *Myth, Symbol and Culture* (New York: Norton, 1971), p. 16.

2. Clifford Geertz, "Ritual and Social Change: A Javanese Example," in William A. Lessa and Evon Z. Vogt, eds., *Reader in Comparative Religion: An Anthropological Approach*, 2nd ed. (New York: Harper & Row, 1965), p. 549.

3. Clifford Geertz, *The Interpretation of Cultures* (New York: Basic Books, 1973), pp. 9, 27.

4. Abraham Heschel, *Who is Man?* (Stanford: Stanford, CA: Stanford University Press, 1968), pp. 50, 52.

5. Max Weber, *The Sociology of Religion* (Boston: Beacon Press, 1964), p. 117.

6. John Wilson, *Public Religion in American Culture* (Philadelphia, PA: Temple University Press, 1979), p. 24.

7. Peter Berger, *The Sacred Canopy: Elements of a Sociological Theory of Religion* (Garden City, NY: Doubleday, 1967), p. 33.

8. Erich Fromm, *Man For Himself* (Greenwich, CT: Fawcett, 1947), p. 47.

9. Heschel, *Who Is Man?*, p. 55.

10. Clifford Geertz, "Religion as a Cultural System," in William A. Lessa and Evon Z. Vogt, eds., *Reader in Comparative Religion*, 4th ed. (New York: Harper and Row, 1979), pp. 80-81.

11. Ibid., p. 83.

12. Ibid., pp. 81, 82. For the distinction between the concepts "model of" and "model for" see p. 81.

13. Ibid., pp. 83, 85.

14. Hugh Dalziel Duncan, *Communication and Social Order* (New York: Bedminster Press, 1962). George Kennedy, in *New Testament Interpretation Through Rhetorical Criticism* (Chapel Hill and London: University of North Carolina Press, 1984), also discusses the rhetorical or persuasive character of political discourse, philosophical systems, and modern science. See p. 158.

15. Geertz, "Religion as a Cultural System," p. 89.

16. James W. Carey, "Mass Communication Research and Cultural Studies: An American View," in James Curran, Michael Gurevitch, and Janet Woollacott, eds., *Mass Communication and Society* (Beverly Hills, CA: Sage, 1979), p. 415.

17. Ibid., pp. 412-13.

18. Geertz, "Religion as a Cultural System," p. 87.

19. Contemporary nonreligious "rituals" provide similar unity and identity to participants. Consider the cohesive function of public ceremonies (e.g., presidential addresses, the renovation of the Statue of Liberty, parades, civic assemblies), popular culture (e.g., Superbowl, Live Aid, Hands Across America, fan clubs), consumption (e.g., shopping and mall cruising), and even television viewing itself. For a discussion of television as ritual, see Gregor Goethals, *The TV Ritual: Worship at the Video Altar* (Boston: Beacon Press, 1981).

20. Sandra S. Sizer, *Gospel Hymns and Social Religion: The Rhetoric of Nineteenth Century Revivalism* (Philadelphia, PA: Temple University Press, 1978).

21. This form is not used by all religious broadcasters; Robertson's "700 Club" follows quite a different pattern, and as I argue in Chapter 9, does not qualify as a religious ritual.

22. See, for example, Stuart Hall and Tony Jefferson, *Resistance Through Rituals* (London: Hutchinson, 1978); Dick Hebdige, *Subculture: The Meaning of Style* (London: Methuen, 1979); Mike Brake, *The Sociology of Youth Culture and Youth Subcultures* (London: Routledge and Kegan Paul, 1980); and Paul Willis, *Profane Culture* (London: Routledge and Kegan Paul, 1978).

23. Sizer, *Gospel Hymns*, p. 52.

24. Robley E. Whitson, *The Coming Convergence in World Religion* (New York: Newman Press, 1971), p. 8; quoted in John H. Morgan, "The Concept of 'Meaning' in Religion and Culture: Toward a Dialogue Between Theology and Anthropology," in J. Morgan, ed., *Understanding Religion and Culture: Anthropological and Theological Perspectives* (Washington, DC: University Press of America, 1979), p. 9.

25. William G. McLoughlin, Jr., *Modern Revivalism: Charles Grandison Finney to Billy Graham* (New York: Ronald Press, 1959), p. 466.

26. Ernest Sandeed develops the concept of parallel institutions in "Fundamentalism and American Identity," *Annals of the American Academy of Political and Social Science* 387 (january 1970): pp. 56-65.

27. Robert Cathcart, "Defining Social Movements by their Rhetorical Form," *Central States Speech Journal* 31 (Winter 1980): p. 268.

28. Ibid., p. 267.

29. Geertz, "Religion as a Cultural System," p. 87.

30. Kenneth Burke's works most relevant to this study are: *Philosophy of Literary Form*, 2nd. ed. (Baton Rouge: Louisiana State University Press, 1967); *Language as Symbolic Action* (Berkeley: University of California Press, 1966); *Counter-Statement* (Berkeley: University of California Press, 1968); *Rhetoric of Motives* (Berkeley: University of California Press, 1969); and *Permanence and Change: An*

Anatomy of Purpose (Berkeley: University of California Press, 1969). For examples of applications of Burke's ideas to the study of social movements and rhetorical criticism, see Leland M. Griffin, "A Dramatic Theory of the Rhetoric of Social Movements," in William H. Reuckart, ed., *Critical Responses to Kenneth Burke* (Minneapolis: University of Minnesota Press, 1969); Leland M. Griffin, "On Studying Social Movements," *Central States Speech Journal* 31 (Winter 1980): pp. 225-232; Herbert W. Simons, "Requirements, Problems, and Strategies: A Theory of Persuasion for Social Movements," *Quarterly Journal of Speech* 56 (February 1970): pp. 1-11; Ralph R. Smith and Russell R. Windes, "The Rhetoric of Mobilization: Implications for the Study of Movements," *Southern Speech Communication Journal* 42 (Fall 1976): pp. 1-19; Dan F. Hahn and Ruth M. Gonchar, "Studying Social Movements: A Rhetorical Methodology," *The Speech Teacher* 20 (1971): pp. 44-52.

31. Burke, *Language as Symbolic Action*, pp. 16-52.

32. Burke, *Rhetoric of Motives*, p. 43.

33. Duncan discusses Burke's dramatism in *Communication and Social Order*, pp. 109-120; see also Burke, *Language as Symbolic Action*, pp. 44-45.

34. Burke, *Rhetoric of Motives*, pp. 58, 177.

35. Ibid., pp. 115, 180; see also his discussion of persuasion as courtship, pp. 177 and 208-211.

36. Ibid., p. 55, for a discussion of consubstantiality and identification.

37. Duncan, *Communication and Social Order*, p. 111.

38. Burke, *Rhetoric of Motives*, p. 25.

39. Identification does not mean identical—to seek to make an identification is to imply an original division or lack of consubstantiality.

40. Sizer, *Gospel Hymns*, p. 17.

41. Statement by Paul Crouch, president of Trinity Broadcasting Network, in a broadcast of his "Praise the Lord" program, October 16, 1986, KTBW, Channel 20, Tacoma, WA.

42. Sizer, *Gospel Hymns*, p. 17.

43. Duncan, *Communication and Social Order*, p. 158.

44. Ibid., p. 165.

45. "Jimmy Swaggert Telecast," October 26, 1986.

46. Burke, *Counter-Statement*, p. 152.

47. Ibid., p. 124.

48. Burke, *Permanence and Change*, p. 50.

49. Burke, *Counter-Statement*, p. 165.

50. Ibid., p. 178.

51. Burke, *Rhetoric of Motives*, pp. 38-39.

52. Duncan, *Communication and Social Order*, p. 165.

53. Burke, *Rhetoric of Motives*, p. 39.

54. Burke, *Philosophy of Literary Form*, p. 1.

55. Sizer, *Gospel Hymns*, pp. 14, 16.

56. Ibid., pp. 18-19.

57. Todd Gitlin, "Television's Screens: Hegemony in Transition," in Michael Apple, ed., *Cultural and Economic Reproduction in Education* (London: Routledge and Kegan Paul, 1982), p. 204.

58. Frankl, *Televangelism*, p. 117.

59. Stewart Hoover concurs with this assessment of the "700 Club." See *Mass Media Religion*, pp. 77-79.

60. George Lipsitz, "'This Ain't No Sideshow': Historians and Media Studies," *Critical Studies in Mass Communication* 5 (1988): p. 150.

61. Dudley Andrew, *Concepts in Film Theory* (New York: Oxford University Press, 1984), p. 15.

62. I refer here to literary New Criticism and to structuralist and poststructuralist textual analysis. Both approaches tend to view cultural forms as synchronic, self-contained systems of meaning and thus to neglect the historical circumstances and social relationships that brought those forms into existence and continue to exert changes upon them. See Stuart Hall, "Recent Developments in Theories of Language and Ideology: A Critical Note," in S. Hall et al., eds. (London: Hutchinson, 1983), pp. 157-162; Fredric Jameson, *The Prison-House of Language: A Critical Accounting of Structuralism and Russian Formalism* (Princeton, NJ: Princeton University Press, 1972); and Richard Johnson, "What is Cultural Studies Anyway?," *Social Text* 16 (1986): pp. 38-80.

63. Johnson, "What is Cultural Studies?" p. 62.

64. Walter Davis, *The Act of Interpretation* (Chicago: University of Chicago Press, 1978), p. 229, emphasis added.

65. Johnson, "What is Cultural Studies?" p. 62.

66. Walter Davis, *Inwardness and Existence: Subjectivity In/And Hegel, Heidegger, Marx and Freud* (Madison: University of Wisconsin Press, 1989), p. 229.

67. Burke, *Counter-Statement*, p. 143.

68. Ibid., p. 142. Fredric Jameson makes a similar argument for narrative, which he calls "a specific mode of thinking the world" and "one of the basic categorical forms through which we apprehend realities in time." Jameson, "The Symbolic Inference; or, Kenneth Burke and Ideological Analysis," *Critical Inquiry* 4 (1978): p. 510.

69. Burke, *Counter-Statement*, p. 143.

70. Ibid., pp. 142-143.

71. Ibid., p. 138.

72. Lipsitz, "Historians and Media Studies, " p. 154.

73. Davis, *Act of Interpretation*, pp. 1-2.

74. Geertz, *Interpretation of Cultures* (New York: Basic Books, 1973).

75. Jean-Paul Sartre, *Search for a Method*, trans. Hazel E. Barnes (New York: Alfred A. Knopf, 1963; reprint ed., New York: Vintage, 1968), pp. 165-166n.

3

The Defense of the Faith: The Dual Historical Projects of Conservative Evangelicalism

Evangelicalism has been "overlooked, or discounted, stereotyped and patronized" by social scientists whose modern biases prevent their taking this religious perspective seriously, according to Warner. He claims, "It is as if evangelicals were denizens of the zoo."[1] The inability to consider evangelicalism as a legitimate contemporary worldview is itself a product of the modernization process. The gulf between contemporary sociological analysis and traditional religious interpretation indicates the extent to which religion has been displaced from the public to private domain. For evangelicals, this is simply another sign of contemporary society's loss of its essential meaning and direction. In the 19th century, science and God had not yet parted company. Far from being exotic, evangelicalism was the dominant form of American religious belief and expression.[2] An analysis of the meaning of contemporary evangelicalism must therefore begin by examining the loss of its cultural hegemony.

Evangelicalism inherited from the Protestant Reformation a belief in the primacy of the Bible as the Word of God and an individuated conception of salvation. By opposing the mediating role of the institutional (Roman) church, clergy, and liturgy, Protestantism established a new understanding of the relationship between worshiper and creator. This new religious perspective placed the individual directly before God and made him or her personally responsible for winning entry into the Kingdom of Heaven. The guide to this journey was the Bible, which had been wrested from Rome's control and made widely accessible through the new medium of printing. Corporate guilt, corporate penance, and corporate redemption—concepts basic to Roman Catholicism—were rejected in the Protestant worldview. Hill contends that Protestantism "popularized the idea of the individual spiritual balance sheet" and created a universe of "individuals fighting for their own salvation, no longer working out its salvation, as it had cultivated its fields, in common."[3] As Hill and other writers have noted, the rise of Protestantism is intimately connected to the development of printing: "Protestantism depended on the new craft of printing. The widespread dissemination of vernacular translations of the Bible, some in pocket editions, made possible individual study of the Scriptures."[4]

Thus, one's ties to the sacred were rerouted around elaborate ecclesiastical structures. Bible reading became a private activity, conducted in the homes of Europe's growing, literate, middle class. Not only were the writings of Protestant reformers such as Luther disseminated through the medium of printing, but the explosive increase of Bibles in vernacular permitted and encouraged new interpretations of the meaning of God's intentions. Protestantism was born and has developed as a religious system highly oriented to "the Word;" its emphasis is more textual than liturgical. Goethals notes this scriptural emphasis in 16th century reformers John Calvin and Urlrich Zwingli who rejected all visual and material supports for belief, including icons and sacred architecture: "The reformers replaced images with the Word, both spoken and written. The Bible was the principal guide to liturgy and to the communication of faith."[5] This doctrine of *sola scriptura* became one of the cardinal tenets of evangelicalism.[6]

Heiler, in an analyis of the history and psychology of prayer, characterizes evangelicalism as a "prophetic" religious form. Prophetic religion holds that God reveals His will through His word, hence, the Bible's centrality in discerning divine intention. Revelation is seen as "an objective, historical fact, a universally binding communication of the divine will" that is made known to believers through Scripture. The believer's "experience of salvation rests on the proclamation of divine revelation;" Christian witness or testimony thus becomes an essential component of the salvific journey.[7] Sin in prophetic religion "lies in a breach of the God-ordained order of moral values, in a revolt against God's holy will." Salvation is the act that heals this separation; it is the "restoration of communion with God."[8] In Burke's terms, salvation occurs through a communicative act (interpretation and testimony of God's will) that creates a sacred identification and establishes a consubstantiality of believers. This prophetic quality of evangelicalism is manifested in its conception of authority, its ethics, its practices, and its attitude toward other symbolic systems.

Modern American evangelicalism grows out of this prophetic, scripturally grounded tradition. Hunter notes that the evangelical worldview is rooted in the Reformation, European and American Puritanism, and the impulses of the Great Awakenings in the U.S., and "has striven to remain doctrinally faithful to this general conservative tradition."[9] Hunter finds in evangelicalism traces of ascetic Protestantism, including the Calvinist doctrine of divine election, German pietism's emphasis on spiritual perfectibility on earth, Methodism's stress on experiential personal conversion, and the Baptist doctrines of personal salvation and a believers' church. These various theological strands, and the way they are interpreted in light of the contemporary cultural order, account for much of the internal tension and division within evangelicalism today.

In the introductory chapter I noted the difficulty of neatly defining evangelicalism and evangelicals, as have many students of the subject.[10] Hunter's definition of the core doctrines and characteristic behavior of evangelicals is useful because it is concise, yet broad enough to include the many variants within the belief system. Evangelicalism holds that the Bible is the inerrant word of God, that Christ is divine, and that salvation is achieved through the efficacy of Christ's life, death, and physical resurrection. Evangelical Christianity is characterized by an "individuated and experiential orientation toward spiritual salvation, and religiosity in general, and by the conviction of the necessity of actively attempting to proselytize all non-believers to the tenets of the evangelical belief system."[11] Evangelical television carries on this tradition of proselytism, although both the form and the goals of this persuasion take on specific characteristics in different religious programs.

REVIVALISM AS RITUAL

To understand contemporary evangelicalism and its use of television as a proselytizing or persuasive tool, we must first consider televangelism's 19th century progenitor—the religious revival. Hunter says the revival was central to religious life in the 1800s and that the expression of religiosity in revivalism "largely accounted for the unity of the style and substance of Protestant life in this period."[12] McLoughlin, Jr. argues that mass religious revivals in the United States have stemmed from a distinct configuration of social conditions: an intense theological reorientation within the churches; inter- and intrachurch conflicts involving prominent religious personalities; a widespread sense of social and spiritual upheaval; and a general feeling among the nonchurched that Christianity was relevant to individual and social problems.[13] That is, revivalism occurs in periods of crisis in the meaning of individual and corporate existence—crises that are related to disjunctures between social institutions and the larger cultural order.

The camp meetings that inaugurated the Second Great Awakening at the turn of the 19th century exhibited the emotionalism, group fervor, and dramatic conversions that have become "part of the inherited lore of American revivalism."[14] The campstyle revivals also signaled an important shift in Protestant belief; the Puritan concept of predestination was being replaced by Arminian ideas of free will through the spread of Methodism, which stressed the role of the individual in achieving his or her salvation. This increased emphasis on the individual in religion corresponded to the increasingly individualistic character of the expanding market economy. Methodist teachings insisted that individuals could attain spiritual "perfection" through the "crisis experience" of conversion. Burke would argue that perfectionism is not the unique property of evangelical Protestantism, but a feature of human existence. Human beings, Burke says, are "separated from [their] natural condition by instruments of [their] own making, goaded by the spirit of hierarchy (or moved by the sense of order) and rotten with perfection."[15] The desire for order, or perfection, and the inevitability of error, lead to guilt. Because guilt is intolerable, Griffin notes, human beings "will dream of salvation, the transformation of their condition, a state of Redemption; will envision, consciously or unconsciously . . . an ideal Order—'heaven,' paradise, the 'good society,' Utopia."[16] Perfectionism infiltrated Protestant thought and practice through the waves of revivalism that swept the country in the first half of the century.[17] According to Pentecostal historian Vinson Synan, "By 1840, perfectionism was becoming one of the central themes of American social, intellectual and religious life."[18]

This shift in theology also signaled changes in the function of revivals and the role of the preacher. Puritanism had seen revivals as spontaneous outpourings of religious sentiment directly initiated by God. By mid-19th century, revivals had taken on a new character. They were consciously orchestrated events intended to instigate the conversion experience. Frankl's work suggests that the revival took on new forms and characteristics under the guidance of Charles Grandison Finney who founded the "modern urban revival." During this period, she argues, revivalism "developed distinctive patterns of organization, complete with specialized roles, routinized traditions, and rituals of conversion as well as distinct beliefs and religious values."[19] That is, revival was rationalized. The preacher acquired a different and more central practice in religious life through this new social institution. He was no longer a pastor tending a flock, but a goad and a beacon on the road to sanctification. This more active role was also characteristic of television ministers. Within the context of prayer, exhortation, and testimony, the congregation and preacher worked together on the task of individual and social salvation. The revival became both the medium for experiencing conversion or rebirth, and a ritual of transformation. To call revivalism a ritual is to consider it as a site for the construction of sacred meaning. The "language" of revivals—prayer, testimony, weeping, moaning, dancing, and so on—symbolically constructed a community and provided a "technique of transcendence."[20]

During the 19th century, revivalism was institutionalized, according to McLoughlin.[21] The process of institutionalization, he argues, created "a simple, almost mechanical outlet for Protestantism's pietistic fervor" which at its most extreme tended toward "empty formalism, bland uniformity, social conformity, and political conservatism."[22] Revivalism—both as an institution and a ritual context—continues to be a key cultural form within evangelicalism. But because religious institutions must fit the social environment in which they operate if they are to survive, contemporary revivalism has evolved historically with the adoption of new media of communication. It has also been forced to adapt to the demands of those media, as the analysis of specific evangelical programs shows.

THE TRANSITION FROM PROGRESS TO APOCALYPSE

The world view of mid-19th century Protestantism was rendered meaningful by its ability to account for the shape of external social reality and the interior landscape of individual existence. A stress on personal piety asceticism and a missionary attitude that made the progress of Christianity identical to that of American civilization and values were supported by and in turn reinforced the values of smalltown mercantilism which then characterized society. This belief in continuing spiritual and social betterment was part of a postmillennial theology[23] that held that America was leading the rest of the world toward Christian perfection—hence, the notion of the "redeemer nation."[24] The evangelical world view was legitimized not only because a majority of Americans held this religious perspective, but also because it offered a sacred explanatory framework for conducting one's daily life; Protestantism seemed to be an accurate representation of reality insofar as social "progress" (the growth of a Christian community through revivals and mission efforts) corresponded to God's plan (redeeming humanity through Christ). The cultural hegemony of evangelicalism was supported and extended through the education system, voluntary associations, and political institutions. In Hunter's words:

> The notion of the quest for a Christian America was .. firmly institutionalized. Local, state, and federal governments, dominated in the main by people who shared this conviction, were thus structured to encourage its ascendance in the culture. . . . the result was the establishment of a uniquely Protestant style of life and work (and therefore, world view) in American society as a whole, even non-Protestant portions of it[25]

Marsden portrays post-Civil War Protestantism as imbued with post-millennial confidence about the inevitability of spiritual progress. All social problems were first and foremost shortcomings of the individual which could be corrected by the social reform that would logically flow from individual spiritual rebirth enacted in revivals and missionary efforts. The guide for correct living was the Bible, seen as "the highest and all-sufficient source of authority."[26] Evangelicals' confidence in the infallibility of Scripture was bolstered by their Baconian view of science, which held that the universe was governed by a rational system of laws created by God. The role of science was to discover those laws which would complement and corroborate biblical teachings. In Marsden's words, "The old order of American Protestantism was based on the interrelationship of faith, science, the Bible, morality, and civilization."[27]

This order was at first shaken and then torn asunder by a series of developments in science, philosophy, and theology, that were in turn connected to societal changes related to industrialization. Darwin's theory of natural selection, new methods of biblical criticism, philosophical idealism, and increasing social problems generated by industrial modernization presented grave challenges to postmillennial optimism. Marsden argues that these developments called forth a "new theology" (liberal Protestantism) that threatened orthodox evangelicalism.[28] The last decades of the 19th century, then, presented a crisis for the evangelical worldview—modernism. Hunter argues that both conservative Protestantism and its liberal counterpart are products of modernism; both were shaped by their particular responses—whether of resistance or accommodation—to the forces of modernization. Conservatives tended toward the former route and liberals to the latter, and this divergence created a major schism in Protestantism in the final decades of the century.

Post-Civil War revivalistic euphoria was short-lived; this is most evident in the growth of premillennial ideas. Premillennialism began to be widely accepted in the 1870s and was popularized by the successful revivals of Dwight L. Moody. Premillennialists believed that the thousand-year reign of peace and progress had not yet occurred and that Christ would return before rather than after the millennium. Thus, the present world was deteriorating materially and spiritually rather than progressing. Adherents of this perspective relied on an elaborate historical schema drawn from a passage of the Book of Daniel in the Old Testament.[29] Called dispensationalism, this conceptual system divides history into radically differentiated eras, or dispensations, that have been preordained by God. Dispensationalism holds that the world is rapidly approaching a cataclysmic encounter between God and Satan. All worldly strife, whether human or natural, is merely a sign of the coming apocalypse, and since it is mandated by God, no human effort can alter or delay its inevitability. The only consolation for Christians (that is, Protestants who have been spiritually reborn) is that they will be spared the horror of the 7-year tribulation by being taken up to Heaven or "raptured" beforehand. Following the tribulation and a terrific battle with Satan, Christ is to return and institute the promised millennium on earth.[30]

This conception of history was persuasive to the extent that it accounted for social and economic problems, made sense of challenges to Christianity associated with modernism (these were the work of the anti-Christ), validated the absolute, prophetic truth of Scripture, and restored to Protestantism a distinctly Christian view of history. These conditions hold for modern evangelicals, a majority of whom hold premillennial, dispensationalist views. It also helps explain many evangelicals' fatalist attitude toward nuclear war.[31] Premillennialism was generally pessimistic about the state of American and worldwide culture. This outlook is evident in Moody's remark: "I look upon this world as a wrecked vessel. God has given me a lifeboat and said to me, 'Moody, save all you can.'" Moody said he found premillennialism an attractive theological concept because it heightened the persuasiveness of evangelism.[32] This pessimism regarding society's future had important theological implications. The already potent individualistic character of American Protestantism became even more pronounced. The aim of evangelism was simply the saving of individual souls, since society at large was already damned. This soul-saving mission in the evangelical tradition is crucial in making sense of the message of modern televangelists, many of whom hold premillennial views. Swaggart's crusades, for example, regularly feature upbeat, joyous songs that proclaim the imminence of rapture. His view of politics and society is similarly grounded in the belief that the apocalypse is near:

> Armageddon is coming . . . They can sign all the peace treaties they
> want. They won't do any good. There are dark days coming . . . My
> Lord! I'm happy about it! He's coming again. I don't care who it
> bothers. I don't care who it troubles. It thrills my soul! [33]

Pat Robertson has historically held premillennialist views, but during
his presidential campaign he seemed to temper some of the harsher
elements of this theological position to appear more palatable to voters who did not share his eschatology. Whether this was pure political
expediency, or an actual evolution of his thought is not clear.[34]

The "Holiness Movement" was another determining factor in
the development of modern evangelicalism. Grounded in Methodist
perfectionism, "holiness" refers to the profound transformative experience whereby an individual is reborn filled with spiritual power. This
conception of sanctification was a feature of Finney's crusades from
1825 to 1835 and quickly spread throughout evangelicalism. Marsden
contends that holiness teachings revolutionized the evangelical movement in the years 1840 to 1870, and by the 1870s had penetrated the
revivalist Protestant tradition. The experience of total purification
came to be called "The Baptism of the Holy Ghost." Sermons and
hymns took up holiness themes and metaphors of total surrender;
being overwhelmed by Jesus and having one's spirit "cleansed" were
common.[35] As Burke says, "Guilt needs Redemption (for who would
not be cleansed)."[36] Moody was an important figure in the growth of
the holiness movement. Holiness teachings were disseminated
through his mass revivals and by other evangelists and teachers connected to Moody through Bible conferences. By 1890, "holiness" was a
regular feature of evangelical theology. To attain salvation, the individual had to undergo the crisis experience of spiritual rebirth; consecra-
tion involved "absolute surrender" which was described by the biblical term "yielding." To "get full of the Holy Spirit," as Moody put it,
was a necessary condition for Christian life, Christian service, and
Christian witness.[37]

THE FUNDAMENTAL SPLIT IN PROTESTANTISM

Hunter characterizes the years from 1890 to 1919 as "the disestablishment of American Protestantism."[38] The impact of modernism—evolutionary theory, higher criticism of the Bible, and idealist philosophy—
infiltrated Protestant denominations. While liberal theologians and
clergy responded by incorporating these new ideas and refashioning
religious practice around the concept of the "Social Gospel" and coop-

erative Christianity, conservative forces responded quite differently. The pervasiveness of premillennial views made the Social Gospel (or social reform) suspect for many orthodox theologians and denominations. Their main preoccupation was saving souls before Christ's return—what Hunter terms a grand "rescue mission."[39] Challenges to the Bible, whether scientific or historical, were met with a retrenchment to biblical inerrancy. Darwinianism and higher criticism also threatened to rob Protestantism of its most basic beliefs and to destroy the supernatural authority of the Word. The way to fight such tendencies was to reassert the divine origins of Scripture; the Bible was not just a metaphor for human history, it was history. Conservatives at first battled to eradicate liberal accommodations to modernism from within the denominations by establishing Bible institutes, new centers of higher education, and numerous publications to propagate orthodox evangelical views.[40] As liberal Protestantism and the Social Gospel gained support among clergy and lay people, some conservatives began arguing for separation from the now corrupted denominations.

The splintering of Protestantism in the late 19th and early 20th centuries had political, as well as theological and ecclesiastical, ramifications. While liberals called for increasing involvement in political and social issues, many conservatives opted for disengagement. Marsden argues that this "Great Reversal" in evangelical thought from 1900 to 1930 is related to the shift from a Calvinist to pietistic tradition (e.g., politics as a way to further the Kingdom versus political action as a temporary, but ultimately futile, restraint on advancing evil), and a shift from postmillennial to premillennial eschatology. Holiness teachings also worked against political involvement because the "infilling" of the Holy Spirit was essentially an individual, rather than a social experience. A primary reason for conservatives' detachment from political action in this period was their hostility to the liberal Social Gospel which appeared to refute the basic tenets of evangelical Christianity. Conservative evangelicals viewed social action as secondary to saving individual souls; liberals seemed to make social reform primary and to take a positive stance toward the emerging modernist cultural order that premillennialist conservatives had already rejected.[41] By the turn of the century, the evangelical revivalist movement was seriously fragmented in addition to being radically separated from liberal Protestantism. The development of Pentecostalism and Fundamentalism were outgrowths of this rupture.

Pentecostalism diverged from other branches of orthodox Protestantism in its view of what constituted sanctification. While adhering to a premillennialist view of history and a belief in the necessity of spiritual rebirth, Pentecostals asserted that the conversion act involved receiving the "gifts" of the Holy Spirit, including the power to heal and to speak in tongues. Pentecostalism is generally an experiential, rather than doctrine-oriented, form of religiosity.[42] Other conservative Protestants rejected this idea, arguing that such gifts were found only in the time of the early apostolic church. Pentecostal groups were soon forced out of the conservative mainstream and formed their own churches in the years 1894 to 1905. Both Swaggart and Robertson are part of the Pentecostal tradition, as are many of the prominent television preachers.

Synan considers this movement, particularly in its formative years, to be a lower class response to the liberalization of Protestantism. It was a move to "keep alive the 'old-time religion' which seemed to be in danger of dying out in American Protestantism."[43] It was also a largely rural phenomenon, strongest in the South and Midwest. The experience of being displaced, first from Protestantism in general, and then from its conservative wing, created for Pentecostals a sense of being dispossessed, which was heightened, no doubt, by their already marginalized social position. Similar to the Mormons, religious outsiderhood constituted an important part of Pentecostals' internal identity.[44] Holiness and Pentecostal groups, says Synan, exhibited this exclusion in their theological beliefs and practices: They "taught a negative social gospel . . . rather than trying to reform society, they rejected it."[45]

Fundamentalism developed under similarly embattled conditions. As conservatives lost control of Protestant teachings and practices, they developed an increasingly separatist mentality. From 1910 to 1915, a group of Bible teachers and evangelists, backed by Southern California oil millionaire Lyman Stewart, published *The Fundamentals*—a collection of articles (in 12 paperback volumes) that spelled out the key teachings and positions of conservative evangelicalism. One-third of the articles defended scriptural authority and attacked higher criticism; one-third dealt with traditional theological questions of sin and salvation; the rest covered a variety of subjects and included attacks on other religions. The authors generally avoided ethical and political issues. Although the books were distributed free to pastors, ministers, missionaries, theology teachers and students, YMCA and YWCA secretaries, Sunday School superintendants, and religious editors (3 million volumes in all), the ideas were largely ignored by the Protestant academy. The primary impact of *The Fundamentals*, according to Marsden, was to become a "symbolic point of reference for identifying a 'fundamentalist' movement"[46] Jerry Falwell is the most prominent contemporary religious broadcaster associated with this tradition. Fundamentalism differs from Pentecostalism in its emphasis on doctrinal purity rather than on religious practices and experience. It also rejects the idea that the gifts of the Holy Spirit are accessible to contemporary Christians. This difference is one of the points of contention within conservative Protestantism, and was one of the main objections among PTL followers to Falwell's taking over the Bakkers' ministry.

Hunter sees the publication of *The Fundamentals* as the conservatives' final assault in the losing battle against modernism's invasion of Protestantism. By 1919, he argues, the split between "Fundamentalists" and "Modernists" was complete.[47] The Scopes trial in 1925, then, was something of an anti-climax. Conservative Protestants had already lost the battle for control of the faith. The highly publicized debate over evolution between Clarence Darrow and William Jennings Bryan did little more than confirm what orthodox Protestants already knew: Their historically central place in American religious life had been formally usurped by forces they believed to be profoundly anti-Christian.

THE CRISIS OF MODERNISM AND THE DEVELOPMENT OF A PARALLEL WORLD VIEW

Marsden views the creation of Fundamentalism as a response to the challenge that modernism presented to religion. Modernism represented the adaptation of religious belief to the exigencies of modern culture, while fundamentalists insisted that culture must conform to the unchanging truths of the Christian belief system. World War I seemed to justify conservatives' cultural pessimism (a pessimism, ironically, that was shared by many "modern" American intellectuals). Premillennialist leaders of the movement drew a causal chain from German theology to liberal politics to evolution and then to world war. They argued that modernist impulses not only led to war, but would also bring about the eventual destruction of civilization. Warnings of imminent cultural catastrophy and denunciations of modernity also characterize much contemporary evangelical rhetoric. In the midst of a world that seemed to be turning from God, or at least from the deity familiar to orthodox Protestants, conservative evangelicalism provided a social and cultural source of identification—a base from which to criticize the faults of modernism. Marsden suggests that early Fundamentalism comprised a "subculture" that created for its members "institutions, mores and social connections that would eventually provide acceptable alternatives to the dominant cultural ethos."[48] As evangelicalism's cultural hegemony waned, so too did its social base. Conservative Protestants looked for a new source of cohesion, which they found by laying greater stress on individual commitment and belief and by asserting the primacy of doctrine:

> Certain key beliefs—inerrancy, anti-evolution, often pre-millennial-ism—gained special importance as touchstones to ascertain whether a person belonged to the movement . . . Exactly correct belief then became proportionately more important to the movement as its social base for cohesiveness decreased.[49]

After 1925, fundamentalists (as most conservative Protestants were then called) were publicly discredited and treated in liberal circles as a social anomaly whose time had passed. It was expected that this outmoded form of religious belief would go the way of horse-drawn vehicles. But, as Sandeen points out, "Fundamentalism, a movement most commonly described as last-ditch reaction and anachronistic, rural anti-intellectualism, has refused to die."[50] Long before the Scopes trial, conservative evangelicals had been building an institutional foundation of schools, publications, Bible conferences, and independent churches outside the liberal domain for the defense and propagation of orthodoxy. Fundamentalism dropped out of the fight inside mainline Protestantism to take root elsewhere. Leaders of the conservative wing in the 1920s and 1930s emphasized working through local congregations and independent Bible institutes and missionary organizations. An internal network of communication was developed through Bible schools (26 were founded in the 1930s), colleges, Fundamentalist publications, mission agencies, Bible conferences and the new medium of radio. Unlike mainline denominations, which saw a decline in church attendance during the Great Depression, Fundamentalism quietly flourished.[51]

This network of communication and organization provided conservative evangelicals with a sense of community and identity separate from mainline liberal Protestantism. McLoughlin maintains that by the mid-1930s there existed two national Protestant religions: liberal Protestantism and pietistic Fundamentalism.[52] The latter created "an institutional framework and culture which provided [believers] with a means of perpetuating their ideological separateness."[53] In the 1940s, tensions within Fundamentalism led to a new schism between hard-line separatists and those who sought to create a broader coalition with evangelical-minded members of mainline denominations. These factions spawned, respectively, the American Council of Christian Churches (ACCC, founded in 1941 by Carl McIntyre) and the National Association of Evangelicals (NAE, created in 1942). The ACCC was a vitriolic challenger to the liberal National Council of Churches; at its peak it claimed 1.5 million members. The NAE, more ecumenical and sedate in style, appealed to the middle-class echelons of conservative Protestantism. This organization created the association of National Religious Broadcasters and the magazine *Christianity Today* and also helped construct a new public identity for conservative Protestants. "Fundamentalist" was dropped in favor of "evangelical" or "neo-Evangelical." By 1952,the NAE claimed 10 million members and represented 30 denominations and churches.[54] The bridge-building activities of the NAE contributed to a new wave of revivalism in the 1950s personified in Billy Graham's rise to national celebrity status. This new phase of religious revitalization issued from a solid institutional framework of schools, publishing houses, journals, radio stations, Bible conferences, missionary alliances, and interchurch evangelizing activities. This institutional support network, according to McLoughlin, meant that "a unified, militant, and prosperous new fundamentalist crusade could be constructed."[55]

THE INSIDER\OUTSIDER PARADOX AND THE USES OF THERAPEUTIC RHETORIC

Sandeen contends that this phenomenon of "parallel institutionalism" has "dominated and shaped" the conservative evangelical movement. Besides the NAE and ACCC, there exists an array of evangelical professional, academic, business, and social associations and societies that parallel similar secular organizations (e.g., Christian Businessmen's Association, Christian Medical Association, Evangelical Press Association, Fellowship of Christian Athletes, etc.). These parallel organizations, as well as evangelical colleges, Bible institutes, and broadcasting ministries, create an identity and structural unity for conservative evangelicals that is simultaneously "inside" and "outside" the larger culture.[56] Marsden argues that the history of evangelical Prostestantism revolves around this inside/outside tension and is manifested in evangelicals' profound ambivalence toward American culture and its "paradoxical tendency to identify sometimes with 'the establishment' and sometimes with 'outsiders'."[57] Religious outsiderhood is a recurring motif in American history, providing a wide array of believers with a point of identification. Adopting an outsider position has proven to be a useful strategy for achieving group cohesion and social status, and for differentiating one's group from the opposition.[58] As Moore notes, however, "insider and outsider identities are rarely unmixed. . . . The assertion that one is an outsider often implies the opposite, and vice versa."[59]

The history of evangelical Protestantism is marked by this paradox; it contains equally powerful impulses toward separation from and accommodation to the larger culture. This is the internal contradiction of a belief system that at one time was central to American society and which was subsequently driven to the margins of social life. Robertson and Swaggart have inherited this contradictory history and draw on the insider/outsider tension to construct their appeals to audiences. Their divergent solutions to this tension reflect the dual historical projects that arose in response to the crisis of modernization and the disestablishment of Protestantism.

Changing historical circumstances demanded creative responses from orthodox Protestants if their belief system was to survive. The splintering of conservative and liberal factions and the proliferation of denominations and churches were signs of a religion in crisis. These were strategies for coping with failure—the failure of postmillennial optimism, the loss of Protestantism's cultural hegemony, and the weakening of religious explanations characteristic of modernization in general. Like other great world religions, Christianity has endured through its ability to adapt to historical change and cultural crisis.[60] In the process, it has developed coherent, persuasive explanations regarding the relationship between Christ's life and teachings and the realm of human conduct. Niebuhr argues that these narratives of "Christ and culture" tend to emphasize either their fundamental opposition, or their basic agreement.[61] The first position holds that there is a radical, irreconcilable gulf between the sacred spiritual, profane, and material worlds; it thus "confronts [humanity] with the challenge of an 'either-or' decision."[62] The second position tries to reconcile these two realms of creation so that culture is the site where Christ's teachings must be made effective.

These general theological explanations have produced variations and syntheses—two of which are important to understanding conservatives' response to the crisis of American Protestantism. The "dualist" synthesis embraces the fundamental opposition between Christ and culture, but also recognizes the authority of both; it accepts that obedience to God entails obedience to human institutions. Because they must obey two authorities who are often in direct disagreement, dualist Christians live in a state of tension. As Niebuhr says, "in the *polarity* and *tension* of Christ and culture, life must be lived precariously and sinfully in the hope of a justification that lies beyond history."[63] This position is exemplified by Swaggart's theology; he advises followers to remain detached from culture because it is not salvageable—they may be in the world, but should not be *of* it.

The "conversionist" synthesis also recognizes an opposition

between Christ and culture, but because culture itself is part of God's creation, Christians are bound to "carry out cultural work in obedience to the Lord."[64] Unlike dualists, who merely endure human life in anticipation of "a transhistorical salvation," conversionists have "a more positive and hopeful attitude toward culture."[65] This key difference is related to their divergent conceptions of the "fall." Dualists see human beings and human culture as essentially, irrevocably corrupt. We are redeemed solely because of God's mercy, not through any action or inherent goodness on our part. Conversionists, on the other hand, see human nature and culture as originally or potentially good because they are God's creations; they become corrupt, however, when humanity fails to recognize God as the source of its goodness. The dualist, who sees "the whole world of human culture as godless and sick unto death," believes it can be redeemed only through literal death and rebirth in the next world.[66] For the conversionist, however, "the problem of culture is . . . the problem of conversion, not of its replacement by a new creation." While such a conversion "is so radical that it amounts to a kind of rebirth," this transformation *can* be accomplished within the realm of human culture.[67] This is Robertson's position, though one that is not without contradictions, given the premillennial elements of his theology.[68] In this way, Robertson straddles the insider\outsider paradox by justifying the authority of his belief "outside" culture in God, while simultaneously calling for its transformation from "inside" culture through Christian action.

The difference between the dualist and conversionist interpretations of the "fall" is particularly important in understanding the two historical projects that have developed within conservative evangelicalism. For orthodox Protestants, the fragmentation of the church, the ascendence of liberal theology, and the secularizing effects of modernization represented failures. They had not only failed to win control of the faith, but also found themselves adrift in a modernizing world that "erodes the plausibility of religious belief and weakens the influence of religious symbols in the social structure and culture at large."[69] The survival of their belief system depended on developing strategies for responding to and coping with this failure. That is, they had to find ways to renegotiate the fit between religious belief and the cultural order.

Payne examined how individuals and groups use "therapeutic rhetoric" to deal with specific instances of failure and with the problem of human fallibility generally. Payne argues that human fallibility "motivates the search for ways of transcendence and repair in self and world."[70] Because one of religion's purposes is to provide answers to the "problem of meaning" (our moral, physical, and intellecual limitations), it necessarily addresses failure's causes, consequences, and solutions. Payne cites Mircea Eliade's description of Christianity as "the religion of 'fallen man'" to suggest that Christian theodicies function to interpret and account for human fallibility.[71] Religious rhetoric becomes "therapeutic" to the extent that it addresses the human failure at the heart of the "problem of meaning."

Payne contends that rhetoric serves a therapeutic function when "the rhetorical activities of the persuader and\or persuadee are addressed to healing or repairing some perceived flaw in self."[72] This perception of failure may also be extended to the individual's relationship to society, or to society as a whole. The theologies of Swaggart and Robertson are therapeutic insofar as they address fallibility at each of these levels. Differences in their rhetorical motives and strategies stem from their divergent conceptions of the sources of failure. Operating from a dualist position, Swaggart believes human beings are *born* fallen. To be embodied—to be part the "the world"—is to be already corrupted. As Niebuhr says, for the dualist "human culture is corrupt; and it includes all human work."[73] There is no redemption in this world because Christ and culture are irreconcilable. The Christian can find salvation only by acknowledging his or her abjectness and awaiting rebirth in the next world. For the dualist, to be human is to be already flawed in one's essence.

The conversionist position of Robertson is less pessimistic because it sees fallenness as a state that can be transcended in this life. Human beings are not born corrupt, but become so by failing to recognize their true relationship to God. For conversionists, Niebuhr argues, "culture is perverted good, not evil."[74] Christians may recover their good nature through the process of conversion or transformation that occurs in *this* world. In this sense, failure and fallenness are not proof of humanity's essential evil, but are states that may be repaired and overcome through worldly action.

These different interpretations of failure and the "fall" produce different rhetorical strategies. Payne notes that therapeutic rhetoric operates by "1) providing a definition of the failure, 2) assigning fault or blame for the failure, and 3) pointing to options for repairing the failure."[75] Further, such rhetoric has certain features and goals:

> The central speakers testify to some previous failure and give personal accounts of their recovery via the doctrine, lifestyle, or product they're trying to sell. These rhetorical appeals communicate techniques for resolving failure that are useful to audiences who must deal with their personal inadequacies.[76]

Both Swaggart and Robertson provide personal testimonies, offer techniques of resolution to their audiences, and do so via symbolic means. Their "therapies" differ because they disagree on the causes, cures, and ways of coping with the malaise.

Payne contends that therapeutic rhetoric can have one or both of two functions: consolation and/or compensation. Both deal with loss or failure, but take different attitudes toward the problem. Consolatory rhetoric seeks "to persuade to a different order of valuation wherein a new perspective on the loss is possible. In consolation, loss is neither denied nor erased." Compensatory rhetoric, in contrast, "tries to balance things to 'get even,' to find another way to achieve the original goals or something like them, or perhaps to set and gain even better goals."[77] While these two functions do not operate totally independently of each other—consolation can pave the way for compensation, for example—Swaggart's rhetoric tends to be organized around consoling followers about humanity's inherent abjection, while Robertson's discourse tends to revolve around compensating for conservative Protestants' displacement as moral guardians of the culture and asserting the possibility of individual and social renewal.

Payne suggests that consolation tends to focus on past conditions and causes of failure and to emphasize "spiritual meanings or orientations over material losses." In contrast, "compensatory discourse stresses self-directed involvements or motives, future consequences or opportunities, and material values and orientations."[78] Robertson's rhetoric, which incorporates the political and social goals of the New Christian Right and the values of the "health and wealth gospel," follows the pattern of compensation. It invites listeners to become actively involved in influencing the direction of their lives and of American society; it points to a bright future when Christians will reclaim social leadership; and it promises that success in one's earthly life is one of the blessings of following the tenets of evangelical Christianity. This rhetoric of compensation is part of a general accommodation to modernization in that Christian values are redefined so as to be compatible with, and achievable within, contemporary society.

Swaggart's rhetoric refuses to redefine traditional evangelical beliefs to conform to modern culture. It neither denies nor erases the basic flaws of humanity. Rather, his rhetoric seeks merely to console listeners in the face of this essential failure. Payne notes that consolatory rhetoric interprets failure in such a way as to make it easier to bear, "or even valuable according to some alternate set of priorities." By emphasizing the necessarily outsider position of true, "Bible-believing Christians," Swaggart creates for himself and his followers a special relationship to failure. In recognizing the unalterable fact of their human fallibility and unworthiness, they possess a unique knowledge and place in God's design. As Payne notes, in consoling rhetoric "one cannot deny the failure and its significance. One can, however, so exaggerate the failure that it is ultimately a product of such great forces that it can be consoled or compensated on another plane altogether."[79] This is the function of the "this world/next world" dichotomy in Swaggart's theology and rhetoric. Human suffering and fallibility are products of forces over which people have no real control; the fall has already occurred and no amount of human effort can reverse that fact. One can only acknowledge one's fallenness and seek redemption in another plane—in the next world which is the true destination of every life's journey. The theologies and rhetoric of Swaggart and Robertson reflect divergent strategies for responding to modernization that coexist uneasily within conservative evangelicalism. These historical strategies are manifested in thematic and stylistic differences between their programs, and are embodied, as I argue, in their contrasting cultural forms.

THE HISTORICAL CRISIS OF MEANING

Evangelicalism was born and has persevered through its capacity to create a persuasive "sacred canopy" that provides for adherents both a model of and a model for reality. The doctrine of *scriptura sola* served to endow nature, history, society, and individual existence with order and significance. Further, it eliminated doubt and ambiguity; the Bible was a factual representation of historical, natural, and spiritual phenomena, and as such was a powerful explanatory tool. Revivalism, premillennialism, and the holiness tradition formed important components of evangelicalism's cosmology. Premillennial eschatology offered an integrated, persuasive interpretation for social conditions in the present, a uniquely Protestant version of the past, and a definitive plan for the future, all based in God's Word. Premillennial theodicy has been compelling in so far as it constructs a predetermined, cosmic order that makes sense of contemporary culture on its own terms. It has therefore acted as an antidote to modernism and relativizes religious belief by making it subservient to cultural and historical contexts. Conservatives' objection to higher criticism and liberal theology, then, is a defense of the very basis of religious belief, rather than a theological difference of opinion.

In this worldview, spiritual rebirth and Christian witness followed from scriptural literalism. Mandated by God as essential expressions of faith and keys to salvation, sanctification and testimony became techniques of transcendence. These rituals reinforced the truth of evangelicalism by constructing a "structure of feeling" that offered an experiential framework for the enactment of belief.[80] Religious revivals and being "baptized in the Holy Ghost" gave communicants a sense of sacred community and a special place in the world that was legitimized by and simultaneously supported covenantal notions of America's role as a redeemer nation. Personal conversion and proselytism were evidence of belonging to the elect and at the same time were necessary for the justification and propagation of the evangelical worldview. The individuated nature of salvation developed in correspondence with the increasingly individualistic character of the expanding market economy: Eternal salvation, like economic survival, was a personal affair, just as sin and financial hardship were individual failings.[81]

This mutually constituting relationship between the shape of religious belief and the fabric of society, which gave significance and legitimacy to both, was eroding by the turn of the century. The scientific and technological rationalism, cultural pluralism, and structural separation of public and private life associated with modernization undermined the evangelical worldview.[82] Evangelicalism's capacity to create a model of reality faced serious challenges, even as it continued to provide what believers felt should be the only proper model for reality. Modernism constituted a crisis for orthodox Protestantism by creating a disjuncture between ethos (social experience) and worldview (belief)—by creating a gap between being and meaning. As Whitson argues, a religion comes into existence at times when a crisis of meaning confronts a community.[83] The Reformation was such a crisis point, as was the birth of the second wing of Protestantism. The evolution of conservative evangelicalism in the 20th century involves the development of strategies for coping with and trying to heal the crisis of meaning associated with modernization. For evangelicals, this crisis involved the potential loss of the symbolic system that had infused their world and their lives with significance.

To lose meaning is to simultaneously lose "being"—to give up the frame of orientation and devotion that tells individuals who they are and what their existence signifies. In fact, this displacement of being and meaning is a characteristic feature of modernity. The loss of traditional and metaphysical explanatory frameworks has been described as scientific "progress" (positivism), as a process of "rationalization" or "bureaucratization" (Weber), as a transition from "Gemeinschaft" to "Gesellschaft" (classical sociology and critical theory), as a product of technological development (Mumford, Innis), and as a necessary feature of capitalist development. Wood suggests that the "meaningless of being" is a product of the rise of capitalism and the birth of the individual "bourgeois subject."[84] Wood argues that precapitalist (and "primitive") societies, grounded in distinct kinds of social organization and, hence, perception, were more integrative systems:

> [These] social formations were distinguished by the common possession of world-views which united the immense diversity of the manifest and unmanifest realms of being within one cosmos within which humanity existed as an integral part continuous with the whole, 'at home.'[85]

In such social formations, "all entities were perceived as entering into complex symbolic relations of religious significance with one another."[86]

With the emergence and subsequent development of capitalism, this unity provided by a cosmic or transcendent system of meaning was gradually altered. The commodification of things in this emerging socioeconomic order (including human labor) offered a new standard for allocating significance. Moreover, this historical process interrupted or exploded the relatively more integrated character of earlier perceptual systems (it prefigured the "death of God" who had been the unifying force behind reality). Under capitalism, according to Wood, "the socially-recognized values (commercial, moral, or whatever) of things change more often than in previous social formations."[87] Harvey notes that this instability is characteristic of modernity:

> The transitoriness of things makes it difficult to preserve any sense of historical continuity. . . . Modernity, therefore, not only entails a ruthless break with any or all preceding historical conditions, but is characterized by a never-ending process of internal ruptures and fragmentations.[88]

The result of this historical development, according to Wood, is "the ceaseless and rapid relativisation of value or meaning."[89] This gives rise to the thoroughly modern perception that existence, or being, is transitory, relative, absurd. Modern philosophies such as existentialism, structuralism and poststructuralism, and contemporary cultural movements like modernism and postmodernism, for example, could develop only after the transitoriness of meaning and being was taken for granted—when perception had become firmly grounded on the premise that "objects should not be perceived as having a stable essence, value or signification. . . . they should not be perceived as pointing to anything beyond themselves *(a transcendent reality, for example.)*"[90]

This "disenchantment of the world," or relativization of meaning, had profound implications for the question of being: It made the "self" a historically new problem. Berman suggests that to be modern is "to find ourselves in an environment that promises adventure, power, joy, growth, transformation of ourselves and the world—and, at the same time, that threatens to destroy everything we have, everything we know, everything we are."[91] Thus, while the gradual dilution of older forms of sociation and symbolic systems can be a liberating experience, it also forces us to turn elsewhere for clues about who we are and how we should act in the world. Given the intensely individualistic ethos of capitalism, one of the places we have turned for such answers is inward. Hunter argues that an increased focus on and concern with the self—what he terms "subjectivization"—is one result of the modernization process. Subjectivization, he says, is "the structural process of being forced to turn inward to find meaningful life patterns and a stable identity."[92] Identity is never a spontaneously self-generated creation, however; it is socially produced via our relationships to others in a concrete time and place. The process of looking inward, then, is necessarily a double gaze, based both on an intensified awareness of others and on a heightened awareness of ourselves as objects of others' observation.[93]

Hunter points out that the question "Who am I?" is an essentially modern one (dating from the Enlightenment). It arises, he says, in a world in which "identity has become deinstitutionalized" so that the "self has become a boundaryless territory to be explored, analyzed, and mapped, an exercise that often requires the assistance of 'experts.'"[94] One of the most important sources of such expertise in contemporary society is the media and cultural industries which offer us a plethora of stories about who we are and who we should be— hence, Riesman's notion of the "other-directed" individual who seeks identity through the dominant contemporary "storytellers"—the mass media.[95] In the early 20 century, Simmel also remarked on this new other dependence among modern urbanites who "cultivate[d] a sham individualism through pursuit of signs of status, fashion, or marks of individual eccentricity."[96] One of the things that distinguishes the modern experience from that of earlier social formations, then, is the extent to which the self has become ephemeral and transitory, based on surface appearances and changing modes of presentation. The loss of apparently stable, universal, cosmic sources of identity has meant that the self must be perpetually reconstituted amid an overwhelming flux of personal and social experiences and symbolic materials. It is not surprising, then, that the self has become the object of such intense scrutiny, nor that modern individuals find it difficult to feel "at home" in the world.

Contemporary symbolic systems therefore have to wrestle with the complexities and anxieties of the "modern self" if they are to retain their significance for people's lives. Evangelicalism must also contend with this shifting ground of personal identity if it is to maintain its capacity to provide a cosmic meaning for reality and individual existence. Televangelism openly deals with this problem of the self in constructing its appeals to viewers. As I argue in the program analysis, Swaggart's crusade program and the "700 Club" offer different interpretations of the source of this problem and propose divergent solutions. Further, the evangelical belief system must operate against a backdrop of the historical process of capitalist modernization that relativizes values, denies transcendental significance, and relegates religion to a personal rather than social, concern.

I am arguing that conservative evangelicalism has not withered away precisely because it continues to respond to many people's desire for transcendent meaning in a persuasive way; it has continued to give believers a sense of their place in history, in society, and in the cosmic order of things. It is an answer—and often a highly persuasive one—to the problem of the self and the relationship of meaning and being. In Geertz's words, the symbolic system of evangelicalism has proven to be able to

> establish powerful, persuasive and long-lasting moods and motivations in [believers] by . . . formulating conceptions of a general order of existence and . . . clothing these conceptions with such an aura of factuality that . . . the moods and motivations seem uniquely realistic. [97]

Although evangelicalism has taken a historically hostile stance toward modernism, it has, of necessity, had to adapt to modernization's pervasive pressures. Modernism's instrumental rationality, cultural pluralism, and private-public dichotomy have had "corrosive consequences for the establishment and maintenance of a religious world view."[98] Conservative evangelicalism has responded to this corrosion with a variety of techniques: attempting to eradicate the contaminating system, emphasizing cultural separatism, building an alternative institutional framework, partial accommodation, and more recently, by forwarding claims of superiority. Such strategies, however, also imply the power of modernism to shape even its opposition. That is, even institutions that resist the modern cultural order must make some accommodation to it if they are to survive. The resiliency of the evangelical belief system indicates the extent to which it continues to supply viable responses to modern (and "postmodern") impulses in social, political, and cultural life. It continues to render reality and existence meaningful for a significant number of people—to fuse individual ethos and worldview in a way that "lend[s] a chronic character to the flow of [one's] activity and the quality of [one's] experience."[99]

Televangelism, then, provides an important site for examining the process whereby evangelicalism legitimates its claims about the nature of reality and existence. It offers us clues about how the evangelical belief system responds to the "problem of meaning"—bafflement, suffering, and evil. And it does so with an urgency related to the powerful, disintegrating impact of modernization. If Harvey is correct that capitalism's most recent transition has dramatically accelerated the ephemerality and disposability of things, people, and values, this acceleration also creates a vertigo of meaningless in consciousness. Questions about being and meaning become even more urgent in a constantly changing cultural order in which "all that is solid melts into air."[100] Evangelical discourse, as expressed in televangelism, must confront this assault upon its claims to offer timeless, universal answers to the questions of being and meaning. It is therefore marked by a passionate defense of transcendent meaning against a world that increasingly denies the significance of such metaphysical symbolic frameworks. Carter, writing about fundamentalist resistance to evolution in the 1920s, points out that orthodox Protestants were not just defending a political ideology or educational perspective, but were also, and primarily, "defending what [they] honestly believed was all that gave meaning to life, 'the faith once delivered to the saints.'"[101] Contemporary conservative evangelicalism and its representative television ministries, I propose, are also engaged in a passionate defense of a symbolic system that makes the lives of believers and viewers meaningful.

NOTES TO CHAPTER 3

1. R. Stephen Warner, "Theoretical Barriers to the Understanding of Evangelical Christianity," *Sociological Analysis* 40 (1979): p. 3.

2. This view is held by most historians of Protestantism. See, for example, Martin A. Marty, "Tensions Within Contemporary Evangelicalism: A Critical Appraisal," in D. F. Wells and J. D. Woodbridge, eds., *The Evangelicals* (Nashville, TN: Abingdon, 1975), pp. 170-188.

3. Christopher Hill, *Reformation to Industrial Revolution, 1530-1780* (New York: Penguin, 1978), p. 40.

4. Ibid., p. 39. See also Neil Postman, *The Disappearance of*

Childhood (New York: Dell, 1982), especially Chapter 2; and Elizabeth Eisenstein, "The Emergence of Print Culture in the West," Journal of Communication 30 (Winter 1985): p. 151.

5. Gregor Goethals, "Religious Communication and Popular Piety," *Journal of Communication* 35 (Winter 1985): p. 151.

6. Sydney Ahlstrom, "From Puritanism to Evangelicalism: A Critical Perspective," in D. F. Wells and J. D. Woodbridge, eds., *The Evangelicals* (Nashville, TN: Abingdon, 1975), pp. 269-289.

7. Vinson Synan, *The Holiness-Pentecostal Movement in the United States* (Grand Rapids, MI: Eerdmans, 1971), p. 58. Freidrich Heiler, *Prayer: A Study in the History and Psychology of Religion*, trans. Samuel McComb (London: Oxford University Press, 1932), p. 154.

8. Ibid., pp. 155, 157.

9. James D. Hunter, *American Evangelicalism: Conservative Religion and the Quandary of Modernity* (New Brunswick, NJ: Rutgers University Press, 1983), p. 7.

10. On the problems of precise definitions and exclusive categories, see Warner, "Theoretical Barriers," pp. 1-2; Hunter, *American Evangelicalism*, pp. 7-9; and Grant Wacker, "The Search of Norman Rockwell: Popular Evangelicalism in Contemporary America," in L.I. Sweet, ed., *The Evangelical Tradition in America* (Mercer, GA: Mercer University Press, 1984), pp. 295-296.

11. Hunter, *American Evangelicalism*, p. 7. George Thomas makes a similar argument in *Revivalism and Cultural Change: Christianity, Nation Building, and the Market in the Nineteenth-Century United States* (Chicago: University of Chicago Press, 1989).

12. Ibid., p. 24.

13. William G. McLoughlin, Jr., *Modern Revivalism: Charles Grandison Finney to Billy Graham* (New York: Ronald Press, 1959), p. 7

14. Razell Frankl, *Televangelism: The Marketing of Popular Religion* (Carbondale: Southern Illinois University Press, 1987), p. 29.

15. Kenneth Burke, "Definition of Man," *The Hudson Review*, XVI (Winter 1963-64): p. 507. Quoted in Leland Griffin, "A Dramatistic Theory of the Rhetoric of Movements," in William Reuckert, ed., *Critical Responses to Kenneth Burke* (Minneapolis: University of Minnesota Press, 1969), p. 457.

16. Griffin, "Rhetoric of Movements, " p. 507.

17. Both McLoughlin, *Modern Revivalism*, and George Marsden, *Fundamentalism and American Culture* (New York: Oxford University Press, 1980), provide good accounts of this period.

18. Synan, *The Holiness-Pentecostal Movement*, p. 25.

19. Frankl, *Televangelism*, p. 23.

20. Sandra Sizer, *Gospel Hymns and Social Religion: The Rhetoric of Nineteenth Century Revivalism* (Philadelphia, PA: Temple University

Press, 1978), p. 19.

21. McLoughlin, *Modern Revivalism*, p. 133.

22. Ibid., p. 13.

23. Premillennial theology holds that the millennium is already in process—that the world is already in the midst of the thousand-year period of holiness under Christ's reign prophesied in Revelation 20.

24. Ernest Tuveson, *Redeemer Nation: The Idea of America's Millennial Role* (Chicago: University of Chicago Press, 1968).

25. Hunter, *American Evangelicalism*, p. 25.

26. Marsden, *Fundamentalism and American Culture*, p. 16.

27. Ibid., p. 17.

28. Ibid., pp. 22-26.

29. From Daniel 9, Verses 25—27, *The New English Bible* (New York: Oxford University Press, 1976), O.T. p. 959.

30. In a historical study of apocalyptic movements and their rhetoric, Ronald Reid claims that apocalyptic visions are appealing in periods when a substantial number of people are dissatisfied with the present and are uncertain about the future. Apocalypse, says Reid, serves to expalin a distressing present and provides reassurance for the future. It does so by identifying a specific hate object or enemy, arousing fears of conspiracy and subversion, legitimizing beliefs by subordinating them to a cosmic plan, and building a strong feeling of commitment among the faithful. Ronald Reid, "Apocalypticism and Typology: Rhetorical Dimensions of a Symbolic Reality," *Quarterly Journal of Speech* 69 (August 1983): pp. 229-248.

31. See William Martin, "Waiting for the End," Atlantic Monthly (June 1982): pp. 31-37; and Grace Halsell, *Prophecy and Politics: Militant Evangelists on the Road to Nuclear War* (Westport, CT: Lawrence Hill, 1986).

32. Marsden, *Fundamentalism and American Culture*, p. 38.

33. Halsell, *Prophecy and Politics*, p. 17, quoted from "Jimmy Swaggart," September 22, 1985.

34. Stephen O'Leary and Michael McFarland, "The Political Use of Mythic Discourse: Prophetic Interpretation in Pat Robertson's Presidential Campaign," *Quarterly Journal of Speech* 75 (1989), pp. 433-452.

35. See Sizer, *Gospel Hymns and Social Religion*, pp. 20-49 on dominant themes in the hymns, and Marsden, *Fundamentalism and American Culture*, pp. 74-75.

36. Kenneth Burke, *Rhetoric of Religion; Studies in Logology* (Berkeley: University of California Press, 1970), p. 5.

37. Marsden, *Fundamentalism and American Culture*, pp. 78-79.

38. Hunter, *American Evangelicalism*, p. 27.

39. Ibid., p. 30.

40. Ibid., p. 31.

41. Marsden, *Fundamentalism and American Culture*, pp. 85-93.

42. Faith healing and glossalalia are two of the gifts acquired when the worshiper is "baptized in the Holy Ghost"; others are wisdom, faith, the ability to work miracles, to prophesy and to interpret tongues. The term *charismatic* is also used to distinguish Christians who hold that the Holy Spirit bestows gifts of healing and speaking in tongues. Charismatic comes from the Greek charisma meaning favor or gift. Not all charismatics are Pentecostal; there is also a growing number of Catholic charismatics. For a history of Pentecostalism and its central beliefs and practices, see Synan, *The Holiness-Pentecostal Movement*. For an interesting discussion of the psychological implications of glossolalia see E. Mansell Pattison, "Ideological Support for the Marginal Middle Class: Faith Healing and Glossolalia, " in I.I. Zaretsky and M.P. Leone, eds., *Religious Movements in Contemporary America* (Princeton, NJ: Princeton University Press, 1974), pp. 498-555.

43. Synan, *Holiness-Pentecostal Movement*, p. 58.

44. R. Laurence Moore, *Religious Outsiders and the Making of Americans* (New York: Oxford University Press, 1986). See especially Chapter One on the Mormons' use of "rhetoric of deviance" to create a common identity.

45. Synan, *Holiness-Pentecostal Movement*, p. 58.

46. Marsden, *Fundamentalism and American Culture*, p.119; see also Hunter, *American Evangelicalism*, pp. 31-32.

47. Hunter, *American Evangelicalism*, p. 32.

48. Marsden, *Fundamentalism and American Culture*, p. 204.

49. Ibid., p. 205.

50. Ernest Sandeen, "Fundamentalism and American Identity," *Annals of the American Academy of Political and Social Science* 387 (1970): p. 57.

51. For a history of Fundamentalism and evangelicalism during this period, see Joel A. Carpenter, "Fundamentalist Institutions and the Rise of Evangelical Protestantism, 1929-1942," *Church History*, 49 (March 1980): pp. 62-75.

52 McLoughlin, *Modern Revivalism*, p. 465.

53. Ibid., p. 466.

54. Ibid., p. 475

55. Ibid., p. 476.

56. Sandeen, "Fundamentalism," p. 61.

57. Marsden, *Fundamentalism and American Culture*, p. 6.

58. R. Laurence Moore, "Insiders and Outsiders in American Historical Narrative and American History," *American Historical*

Review 87 (April 1982): pp. 390-412; Moore, *Religious Outsiders and the Making of Americans*; Sizer, *Gospel Hymns*; Luther Gerlach and Virginia Hine, *People Power, Change: Movements of Social Transformation* (Indianapolis: Bobbs Merrrill, 1970).

59. Moore, "Insiders and Outsiders," p. 398.

60. For a discussion of this evolutionary capacity of Christianity (and Islam) on a grand historical scale, see Samir Amin, *Eurocentrism* (New York: Monthly Review Press, 1989).

61. H. Richard Niebuhr, *Christ and Culture* (New York: Harper and Row, 1951, 1956), pp. 40-41.

62. Ibid., p.40.

63. Ibid., p. 43.

64. Ibid., p. 191.

65. Ibid., pp. 43, 191.

66. Ibid., p. 156.

67. Ibid., p. 194.

68. O'Leary and McFarland, "Political Use of Mythic Discourse."

69. Hunter, American Evangelicalism, p. 4.

70. David Payne, *Coping With Failure, The Therapeutic Uses of Rhetoric* (Columbia, SC: University of South Carolina Press, 1989), p. 3.

71. Ibid., p. 6.

72. Ibid., p. 32.

73. Ibid., p. 153.

74. Niebuhr, *Christ and Culture*, p. 194.

75. Payne, *Coping with Failure*, p. 53.

76. Ibid., pp. 12-13.

77. Ibid., p. 42.

78. Ibid., p. 45

79. Ibid., p. 153.

80. This phrase comes from Raymond Williams and refers to "meanings and values as they are actively lived and felt, and the relations between these and formal or systematic beliefs." In *Marxism and Literature* (Oxford: Oxford University Press, 1977), p. 132.

81. Schultze suggests that this deeply entrenched individualist ethos in Protestantism also works against any serious self-regulation in religious broadcasting; as he says, "American Protestantism is almost thoroughly individualistic and increasingly entrepreneurial." Quoted in Randy Frame, "Surviving the Slump," *Christianity Today*, February 3, 1989, p. 33.

82. See Hunter, American Evangelicalism, Chapter 2.

83. Robley E. Whitson, *The Coming Convergence in World Religion* (New York: Newman Press, 1971), p.8.

84. Philip Wood, "From Existentialism to Poststructuralism, and the Coming of the Postindustrial Society," unpublished manuscript,

Seattle, WA, 1987.

85. Ibid., p. 7.

86. Ibid., p. 8.

87. Ibid., p. 11.

88. David Harvey, *The Condition of Postmodernity* (Oxford: Basil Blackwell, 1989), pp. 11-12.

89. Wood, "From Existentialism to Poststructuralism," p. 11.

90. Ibid., p. 13, emphasis mine.

91. Marshall Berman, *All That is Solid Melts Into Air: The Experience of Modernity* (New York: Simon and Schuster, 1982), p. 15.

92. Hunter, *American Evangelicalism*, pp. 92, 93.

93. Sartre, of course, examines this phenomenon in depth in *Being and Nothingness*, trans. Hazel E. Barnes (New York: Philosophical Library, 1956), pp. 252-302.

94. Hunter, *American Evangelicalism*, p. 94.

95. David Riesman in collaboration with Reuel Denny and Nathan Glazer, *The Lonely Crowd: A Study of the Changing American Character* (New Haven, CT: Yale Universtiy Press, 1950).

96. Georg Simmel, "The Metropolis and Mental Life," in Donald N. Levine, ed., *On Individuality and Social Form* (Chicago: University of Chicago Press, 1971). Quoted in Harvey, *The Condition of Postmodernity*, p. 26.

97. Clifford Geertz, "Religion as a Cultural System," in William A. Lessa and Evon Z. Vogt, eds., *Reader in Comparative Religion*, 4th ed. (New York: Harper and Row, 1979), pp. 80-81.

98. Hunter, *American Evangelicalism*, p. 14.

99. Geertz, " Religion as a Cultural System," p. 82.

100. This is the title of Marshall Berman's book as well as a phrase that Marx used to describe the ephemerality of capitalist modernization in the "Communist Manifesto." Karl Marx and Friedrich Engels, "Manifesto of the Communist Party," in Lewis Feuer, ed., *Basic Writings on Politics and Philosophy* (Garden City, NY: Anchor Books, 1959), p. 10.

101. Paul A. Carter, "The Fundamentalist Defense of Faith," in J. Braeman, R. Bremner, and D. Brody, eds., *Change and Continuity in Twentieth-Century America: The 1920's* (Columbus: Ohio State University Press, 1968), p. 212.

4

The Struggle Over Symbolic Production

THE RESURGENCE OF FUNDAMENTALISM

The New Christian Right is rooted in the evangelical past. As Marsden and other writers have pointed out, 19th-century evangelicalism was characterized by racism, a hostility to Native Americans, an imperialist mentality, superpatriotism, a pro-militarist stance, and a deep suspicion of "foreign" ideologies such as Catholicism and socialism. Pierard argues that 19th-century evangelicals "had become deeply involved in what today would be called 'rightist extremism' long before Fundamentalism emerged in the period after World War I."[1] Conservative Protestants' withdrawal from politics in the decades between the world wars was a temporary secession. While they refrained from organized political action, they maintained intensely conservative views. The Cold War, McCarthyism, and Eisenhower's election provided a ground for the reflowering of evangelical activism; indeed, Ribuffo claims that the New Christian Right is part of a general revival of evangelicalism that began after WWII.[2] "Neo-evangelicalism" fluorished under the "genteel conservativism" of the Eisenhower years. It took the upheavals of the late 1960s and early 1970s, and general confusion within mainline Protestantism, to create a climate conducive to the creation of a new conservative Christian "movement."

The "resurgence of Fundamentalism" was temporarily eclipsed by a brief revival of liberal Protestantism in the 1960s—a decade that provoked deep reassessments of religious faith and practice for many members of mainline denominations.[3] Liberal clergy and laity became increasingly involved in social and political issues (especially in the Civil Rights and anti-war movements), bringing a temporary renewal of the Social Gospel. Conservative Protestants, historically at odds with this orientation, kept a critical distance from both movements.[4] For them, the 1960s represented a serious challenge to traditional Christian values. Supreme Court rulings in 1962 and 1963 against school prayer and Bible reading, in particular, were interpreted as a dangerous severing of religion from society, and evangelicals responded accordingly.[5] The defeat in Vietnam, Watergate, rising rates of drug use, teenage pregnancy and divorce, the growth of the pornography industry, and an increase in sex and violence on television reinforced conservative Christians' view that American society was undergoing a moral and spiritual crisis. The Supreme Court's decision in 1973 to legalize abortion was taken as a particularly devastating renunciation of evangelical values.[6]

These developments seemed to constitute a systematic assault on the nuclear family—an institution held by evangelicals to be central to a proper Christian life. By 1976, the political right, headed by men like Paul Weyrich, Howard Phillips, and Richard Viguerie, established contacts with key evangelical leaders. It was this coalition, aided by Viguerie's sophisticated fundraising techniques and interlocking organizational networks, that set the stage for the birth of the New Christian Right. The NCR's most visible organizations—the Moral Majority (now the Liberty Foundation), the Religious Roundtable, and Christian Voice—were all formed in 1979.

Wacker contends that the worldview of the NCR is organized around the notion of "Christian Civilization"—an "explicit set of social and cultural commitments" that were dominant in the 19th century when evangelicalism was the primary belief system in America.[7] "Christian Civilization," he argues, is "not so much a list of discrete ideals as a coherent world view, a way of seeing reality." This worldview is constructed on the belief that there exists a set of "moral absolutes" explicitly and transparently revealed in Scripture that should underpin society's laws, institutions, and public policies.[8] Social changes in the 1960s and early 1970s, perceived as a direct threat to the "Christian Civilization" ideal, evoked widespread dissatisfaction among conservative evangelicals. Wacker argues that it is the "Evangelical Right" that identifies most strongly with the values of "Christian Civilization," and that it is this faction of evangelicalism that has experienced the greatest growth in the last 20 years. The "Christian Civilization" ideal informs Robertson's worldview and is a central theme of the "700 Club." As he stated in one program, "I think we should be a biblically-based nation. There has got to be some unifying ethic for society."[9] This statement reflects Robertson's conversionist perspective. While Swaggart agrees that the Bible should guide one's life, he tends to make this a personal, rather than social, imperative because his dualist stance places spiritual and worldly concerns in opposition.

The resurgence of conservative evangelicalism has been noted in the popular press and in public polls. It is evident as well in the growth of the evangelical publishing industry, in the increase in private Christian schools and colleges, in the creation of popular organizations and lobbying groups, in the success of numerous grass roots political campaigns, and in the growth of the television ministries in the last 10 years.[10] I believe it is no coincidence that conservative evangelicalism has once again become a significant, vocal religious force in American culture. This perspective was born in a climate of social and spiritual crisis. It has been forced to develop its ideological and material resources in opposition to the dominant currents and structures of modern society, and has therefore become highly sensitive to threats to the maintenance of its worldview.

Hunter offers a provocative interpretation of why evangelicalism has sucessfully survived many of the secularizing pressures of modernism. He suggests that adherents of this religious perspective have been able to maintain their worldview, or symbolic system, because as a whole, evangelicals have been

> located furthest from key structural pressures of modernity: high levels of education, high mobility-inducing income levels, urbanization, and the public sphere of work. The relative isolation of Evangelicals from these factors mitigates the threats of the world-disaffirming qualities of modernity. Orthodox beliefs and more demanding religious practices are much more easily sustained in this situation.[11]

Conservative evangelicals are heavily represented in the South and Midwest in rural areas and small towns. Since World War II, these peripheries have come into increasing contact with forces of modernization. Economic and industrial development, black civil rights struggles, and the universalization of television have eroded many of the boundaries that had separated orthodox Protestants from "the world." Many analysts of the New Christian Right suggest that its social base is greatest in these newly modernizing areas. Guth argues: "that the current religious militance draws much of its strength from the rapidly modernizing regions of the South and West hints in some way the processes of modernization and secularization may be responsible for the movement."[12] Conservative Christians' decision to publicly and vigorously challenge the legitimacy of modernism and secular humanism suggests that the traditional buffer zones surrounding the evangelical worldview have lost some of their protective power. The key institutions through which evangelicalism has been maintained and propagated have, in the last 30 years, increasingly come under pressure from the disaffirming pressures of modernization.

Conservative evangelicals' original response to the crisis of modernism was to disenfranchise themselves from the broader society. As Marsden says, the pietistic element of 19thcentury revivalism required a separation from "worldliness and apostasy."[13] This ideological separatism provided evangelicalism with the means to preserve its belief system and construct alternative religious institutions and practices. At the same time, conservative evangelicals' geographical and social separation from mainstream society permitted the maintenance of a distinct world outlook. By the 1950s, Hunter says, evangelicalism had crafted a "cognitive defense" against modernity "within which the meaning of conservative Protestantism could be plausibly maintained."[14] The concept of separation has gradually taken on a new meaning for many evangelicals, however, reflecting a theological shift from a dualist to a conversionist perspective.

Before the 1940s, separation was defined negatively: The world is sinful so Christians, as individuals, must avoid its seductions while obeying its laws. After World War II, as many evangelicals reaped the benefits of postwar economic growth, separation began to be defined differently: Secularism, a by-product of modernism, is sinful, so conservative Christians, as an organized body, must fight to replace it with evangelical values and institutions. That is, they must work within culture to reform it. This is the characteristic view of the NCR and of Robertson, while Swaggart's dualist theology continues to insist that separation from the world is still the best defense against modern values. This shift in the meaning of separation has had consequences for the extent to which evangelicals have been willing to engage in social and political activity.[15] The creation of the Religious Roundtable and the Moral Majority are two manifestations of this increased political involvement; the explicitly political content of the "700 Club," Falwell's "Old Time Gospel Hour," and much of TBN's programming is another.[16]

SYMBOLIC STRUGGLE AND THE MAKING OF THE NEW CHRISTIAN RIGHT

Because the maintenance and propagation of conservative evangelicalism depends on perpetuating its symbol system, the battle against modernism and secularization necessarily takes symbolic form. Heinz contends that the New Christian Right is engaged in a struggle to create a "countermythology" to combat the "mythologies" of secular humanism and liberal Christianity.[17] Conservative evangelicals identify secular humanism as a source of corruption and godlessness leading to a wide array of social ills from abortion to homosexuality. Secular humanism is seen as particularly pervasive and dangerous because it informs the "cultural assumptions of contemporary intellectuals who significantly control symbol production."[18] Hunter's analysis supports this argument. He contends that modernism is "irregularly distributed in society" and is concentrated in urban centers, the academy, the professions, and the public sphere generally, which are the primary sites of symbolic production (e.g., education, media, law, public policy, etc.).[19] Modernism—and its embodiment in the ideology and practice of these powerful symbol producers—constitutes a threat to evangelical belief because its "symbols and its structures are deeply contrary to [the] religious, supernaturalistic assumptions" on which evangelicalism rests.[20] Heinz proposes that the various mythologies offered by conservative evangelicalism, liberal Christianity, and secular humanism can be understood as contending interpretations or "stories" about American history and culture. The National Council of Churches (the organizational arm of liberal Protestantism) has also taken this position. In 1981, an NCC report titled "Christianity and Crisis" viewed the current liberal-conservative schism in Protestantism as "a contest over opposing American stories" that are played out through the use of "rhetorical and political symbols."[21]

In the current struggle against modernism, conservative evangelicalism has developed a new strategy. Rather than retreating to safer ground and carving out relatively protected social spaces within which to preserve and practice their beliefs, many evangelicals are challenging modernism on its own ground—that of symbolic production. I believe that this new strategy was adopted for several reasons: The forces and structures of modernization have penetrated nearly every available social space, thus posing a greater threat to the evangelical worldview; conservative Protestants have discovered allies among other social groups similarly dismayed by the disintegration of traditional values (e.g. conservative Catholics, Mormons, and orthodox Jews); and evangelicals have recognized the potential power inherent in the control of symbolic creation (communication), partly through their successful use of print and broadcast media. As Heinz notes:

> If the [New Christian Right] is engaged in a contest over the meaning of America's story, and if public symbols are the key instruments through which overarching systems of meaning are discovered and constructed, then gaining access to symbol production (generation, selection, definition, dissemination and control) is indispensable.[22]

Direct mail technology, the expansion of religious broadcasting, and skillful manipulation of the secular media have given Christian Right activists broad access to the production of public symbols or "stories" about the nature of society. But access alone is not enough. For the story told by the NCR to be persuasive, it must speak to and about the experiences of significant numbers of Americans. Wuthnow contends that conservative evangelicals have renewed their interest in politics because the political climate of the 1970s was hospitable to their moral perspective. Evangelicalism has historically been opposed to the separation of public and private morality. This is one of the bases of its hostility to modernism. Wuthnow suggests that Vietnam, Watergate, the Supreme Court decision on abortion, and the election of Jimmy Carter provoked a national reconsideration of the public/private relationship through which "morality came to be viewed as a public issue rather than in strictly private terms."[23] As debates about morality were played out in the public arena (e.g., in the media), evangelicals felt more at home in society: "They found a version of their view being expressed in far quarters, including the nation's major news media and the White House itself."[24] Carter's election, in particular, was seen as a symbolic victory among evangelicals; it shifted their religious perspective from the margins of social life to its center. Their values and beliefs were suddenly treated with respect by the secular media which previously had relegated orthodox Protestantism to cult status. By recognizing the evangelical worldview as a legitimate public perspective, the secular media helped constitute conservative evangelicalism as a movement. As Heinz argues:

> The national attention that evangelicalism received in the 1970s forged a symbolic link between their own identity and that of the larger society, giving them a sense of political entitlement which made it more conceivable to speak out on moral issues. Evangelicals perceived themselves as having a special message to bring to the American people.[25]

The reconnection of public and private morality gave conservative evangelicals a platform from which to speak, and it is in terms of morality that the NCR has thrown itself into politics. Indeed, the unity of the New Christian Right derives from breaking down the barriers that had separated politics, morality, and religion. "Evangelicals' commitment to the preservation of traditional morality, together with the growing politicitization of morality more generally, provided the symbolic linkage necessary to legitimate evangelicals' awakening interest in politics."[26] It is the task of the New Christian Right to maintain this symbolic link. Religious broadcasters such as Robertson, who are identified with the NCR, actively reconstitute the connection between politics and Christian morality. Programs such as the "700 Club" encourage political activism in terms of moral imperatives that derive from divine mandates. The tenets of Christian Civilization are forwarded as pillars of public morality and the NCR's political agenda is legitimized by linking its moral claims to the public interest.

The success of any modern social movement depends on building a coalition around clearly identified issues. A movement must also have a clearly identifiable opposition if it is to create "enjoinment in the moral arena." Movements such as the NCR therefore have to minimize differences "inside" while enhancing differences with those who are "outside" in order to create consubstantiality. The New Christian Right creates this unity among constituents by stressing general moral issues and downplaying specific internal divisions. As Wuthnow notes, "Morality was the one issue on which evangelicals agreed. They remained deeply divided in many other ways—theologically, denominationally, geographically."[27] Tim LeHaye, an outspoken leader of the NCR, publicly acknowledged the importance of minimizing such divisions. In an anti-homosexual campaign in California, he said: "Knowing pastors as we did, we all recognized that the only way to organize them was to make it clear that our basis of cooperation was moral, not theological."[28]

The significant theological differences within evangelicalism (e.g., Fundamentalists versus Pentecostals, charismatics versus non-charismatics, denominational disputes and demographical distinctions) are rarely addressed by NCR activists (such differences did surface, however, in the PTL scandal). Religious broadcasters who are active in the New Christian Right are part of this coalition-building enterprise. According to Horsfield, the Moral Majority was initially successful because it was able to organize previously divergent and disenfranchised groups of conservative Christians around a moral consensus. Falwell's campaign demonstrated "the potential of television and its associated media to bring together elements of society that previously had been scattered" and to unite them "in a potentially dramatic way."[29] As I show in the program analysis, Robertson's message echoes the agenda of the New Christian Right. The "700 Club" seeks to bridge divisions among conservative evangelicals and to create a political coalition around moral issues.[30] Swaggart is not in the business of coalition building, either religious or political. He is creating a consubstantiality of the "elect" based on an exclusionary theology. Swaggart's followers are not out to save the world, but to save their eternal souls. Robertson tries to convince viewers that these goals are identical.

The key sites of moral contestation (and therefore of symbolic production) for the New Christian Right are the family, the education system, and the mass media. Battles to influence or control public school curricula (e.g., teaching creationism alongside evolution, controlling availability of reading material, restoring school prayer, prohibiting homosexual teachers) and to promote "pro-family" legislation (e.g., restricting teenage contraception, opposing the Equal Rights Amendment and homosexuality, prohibiting abortion, etc.) are struggles over the "implanting, development and maintenance of symbolic universes."[31] Campaigns against the content of popular culture (e.g., Coalition for Better TV, Accuracy in Media, the American Family Association, Focus on the Family) are also aimed at influencing popular symbolic meanings. The development and growth of evangelical broadcasting, then, is a powerful, important tool in the contest among American mythologies. Developing their own forms of television, in particular, gives conservative evangelicals crucial access to symbolic production because, in their eyes, commercial TV has been the primary means "through which secular humanism was being implanted in the public consciousness."[32] Evangelical broadcasters frequently stress the need for Christian television to counteract the anti-religious messages of secular broadcasting.[33]

If, as Heinz says, secularization is "the process by which more and more sectors of society and culture are withdrawn from the domination or interpretive power of religious symbols,"[34] evangelicals seek to reverse this process—to recapture and redefine areas of social and cultural life that have been penetrated by secular ideology. Religious television is an important component of this process; evangelical programming offers an alternative narrative or story about the relationship between individual action and social morality. Heinz argues that "relating to symbols by drawing meaning from them and attempting to disseminate such meaning is a significant form of expressive social action."[35] As such, televangelism plays a vital role in evangelicalism's struggle to define itself publicly, to propagate its belief system, and to perpetuate itself historically. As Heinz notes: "Seizing access to or control of symbol production gives a social movement the opportunity to create an alternative world through the power of symbols."[36]

THE SYMBOLIC CHARACTER OF COMMITMENT

The Bible, or the primacy of the Word, is the heart of the evangelical symbol system. As an "ultimate" term, the Bible acts as a reference point that explains all natural and social phenomena; it is the primary interpretive tool for individual and collective questions about the nature of society, as well as the chief guide for moral action. As Burke says, an ultimate term functions to explain the relationships among all other terms. The popular evangelical child's prayer, for example, exhibits this function: "Jesus loves me, this I know, because the Bible tells me so." Marsden argues that the notion of *scriptura sola*, which informs Protestantism and has become paramount in evangelicalism, serves to eliminate ambiguity and moral doubt.[37] It permanently defines truth and one's relationship to it. Bob Slosser, president of CBN University, expresses this absolute conviction: "If you're going to take a position, then the Scripture gives you a true position."[38] In such a worldview, transitions are never gradual, but are radical conversions from one state (sin and error) to another (salvation and truth). An ultimate term must also function to spell out the terms of authority in a given social order or subculture. Marsden points out that because evangelicalism is founded on a highly individuated conception of salvation, it lacks a well-defined tradition of institutionalized authority. The absence of institutional guides to personal action places a greater weight on the inerrancy or infallible authority of Scripture.[39]

Appealing to the Bible is a necessary, but not sufficient condition for belonging to the evangelical community. One must also be born again or "choose Jesus" as one's "personal savior." A correct Christian life, and thus salvation, is impossible without this crucial commitment. Gerlach and Hine, in a study of Pentecostalism and of the Black Power movement, argue that the act of commitment plays a major formative role in determining belonging in social movements.[40] Commitment arises from "bridge-burning acts" such as being spiritually reborn. This type of commitment is

> a psycho-social state . . . generated by an act or an experience which separates a convert in some significant way from the established order (or his previous place in it), identifies him with a new set of values, and commits him to changed patterns of behavior.[41]

The act of commitment or rebirth acquires divine significance for evangelicals because it refers back to scriptural mandates.[42] Being born again thus legitimates individual experience, places the believer within a symbolic system and community, and reasserts the authority of the Bible. As Gerlach and Hine note, an act of commitment gives the individual "a sense of finality—of having got firm hold on a belief system or conceptual framework that fully satisfies the human need for explanation and meaning."[43] Jim Whelan, CBN news director, displays this sense of finality:

> We begin with the premise that the center of our universe and that the center of meaning is God through Jesus Christ. It's what gives meaning to our existence. We therefore begin with not only a moral framework but also with a philosophical true north so there's a basis for our values.[44]

Gerlach and Hine contend, and I agree, that the certitude surrounding such acts of commitment cannot be understood as effects or character traits associated abstractly with "authoritarian" or "dogmatic" personalities. Rather, the "cognitive closure" that occurs with a profound act of commitment must be examined in its specific social context and related to the particular symbolic universe that calls forth and is upheld by that act.[45] In the case of conservative evangelicalism, being born again is a transformative experience that simultaneously creates for the believer a personal identity, locates her or him within a consubstantiality of other worshipers, and fuses individual ethos with religious worldview.

THE DICHOTOMY OF INSIDERS AND OUTSIDERS

Consubstantiality, Burke points out, implies an original social division: It requires an "us" and a "them." Evangelicalism rests on a profound division of the saved from the damned, radically separated by the act of spiritual rebirth. Hence, one is either a Christian or a humanist, but never both. Marsden argues that the revivalist tradition in conservative Protestantism "disposed people to think in terms of fundamental dichotomies—between the saved and the lost, the spiritual and the worldly, absolute truth and error." He notes that this belief system, based on a "fixed antithesis between truth and error, allowed little room for historical and developmental views."[46] Gerlach and Hine contend that all modern social movements exhibit this dichotomizing tendency because it creates a clear definition of the opposition and the elect and establishes the terms of belonging.[47]

Wacker also sees a tendency within the Evangelical Right to draw absolute lines between proper and improper belief and conduct. Conservative evangelicals, he says, hold that for every moral question there is only one morally correct answer that "can be discerned with absolute clarity and certainty."[48] Wacker locates this absolutism in evangelicalism's 19th century roots when adherents "were strongly disposed to consider themselves the moral custodians of the culture." He argues that conservative Protestants adopted this custodial position "in direct proportion to the degree that they felt themselves alienated from [the larger culture]."[49] As evangelicals found themselves increasingly at odds with American society, the need to clearly identify the beliefs that set them apart became more urgent. Hence, the "explicit identification of the nature of the dichotomy between worldliness and spirituality" (e.g., strict prohibitions against sensual pleasure and participation in popular culture). Abstinence from such indulgences, according to Marsden, "became the chief symbols of the spiritual separation of the individual from the world."[50] This interpretation of separation is central to Swaggart's dualist theology. Robertson's conversionist stance, on the other hand, tries to overcome this separation by transforming the world to conform to his beliefs. Both positions, however, reflect the insider/outsider tension within conservative evangelicalism.

Moore contends that "religious struggles engage people in elaborate strategies that on each side entail affirmation and denial, advancement and repression, of a set of cultural options."[51] For conservative evangelicals, these options circulate around the insider/outsider paradox. The experience of being an "outsider" is an important basis for cohesion, for fashioning a sense of community capable of withstanding the pressures of the dominant culture. Conservative Protestants certainly found themselves at odds with the direction of the dominant culture in the 1960s and early 1970s. The call by many for a return to "Christian values" and for a renegotiation of the relationship between politics and religion grows out of a historical belief in their role as custodians of social morality. The appeals of evangelical leaders were persuasive to many people precisely because they issued from an absolute and coherent set of beliefs.

Liberal Christianity, which had accommodated social changes in the last 20 years by reinterpreting or compromising doctrinal positions, began to lose much of its explanatory power and distinct message.[52] It appeared to many conservative Christians that liberal theology was becoming indistinguishable from New Age philosophies and the human potential movement. Conservative evangelicalism was strategically positioned to fill the vacuum created by the faltering of liberal Christianity.

Conservative Christians moved into politics and justified their actions by referring to their moral custodial role. The belief that Christians should be the leaders of American (and universal) morality is a recurring them in televangelism. Swaggart, for example, admonishes his viewers to be the "lights of the world" in order to guide the rest of humanity to salvation. In a program meant to raise money for his worldwide evangelization efforts, Swaggart repeatedly told those viewers who were willing to give money that they were helping him "take these countries for Christ." He also warned those who failed to give to the ministry that they were "sending people to hell" because his programs would be taken off the air.[53] Although both men draw on the historical missionary impulse of evangelicalism, Swaggart generally emphasizes the saving of individual souls, while Robertson encourages cultural transformation through Christian action. As he told an interviewer:

> I have always thought that Christians should get involved in public life. . . . The way you lead is from service. If we serve the people with knowledge and compassion and with care, that's the way we ought to take over leadership.[54]

EVANGELICALISM AND THE PROBLEM OF THE SELF

To be effective, contemporary evangelicalism must offer persuasive answers to the modern "problem of the self." The endurance of this religious perspective, Wacker says, is one response to people's "deep bewilderment about the reasons for the faltering of the American Dream."[55] Marsden proposes that fundamentalist Protestantism has been successful precisely because of its "marked divergence from many prevalent twentieth-century trends in preserving a decisive basis for authority in a culture that has lost most of its other moorings."[56] Evangelicalism has tackled the erosion of individual and social meaning by identifying the causes of this modern malaise and by offering explicit solutions. But in confronting the problem of subjectivization, evangelicalism has also implicitly accommodated modernism. The growth of Christian self-help literature, counseling centers, encounter-style retreats, and lifestyle programming is a contemporary phenomenon—one that would have been utterly foreign to 19th century evangelicals. While the solutions to emotional and psychological problems are always defined in spiritual terms, the fact that these difficulties are addressed at all indicates an interpenetration of modernism and orthodox Protestantism.[57]

This particular accommodation to modernism is not uniformly distributed within conservative evangelicalism, however. Swaggart, for example, frequently denounces Christian psychology as a sign that people have rejected God's solutions for their problems and that by so doing Christians have capitulated to the demands of "the World." Robertson's "700 Club," on the other hand, features regular advice segments on how to cope with problems such as depression, obesity, sexual dysfunctions, divorce, and so on. The type of symbolic healing offered by these two programs is related to where they locate the source of the self's division: Swaggart finds it in human nature; Robertson locates it in the corruption of human culture.

I believe that much of the persuasive power of the evangelical belief system lies in its creative responses to the problem of the self and in its ability to make sense of the difficulties of modern life by incorporating these into a coherent symbolic system. Conservative evangelicalism offers a cosmic framework that responds to profound questions about the relationship between society and individual existence at a time when such questions seem to have become increasingly urgent for people both inside and outside its boundaries. Heinz argues that a successful social movement is organized around "symbolic dimensions which promise revitalization, new direction, or legitimation for a particular way of life in a time of bewilderment or loss."[58] A religious movement is particularly well-equipped to respond to such crises because "when symbols are interpreted or experienced as religious, they gain a larger resonance." Conservative evangelicalism has managed to win support and propagate its values because it "has tapped into symbols that turn out to be powerfully resonant in the lives of many people."[59] This study is concerned with the form and substance of those symbols as they are manifested in televangelism and with discovering how and why they resonate for viewers. Heinz argues that it is crucial to listen to "the public stories that are currently being recommended to give meaning and purpose to the American experience" as well as to ask, "When its symbols have been put together, what is the nature of the symbolic universe toward which the NCR points?"[60] I propose that within conservative evangelicalism, there are actually two stories that point to conflicting symbolic universes. The analysis of "Jimmy Swaggart" and the "700 Club" attempts to flesh out and interpret those stories.

NOTES TO CHAPTER 4

1. Richard Pierard, "The New Religious Right in American Politics," in George Marsden, ed., *Evangelicalism in Modern America* (Grand Rapids, MI: Eerdman's, 1984), p. 163.

2. Leo Ribuffo, "Liberals and that Old-time Religion," *Nation,* November 29, 1980, pp. 570-573.

3. Sidney Ahlstrom, "The Radical Turn in Theology and Ethics: Why it Occurred in the 1960s," *Annals of the American Academy of Political and Social Science* 387 (1970): pp. 1-13.

4. Falwell, for example, opposed the early Civil Rights movement on the grounds that it was a political, rather than a religious, concern. His later entry into politics indicates a change in evangelicals' sentiments regarding the relationship between religion and politics. See Frances FitzGerald, *Cities on a Hill: A Journey Through Contemporary American Cultures* (New York: Simon & Schuster, 1986), p. 129.

5. See George H. Williams and Rodney L. Peterson, "Evangelicals: Society, the State, the Nation," in David F. Wells and John D. Woodbridge, eds., *The Evangelicals* (Nashville, TN: Abingdon, 1975), pp. 203-231.

6. This view is held by many students of Evangelicalism. See Jeffrey K. Hadden, "Soul-Saving Via Video," and Leonard I. Sweet, "The 1960s: The Crises of Liberal Christianity and the Public Emergence of Evangelicalism," in Wells and Woodbridge, eds., *The Evangelicals*, pp. 29-45.

7. Grant Wacker, "The Search for Norman Rockwell: Popular Evangelicalism in Contemparary America," in G. Marsden, ed., *Evangelicalism in Modern America* (Grand Rapids, MI: Eerdmans 1984), p. 297.

8. Ibid., pp. 298-99.

9. Quoted in Pat Aufderheide, "The Next Voice You Hear," *Progressive*, September 29, 1985, p. 34.

10. For an overview of the growth of evangelicals' use of media see Richard N. Ostling, "Evangelical Publishing and Broadcasting," in G. Marsden, ed., *Evangelicalism in Modern America* (Grand Rapids, MI Eerdmans, 1984), pp. 46-55. See also Deborah Huntington and Ruth Kaplan, "Whose Gold is Behind the Altar:? Corporate Ties to Evangelicals," *Contemporary Marxism* 4 (Winter 1981-82): pp. 62-94 and Erling Jorstad, "The New Christian Right," *Theology Today, 39* (1981): pp. 193-200.

11. James Hunter, *American Evangelicalism: Conservative Religion and the Quandary of Modernity* (New Brunswick, NJ: Rutgers University Press, 1983), p. 130. He also offers a detailed demographic profile o

evangelicals on pp. 49-60.

12. James L. Guth, "The Politics of the 'Evangelical Right': An Interpretive Essay," paper presented to the American Political Science Association Annual Meeting, September 1981, p. 1. Quoted in Michael Lienesch, "Right-wing Religion: Christian Conservatism as a Political Movement," *Political Science Quarterly*, 97 (1982): p. 412.

13. Marsden, "From Fundamentalism to Evangelicalism: A Historical Analysis," in Wells and Woodbridge, eds., *The Evangelicals*, p. 134.

14. Hunter, *American Evangelicalism*, p. 45.

15. Ibid., pp. 47-48.

16. For an assessment of this increased political activism see Pierard, "The New Religious Right," and Robert Wuthnow, "The Political Rebirth of American Evangelicals, "in R. Liebman and R. Wuthnow, eds., *The New Christian Right: Mobilization and Legitimation* (New York: Aldine, 1983), pp. 133-137.

17. Donald Heinz, "The Struggle to Redefine America," in R. Liebman and R. Wuthnow, eds., *The New Christian Right*, pp. 133-137.

18. Ibid., p. 135.

19. Hunter, *American Evangelicalism*, p. 130.

20. Ibid., p. 131.

21. Heinz, "The Struggle," p. 135, quoted from "The Remaking of America," *Christianity and Crisis*, July 20, 1981, pp. 207-210.

22. Ibid., p. 137.

23. Wuthnow, "The Political Rebirth of American Evangelicals," p. 176.

24. Ibid., p. 177.

25. Ibid.

26. Ibid., p. 179.

27. Ibid., p. 178.

28. Ibid.

29. Horsfield, *Religious Television*, p. 155.

30. Stewart Hoover's study of CBN supports this argument. See his *Mass Media Religion: The Social Sources of the Electronic Church* (Newbury Park, CA: Sage, 1988).

31. Heinz, "The Struggle to Redefine America," p. 143.

32. Ibid., p. 138.

33. Robertson's view of commercial television is typical of religious broadcasters: "I don't think there's any question that (network) television has brought about a lessening of the moral perception of our nation." Quoted in Kenneth Clark, "The $70 Miracle Named CBN," *Chicago Tribune*, July 26, 1985, p. 3.

34. Heinz, "The Struggle to Redefine America," p. 143.

35. Ibid., p. 144

36. Ibid., p. 147.

37. Marsden, *Fundamentalism and American Culture*, pp. 224-225.

38. Kenneth R. Clark, "'Christian News' a CBN Objective," *Chicago Tribune*, June 26, 1985, Sec. 5, p. 3.

39. Marsden, *Fundamentalism and American Culture*, p. 136.

40. Luther Gerlach and Virginia Hine, *People Power, Change: Movements of Social Transformation* (Indianapolis, IN: Bobbs Merrill, 1970).

41. Ibid., p. xvii.

42. A central biblical passage for evangelical Christians is John 3:3: "Jesus said, 'In truth, in very truth, I tell you, unless a man has been born over again he cannot see the Kingdom of God'." *New English Bible*, N.T., p. 111.

43. Gerlach and Hine, *People, Power, Change*, p. 161.

44. K. Clark, "Christian News."

45. Gerlach and Hine, *People, Power, Change*, p. 161.

46. Marsden, "From Fundamentalism to Evangelicalism," p. 137.

47. Gerlach and Hine, *People, Power, Change*, pp. 174-175.

48. Wacker, "Popular Evangelicalism," p. 298.

49. Ibid., p. 312.

50. Marsden, *Fundamentalism and American Culture*, p. 134.

51. R. Laurence Moore, *Religious Outsiders and the Making of Americans* (New York: Oxford University Press, 1986), p. xii.

52. See Sweet, "The 1960s," for a more in-depth discussion of the transformation of liberal Christianity.

53. "Jimmy Swaggart Telecast," special episode titled "Partners in the Harvest," March 15, 1987.

54. K. Clark, "$70 Miracle," p. 3.

55. Wacker, "Popular Evangelicalism," p. 306.

56. Marsden, "From Fundamentalism to Evangelicalism," pp. 138-139.

57. Hunter discusses this trend in *American Evangelicalism*, pp. 94-98.

58. Heinz, "The Struggle to Redefine America," p. 144.

59. Ibid., p. 145.

60. Ibid., pp. 147-48.

5

The Symbolic Universe of Evangelical Television

THE RISE OF EVANGELICAL TELEVISION

Unlike orthodox evangelicalism, which has been displaced from the center of American religious life to a peripheral position, televangelism has migrated from the margins of religious television in the 1950s to a position of overwhelming dominance today. This success story is the result of governmental policy decisions, the economic structure of the television industry, and shrewd business practices by evangelical broadcasters.[1]

In the early years of television, the networks offered free air time to mainline denominations in fulfillment of the Federal Communication Commission mandate to operate in the "public interest." Besides this "sustaining time," networks provided religious programmers with technical support. Mainline denominations fulfilled their part of the bargain by producing noncontroversial, generalized "Christian" programming (usually in the form of televised religious services or a "talking heads" format). This arrangement benefited both parties; mainliners retained their hegemony over the content of religious communication, while fitting into networks' overall strategy of avoiding controversy. Television, after all, was conceived as a commercial medium to attract the broadest possible audience and was born and became a national medium in the heyday of the Cold War and McCarthyism.

The partnership of networks and mainline denominations

97

effectively eliminated other religious perspectives. Orthodox Protestant groups, who by this time were accustomed to a marginal status, were forced to be more creative in getting their views on the new medium. Some of the larger conservative denominations (including the Southern Baptist Convention, Seventh Day Adventists and the Lutheran Missouri Synod) devised alternative methods of acquiring exposure by buying air time from local stations and producing programs with members' donations. Smaller orthodox denominations and individual evangelists, who lacked the financial resources of large memberships, looked to the example of earlier radio evangelists.[2] According to Horsfield, the pioneers of evangelical TV programming who ultimately survived were aggressive and highly competitive; they developed a program structure built around preachers who had the charisma to elicit audience support. (Rex Humbard went on the air in 1953, Oral Roberts aired for the first time in 1956, Falwell followed in 1957, and Billy Graham's crusades were telecast throughout the decade.) This arrangement of buying air time from local stations enabled evangelical broadcasters to circumvent the network-mainliner monopoly. By 1959, this type of religious programming constituted a little more than half (53%) of all religious shows on television.[3]

Paid-time religious programs—the vast majority of which are evangelical in perspective—came to dominate in the 1960s and 1970s because of changes in FCC regulations and in the structure of the television industry. In 1960, the FCC released guidelines saying that there was no difference, in terms of serving the public interest, between sustaining-time and paid-time religious programming. Thus, stations were released from the obligation to provide free religious air time. The Commission also removed restrictions on the amount of solicitation permitted on "noncommercial" programs; this meant that TV stations could pack more advertising into religious shows, making them highly profitable. Finally, the FCC guidelines exempted religious programming from the restraints of the Fairness Doctrine, saying that "religion has not yet reached the level of social controversy."[4] This freed stations from any responsibility for the content of religious programs; religious broadcasters could therefore tackle any political or social issues without forcing stations to "balance" these viewpoints with other programming.

This governmental policy revision made paid-time religious programming extremely profitable and particularly attractive to independent stations seeking to compete with network affiliates. As Horsfield notes, the FCC put religious TV into the domain of the economic marketplace, thus "giving a distinct advantage to those expressions of religious faith that are economically competitive."[5] This profit imperative dovetails with the general economic structure of commercial television. As competition within the TV industry grew due to the increase in independent stations in the 1960s and the growth in UHF and cable stations in the 1970s and 1980s, evangelical broadcasters pursued their strategy of purchasing nonnetwork air time. Robertson went on the air in 1961; Swaggart, Schuller, Bakker, and a host of others began broadcasting in the 1970s. Today, the great majority of paid-time religious programming is aired on unaffiliated and cable stations. TV ministries also began buying stations and developing their own networks in the 1960s and 1970s. By 1977, 92 % of religious television was paid-time programming, and local religious shows had been virtually eliminated. The largest evangelical broadcasters had also achieved a pronounced dominance in religious TV; the 10 major programs constituted more than half of all national airings in 1979.[6] Most religious programmers belong to the evangelical association of National Religious Broadcasters (NRB), whose membership increased tenfold between 1968 and 1985.[7] The NRB's National Directory of Religious Broadcasting included 96 TV stations and 1,043 radio stationsin 1985; by 1989 those numbers had grown to 336 TV and 1,485 radio stations.[8] According to Horsfield, NRB members hold a near monopoly over religious air time in the United States due to their "cutthroat purchase of time."[9]

The growth of evangelical television ministries in the 1960s and 1970s had implications extending beyond the broadcasting industry. As this type of religious programming came to dominate the airwaves, it gave evangelicals a broader base for the production of public symbols. The increased visibility of prominent TV preachers and evangelical leaders helped create the perception that evangelicalism was a viable and growing religious force. The television ministries also gave viewers a sense of identification with the wider evangelical community, thus reinforcing audience members' personal commitment to that belief system. Research in the last 20 years indicates that conservative churches have grown much more than have liberal denominations.[10] Televangelism did not produce this growth by itself, but it has helped unify conservative evangelicals through the creation of national celebrities and charismatic televangelists who command the loyalty of large audiences. Further, as this religious perspective acquired dominance in television broadcasting, it heightened the perception in the TV industry, and in the wider society, that evangelicalism constituted a "social movement." As I suggested earlier, a movement comes into being only when it is perceived as such by outsiders. For such a perception to develop, a social movement must be constituted in the realm of public symbols. Symbolic production, then, is a key function of evangelical television.

According to Horsfield, the interplay of public perception, the commercial television industry, evangelical activism, and TV ministries have contributed to evangelicalism's move from a marginalized to a more central position in society. In the 1960s, he says,

> evangelicalism as a whole began to shift away from the fringes of American society into the country's religious mainstream, shifting the relative power relation of the television industry away from the mainline broadcasters and their viewpoint to the evangelical broadcasters and their approach to television.[11]

Evangelical broadcasters were therefore accorded greater power and influence in the realm of symbolic production at the expense of other religious perspectives. Further, because viewers generously supported this programming, televangelists were able to build wealthy media empires and employ the latest computer technology to enhance their fund-raising capabilities. Computerization (the use of sophisticated direct mail techniques and telephone banks) has also made possible the well-organized power bases on which television ministries rely and prosper.[12]

THE "INTIMATE" MEDIUM AND THE PARASOCIAL RELATIONSHIP

Personalized mailings and phone banks are also employed to constitute a quasi-personal relationship between TV preachers and audiences. Pseudo-dialogic qualities incorporated into evangelical programming help establish an identification between televangelists and viewers and solidify the audience's connection to evangelical beliefs. Merton found that this use of fabricated "dialogue" in a Kate Smith bond drive in 1943 gave her a degree of interaction and flexibility in shaping appeals that is normally missing from mass mediated communication. Such "reciprocal interplay," Merton said, reinforced listeners' sense of being appealed to personally, binding together the audience and performer.[13] One of the striking qualities of television is its ability to produce a feeling of intimacy between viewers and performers, both real (as in the case of "Uncle" Walter Cronkite) and fictional (witness the volume of mail sent to TV characters). Such personal identification with people who are actually strangers results in part from television being an "intimate" medium: Programs and personalities invade or are invited into our homes—our most private spaces.[14] The serial nature of most television programming also creates a sense of intimacy and familiarity with TV characters; we watch these people daily or weekly and over time come to feel we know and understand their personal lives, weaknesses, motives, and so on.[15]

Television's ability to create this "intimacy at a distance," according to Horton and Wohl, is based on an "illusion of face-to-face relationship with the performer."[16] This is particularly true of programs such as talk shows that are based on conversation. By employing strategies that mimic reallife conversation, the TV host or interviewer (the authors use the term "persona") invites viewers to join in the program's action and message. Such strategies include using "subjective camera" techniques, creating a casual atmosphere on the set, blurring the line between the host and viewers, attributing special character traits to cast members, and addressing the viewing audience directly. (These devices are used extensively in the "700 Club," less so in Swaggart's crusade program.) Horton and Wohl call this simulated conversation "para-social interaction," which consciously employs the qualities that we usually associate with interactions in our primary social groups. The authors propose that through such strategies, television personalities (e.g., interviewers, talk show hosts, announcers, etc.)—"whose existence is a function of the media themselves"—are able to achieve a singular intimacy with their largely anonymous audience. This intimacy is "extremely influential with, and satisfying for, the great numbers who willingly receive it and share in it."[17]

The regularity of Sunday programs and weekday shows also permits televangelists (and TV personalities generally) to offer the audience a continuing relationship that enhances the feeling of intimacy between viewers and performer. Religious broadcasters promote this relationship by revealing personal information and anecdotes: Swaggart tells and retells the story of his childhood conversion and relates instances of God's presence in his life; Robertson refers to his family, his military and boxing experience, and his friendships with important public figures. The programs also encourage regular, repeated contact between performer and viewer. Swaggart's sermons are often presented in two or threepart segments aired on successive Sundays with next week's sermon topic mentioned at the end of each show. The "700 Club" closes with previews of the next day's show, and special broadcasts (such as Robertson's 1987 trip to Israel) are heavily promoted beforehand. Because regular viewers are the most generous donors, religious broadcasters must devise strategies that encourage repeated contact. The structure of serial programming itself (which originated with serialized accounts in the print media) cultivates familiarity; the performer's "appearance is a regular and dependable event, to be counted on, planned for, and integrated into the routines of daily life."[18]

The relationship between viewer and performer therefore

acquires a history, and through an "accumulation of shared past experiences gives additional meaning to the present performance."[19] Jim
Bakker's resignation from PTL, for example, was interpreted differently by his regular audience than by nonviewers. Loyal audience members were initially far less critical of Bakker, and a majority believed
the devil, rather than Bakker, was responsible for his fall into
adultery.[20] Longtime viewers had already "participated" in his and
Tammy's on-air marital crises, supported Tammy through her breakdown and drug addiction, and exhibited their feelings for the couple
by increasing donations after Bakker stepped down. Many devoted followers of Swaggart were similarly forgiving. Swaggart drew on that
ongoing relationship with his viewers in asking for their understanding and absolution during his crisis. Noncelebrity guests, studio audience members, and call-in viewers on the "700 Club" often express
"love" for Robertson and his co-hosts; the basis of this emotional connection is their previous viewing experiences. For example, many
viewers sent birthday cards to former co-host Danuta Soderman as if
she were a personal acquaintance. Viewers' affinity for Robertson created a serious problem for the show when he left the air briefly to run
for president. Oral Roberts's ability to raise $8 million by suggesting
the money would prevent his being "called home" by God attests to
the degree of personal devotion television ministers command from
their audiences.

The immediacy and intimacy of television that brings televangelists into people's homes creates an "evocative relationship"
between the viewer and broadcaster, according to Horsfield.
Evangelical programming utilizes and capitalizes on this capacity by
both addressing and appealing to viewers' personal concerns.[21] Fore
suggests that the success of the "electronic church" stems from its
having "developed an extremely accurate diagnosis of the spiritual
hunger" of its audience.[22] Because the television medium is ultimately
a one-way communication, however, religious broadcasters cannot
achieve actual intimacy with their audience. Rather, the parasocial
relationship effected between the TV performer and viewers is a simu-
lation: "The interaction . . . is one-sided, nondialectical, controlled by
the performer, and not susceptible to mutual development."[23] The
one-sided nature of communication between programmers and audiences is particularly transparent in the use of phone banks and computerized mail systems. Viewers are continually invited by religious
broadcasters to call in their prayer requests, testimony, and pledges,
but their calls are received by trained "prayer counselors," not by
Robertson et al. When Robertson asks viewers to phone in and
express their opinions on specific political issues, they reach a computer that merely records that a call has been made.[24] Requests for

prayers are systematically categorized according to the type of problem mentioned. A viewer who asks for prayers for her alcoholic husband will then receive a letter referring to her by name and signed by the TV minister that discusses her specific troubles. The letter most often asks for funds to help the TV ministry combat that particular social or individual ill.[25]

While not all callers respond to these techniques by sending donations, enough do to keep religious broadcasters in business. Further, in a world in which most of our daily contacts are impersonal, it must be somewhat heartening to have one's problems recognized and responded to. Many callers probably do not consider the elaborate computer technology that mediates their relationship with their favorite televangelist. The relationship or identification between religious TV personalities and their audiences, then, is a completely mediated one, based on an illusion of personal interaction. In Horsfield's view:

> [the] implied intimacy is basically dishonest. The presentation of the broadcaster as a compassionate friend is actually a selective, edited, and cultivated message neatly honed by market research and designed to evoke a particular response.[26]

RELIGIOUS COMMUNICATION AND MASS MEDIA

While one of the responses desired by religious broadcasters is continued financial support, this is not their sole aim. In fact, television preachers and program hosts generally insist that donations are merely a means to the real end of their broadcasts: the saving of souls for Christ. Horsfield and Schultze contend that the majority of evangelical broadcasters share a utilitarian attitude toward media technology, whereby television and radio are simply megaphones for the Gospel message rather than complex social and technological formations that mediate both the Christian message and the nature of the relationship between preachers and the faithful.[27] This hypodermic view of television's effects leads televangelists to equate the size of the audience with the number of souls saved. This attitude toward mass communication is part of evangelicalism's history. The use of mass media to disseminate and amplify religious messages, as we have seen, is as old as Protestantism. The Reformation was tied to the printing press; the Bible was the first book (in 1456) to be mass produced.

Nord argues that the development of a mass press in the United States actually originated in the evangelical movement's goal to reach all Americans with the Gospel message.[28] In the two decades before the birth of the Penny Press, the American Bible Society and American Tract Society pioneered in the development of new printing technology and distribution techniques that are usually assumed to have originated with mass circulation newspapers. Designed to reach the widest audience possible, the tracts and Bibles produced by these evangelical publishers instituted formats and styles that would cut across divisions of class and denomination. That is, the gospel message was simplified and standardized. Bibles were printed without comment, tracts were crafted to be "plain," "entertaining," "interesting," "unassuming," and noncontroversial.[29] These are the same qualities that came to be linked with popular journalism and literature (and later with radio and television programming). Further, like the Penny papers, these publications were made affordable to a mass audience. As an American Tract Society noted: "Perhaps in no way can the message of the Gospel be conveyed *to more individuals at less expense*".[30]

Contemporary televangelists thus draw on a lengthy historical tradition of adopting mass media for religious purposes. Religious services began to be regularly broadcast within two months of radio's birth as a mass medium in 1920, and one of the first offerings on television in 1940 was an Easter Sunday service.[31] Contemporary TV preachers employ television for evangelism with the same attitude that compelled their 19th-century counterparts to utilize new printing technology. Nord points to an American Bible Society report that spoke of "the Christian obligation to use the 'mighty engine' of print just as God himself had used the written word to reveal himself to man."[32]

Fashioning a religious message for a mass medium to appeal to a mass audience places important constraints on the nature of that message, however. Religious broadcasters' dependence on continued audience support and their adoption of commercial television's competitive strategies have had profound consequences for the character of evangelical discourse. In learning how to locate and target specific Christian "markets," broadcasters have also been forced to shape their communication in ways that appeal to those targeted groups, or, as Fore says, they have "become captive to the commercial broadcasting system and its demands."[33] This has led, in many cases, to a transformation and dilution of the evangelical message. Mainline denominational programmers, who did not have to worry about audience shares or viewer support, could assume that people who watched their shows were interested in the message independently of the format. Producers of paid-time programming cannot make such assumptions; if ratings drop, so does their income and likelihood of staying on the air. Holding viewers' interest is therefore a primary concern for evangelical broadcasters. Because the maintenance of interest (e.g., ratings) is also essential in commercial broadcasting, religious programmers found a logical model for their programs in the techniques and formats of secular television. Successful televangelists, says Horsfield, are those who can structure an appealing "message package" and build an organization "capable of generating mass support."[34] Dependence on a mass audience, Horsfield notes,

> means that the Gospel must not only be proclaimed, but it must be proclaimed in such a way that it meets with the approval of a large share of one's audience . . . [and thereby] triggers the audience's desire to give.[35]

Evangelical broadcasters, in their pursuit of large audiences, have learned to obey the first commandment of television: "Thou Shalt Not Bore." One religious broadcaster contends that an emphasis on entertainment "flows from the natural demands of the visual medium," hence, the obsolescence of the mainline denominational program with its "spiritual talking head."[36] Television has taught us to expect visual appeal. Evangelical broadcasters try to fulfill that expectation and to match commercial television's emphasis on entertainment at the expense of information. Much televangelism therefore incorporates and highlights the spectacular, celebrity images of luxury and dramatic transformations; in this sense, it is very much like secular television. Like commercial television, most Christian programming offers immediate gratification and simple solutions to complex problems: lives are transformed, serious illnesses cured, souls redeemed in the span of 30 or 60 minutes. Like much commercial television programming, religious programs also simplify complicated political and social issues to make them palatable for mass consumption. Celebrity guests attribute their fame and riches to their "decisions for Christ." Ordinary people testify to having been saved by watching the "700 Club" or cured by Robertson's "Word of Knowledge." As Fore argues, "the electronic church is great show business, a terrific audience grabber, and very much in tune with the times." But, like Schultze and many critics of evangelical television, Fore questions its theological motives and relevance; the popularity of the "electronic church," he suggests, "is more a sign that it has become just a part of TV's entertainment package with a religious gloss than it is the good news of the Christian faith."[37]

Although evangelical programs tend to propose that solutions to most social problems are ultimately personal—society will improve when individuals are reborn and lead Christian lives—there are important differences within this perspective. Swaggart is concerned almost exclusively with individual salvation because he believes society is already doomed. Robertson sees Christians as the moral custodians of society so that personal salvation is the first step toward reestablishing "Christian Civilization." Both orientations are grounded in the insider/outsider paradox and reflect the dualist and conversionist theologies held by Swaggart and Robertson. Swaggart constructs a community "outside" the world; Robertson forges a community of future "insiders" who will reverse society's moral decay. In both cases, however, issues are presented in absolute terms. One is a "Christian" or a godless humanist, good or evil, saved or damned. Solutions to social ills are equally dichotomized. In this worldview, the complexities of cultural difference, the international economic structure, class antagonisms, and structural inequality simply disappear.

In this respect, religious programming is not too different from secular television. Drama and comedy series are structured on a principle of closure that reduces all problems to personal difficulties and solves them within the space of a program.[38] Television news simplifies social reality by reducing it to isolated "events," turning deep social conflicts into disputes between prominent personalities, and dramatizing rather than analyzing issues.[39] If televangelism offers an alternative story to counteract the dominant narrative of secular society, the packaging of both tales is strikingly similar. Rather than devise new formats and genres to convey the evangelical message, religious broadcasters have for the most part simply borrowed the conventions of commercial television. The creation of 24-hour Christian television networks has exacerbated this problem because of the medium's enormous appetite for programming. Trinity Broadcasting Network (TBN), for example, features Christianized game shows, children's programs, morning exercise workouts for women, soap operas, variety programs, and music videos for young people ("Real Videos"). Besides its flagship "700 Club," CBN has produced a children's show, a soap opera, and a news program, and filled out the rest of its broadcast day with reruns of "wholesome" family shows such as "Father Knows Best." CBN's development of the Family Channel is a continuation of that strategy. This move toward variety in programming, according to Bisset, indicates that Christian television is a "creative medium"—one that understands that mass evangelism must be entertaining if it is to be effective.[40] It may be, however, that in the process, Christian television has become most effective at entertaining. The use of standard television formats filled with religious content tends to blur the line between "Christian" and secular TV. Horsfield and other critics of televangelism argue that this type of programming necessarily deemphasizes the mystical, sacramental, and liturgical elements of Christianity, prevents the formation of genuine Christian community by "privatizing" religious worship, and robs the Christian message of its critical edge by reproducing the culture-affirming qualities of commmercial television.[41] I address these criticisms in more detail in the program analysis.

It is important to note divergences from this wholesale adoption of commercial television formats. Certainly, the talk show/news magazine format of the "700 Club" has been largely determined by its secular counterparts. Many televangelists are avid promoters of a "health and wealth Gospel" (e.g., Robertson, the Bakkers, Roberts, Kenneth Copel, and others) that is highly compatible with the values of consumer culture. Robert Schuller extols a mixture of religion, popular psychology, and positive thinking that mirrors the affirmative, upbeat tone of much commercial programming. A minority of televangelists, however, preach a version of evangelicalism that retains some of the historical tension between spirituality and the world, and some also draw on cultural forms and traditions that precede television.

Swaggart is a prominent example of this latter perspective. Not only does he frequently and vehemently denounce the fusion of popular culture and evangelism, but his crusade program is less dependent on standard television formats. Swaggart's program originates in the cultural form of the 19th century camp meetings and urban revivals. It is an edited version of a live crusade, set not in a television studio, but in civic auditoriums and arenas in major cities. These were also the sites of the mass revivals of Finney and Moody. The Swaggart crusade does include entertainment (country music with a gospel message), but the use of music here dates back to the old-style revivals. Indeed, Moody established himself as a preacher in partnership with musician Ira Sankey, who opened their crusades with inspirational gospel hymns.[42] The function of the music in such settings was integrated into the aims of revivalism: it was intended to buoy the emotions and spirituality of the audience and prepare listeners to accept the Holy Spirit. Swaggart's program opens with gospel music that is intended to excite audience emotions, to bring the congregation to its feet, and to open listeners to the evangelist's message. The form of the crusade program—gospel music, sermon, and altar call—is prefigured by that of the urban revival. Television is employed as a means for conveying that religious ritual to the viewing audience—to recreate for the viewer the emotionalism and interaction between preacher and congregation that characterized 19thcentury camp meetings and revivals. Grounding his services in this traditional cultural form permits Swaggart to retain some of the historical tension and separation between evangelicalism and "the world" in a way that is not possible for religious programming that embraces television's standard formats. Shows such as the "700 Club," in contrast, are developed wholly within televisual discourse and are "Christian" only insofar as they insert religious content into the forms dictated by that discourse. This type of program more actively integrates the evangelical belief system and the values of modern culture.

THE AUDIENCE FOR EVANGELICAL TELEVISION

The strategies of evangelical television cannot be examined apart from the people it addresses. Contrary to claims by religious broadcasters, research indicates that the audience for televangelism stabilized or tapered off after peaking in 1977, and suffered significant a decline following the scandals of 1987 and 1988.[43] The Annenberg study in 1984 estimated that 13.3 million Americans tune in to religious television each week; this figure includes programming by mainline denominations as well as by prominent TV ministries.[44] It does not take into account multiple viewing—an important consideration since many respondents in the study said they watch more than one program per week. Nor does it account for those people who watch without agreeing with the viewpoints espoused by a particular program (I certainly am not the only "unpersuaded" viewer in the audience). Horsfield also points out that the total audience for televangelism is relatively small compared to the drawing power of most commercial programming. In 1981, for example, only five religious programs reached over 1% of the viewing population (these were Swaggart, Roberts, Schuller, Humbard, and "Day of Discovery").[45] The potential social impact of televangelism, therefore, lies not so much in the number of viewers it attracts, but in its ability to transform audience members into social actors—to "coalesce an audience around a social or political issue."[46]

Research also shows a strong correlation between the characteristics of religious television audiences and those of the evangelical population as a whole. Viewers of evangelical programs are disproportionately Southern, female, 50 years or older, rural, have modest incomes, and a lower than average education.[47] A 1978 Gallup poll found that viewers of this programming are more likely to hold beliefs and engage in practices associated with conservative evangelicalism (e.g., to have had a conversion experience, to hold that the Bible is the inerrant word of God, to believe in a personal devil, and to read the Bible, attend church, and talk about their faith more often).[48] Further, a majority of evangelical Christians do not watch religious television; the audience for televangelism therefore constitutes "a subculture within evangelicalism."[49] All available studies indicate that for the most part, televangelism primarily reaches those who have previously committed themselves to evangelical beliefs and practices. That is, television preachers speak to and are supported by the already converted. As Horsfield says, "It is apparent . . . from the dominant characteristics of the audience that, for the most part, the broadcasters are not reaching outsiders but insiders."[50] The fierce competition among TV ministries for viewers and supporters suggests they are aware that their audience is not infinite.[51] Horsfield argued in 1981 that evangelical broadcasting was already approaching its audience saturation point.[52] Paul Virts, CBN's director of marketing, agrees that the decline in viewership and donations is a result of the glut of evangelical programming: "Things peaked around 1985. Since then we've seen a lot of donor fatigue."[53]

Critics of televangelism often cite its failure to fulfill its stated goal of bringing new converts to Christ. TV preachers respond by arguing that the conversion rate is dependent on expanding their operations to reach a bigger audience. This reasoning, I believe, is flawed. The ceiling on the potential audience for televangelism does not depend on technological enhancements or refinements in persuasive appeals, but on the nature of the fit between the evangelical belief system and the reality of people's lives. For televangelism and orthodox Protestantism to be persuasive they must offer adequate interpretations of individual and social existence. Rationalism, cultural pluralism, and the split between public and private life have so thoroughly penetrated the ideological assumptions of most Americans that the road to salvation offered by evangelicalism is no longer open for the majority of people. Televangelism speaks largely to "insiders" because "outsiders" are, and will continue to be, immune to its message.

The persuasive strategies of evangelical programming must therefore aim at capturing a greater share of the evangelical "market" and holding those viewers it has already attracted. To attain these ends, religious broadcasters must be highly sensitive to the values, beliefs, and desires of their audiences. In the competitive world of television today, achieving a unity between the "voice within" and the "voice without" requires sophisticated demographic research; evangelical programmers' support for and cooperation in the Annenberg study was no doubt motivated by their need for accurate marketing information.[54] In that study, viewers of religious programs said they received the most "gratification" from the sermons, preaching, and music, and from the experience of "having your spirits lifted" and "feeling close to God."[55] Because these "needs" are highly generalized, individual televangelists must try to devise specific programming strategies to fulfill such desires in ways compatible with the characteristics of their target market. Differences in evangelical programs are not limited to format, but also stem from differences in audience makeup and the perspectives of the preachers. Swaggart, for example, is highly critical of the "health and wealth gospel" promoted by Robertson, Copeland, and others. Similarly, a viewer who embraces Schuller's positive thinking theology would be uncomfortable with Swaggart's denunciations of popular psychology. Fundamentalists who are at home with Falwell's sermons would probably reject Swaggart's insistence that being "baptized in the Spirit" requires speaking in tongues. The audiences for these programs are thus not homogenous, monolithic, nor interchangeable. Televangelists must employ formats and construct appeals that take into account the predispositions or patterns of experience of the people who watch them; this constitutes the importance of examining the connection between history and cultural form to understand the appeal of specific shows.

Analyzing the structure of appeal in Swaggart's crusade and in the "700 Club" requires a consideration of the intended audience of each program, the ideological and theological perspectives of Robertson and Swaggart, the way in which the evangelical tradition has been wedded to the televisual medium, and the distinct persuasive strategies employed to create an identification between televangelists and viewers. All of these characteristics come together in the cultural form of specific programs. As Robertson says, "Communication by mass media is not the same as direct personal contact between pulpit and pew."[56] The intervention of the television medium affects the substance of the evangelical message, the method of preaching (or techniques of persuasion), and the nature of the relationship between speaker and listener. Televised evangelism requires persuasive strategies that are quite distinct from those of the 19th century revivals. If, as research seems to indicate, the audience for televangelism is finite, and if the parameters of that audience are constituted by the tension between modernism and the evangelical belief system, then televangelists are forced to compete with each other for survival. To stay on the air, television preachers must elicit support from their viewers in the form of donations. Evoking this kind of devotion requires persuasion, and persuasion is achieved by creating identification between speaker and listener. Identification works by establishing a connection between being and meaning that is grounded in people's understanding of themselves and the world. Persuasion is therefore a social relationship rather than a communicative technique. In the case of televangelism, persuasion is effected through the communion of beliefs of the preacher and his audience. While both Swaggart and Robertson are evangelical Christians, their perspectives are markedly different. So too are their audiences and their persuasive strategies. In the program analysis I examine the relationship between the substance of each broadcaster's beliefs and the way in which they structure appeals to achieve identification with their audiences. Swaggart's program and the "700 Club" propose divergent—if not overtly opposing—solutions to the problems of meaning that reflect deep tensions within evangelicalism itself, and within contemporary society.

NOTES TO CHAPTER 5

1. This argument owes much to Peter Horsfield's *Religious Television: The American Experience* (New York: Longman, 1984).

2. Evangelical radio's history is treated in Richard Ostling, "Evangelical Publishing and Broadcasting," in G. Marsden, ed., *Evangelicalism in Modern America* (Grand Rapids, MI: Eerdmans, 1984), and in James Hunter, *American Evangelicalism: Conservative Religion and the Quandary of Modernity* (New Brunswick, NJ: Rutgers University Press, 1983), pp. 44-45.

3. Horsfield, *Religious Television*, p. 7.

4. Ibid., p. 14.

5. Ibid., p. 15.

6. Ibid., p. 7.

7. Quentin Schultze, "The Mythos of the Electronic Church," *Critical Studies in Mass Communication* 4 (1987): p. 246. In 1968, 104 organizations were affiliated with the NRB; in 1985, that number was 1,050.

8. Peter Applebome, "Scandals Aside, TV Preachers Thrive," *New York Times*, October 8, 1989, p. A24.

9. Horsfield, *Religious Television*, p. 10.

10. Dean Kelley, *Why Conservative Churches Are Growing* (New York: Harper & Row, 1972).

11. Horsfield, *Religious Television*, p. 17.

12. Ibid., p. 19; also see Jeffrey Hadden and Charles E. Swann, *Prime Time Preachers: The Rising Power of Televangelism* (Reading, MA: Addison Wesley, 1981), pp. 106-124.

13. Robert Merton with Marjorie Fiske and Alberta Curtis, *Mass Persuasion: The Social Psychology of a War Bond Drive* (Westport, CT: Greenwood Press, 1946), pp. 38-40.

14. Raymond Williams discusses the social context of the development of television which prescribed that the medium would be centrally produced, yet received in the privatized sphere of individual homes. The mode of reception or, to use a more active term, con-

sumption, inevitably affects how we perceive and make sense of media messages. See Williams, *Television, Technology and Cultural Form* (New York: Schocken Books, 1975), pp. 26-31.

15. See M. S. Piccirrillo, "On the Authenticity of Televisual Experience: A Critical Exploration of Para-social Closure," *Critical Studies in Mass Communication* 3 (1986): pp. 337-355; and Razelle Frankl, *Televangelism: The Marketing of Popular Religion* (Carbondale: Southern Illinois University Press, 1987), pp. 91-96.

16. Donald Horton and R. Richard Wohl, "Mass Communicaton and Para-Social Interaction: Observations of Intimacy at a Distance," in J.E. Combs and M.W. Mansfield, eds., *Drama in Life: The Uses of Communication in Society* (New York: Hastings House, 1976), p. 212.

17. Ibid., pp. 212-213.

18. Ibid., p. 213.,

19. Ibid., p. 214.

20. Adam Clymer, "Survey Finds Many Skeptics Among Evangelical Viewers," *New York Times*, March 31, 1987, pp. 1, 14.

21. Horsfield, *Religious Television*, p. 61.

22. William Fore, *Television and Religion* (Minneapolis: Augsburg, 1987), p. 110.

23. Horton and Wohl, "Para-Social Interaction," p. 212.

24. I responded to one poll on the SDI defense system and reached a recorded message by AT & T. Over 13,000 calls were placed during the program, according to Robertson; 96% favored implementing "Star Wars". "700 Club," February 16, 1987.

25. See Horsfield, "Evangelism by Mail: Letters from the Broadcasters," *Journal of Communication* 35, (Winter 1985): pp. 89-97; and Jeffrey Hadden, "Soul saving Via Video," *Christian Century*, May 28, 1980, pp. 609-613.

26. Horsfield, *Religious Television*, p. 61.

27. Ibid., p. 86; Schultze, in "Mythos of the "Electronic Church," makes a similar arguement in looking at the 'technological optimism" that is deeply embedded in American history and perceptions.

28. David Pual Nord, "The Evangelical Origins of the Mass Media, 1810-1835, "*Journalism Monographs* 88 (1984): entire issue.

29. Ibid., pp. 5-6, 21.

30. Ibid., p. 22, note 82.

31. Horsfield, *Religious Television*, p. 68.

32. Nord, "Evangelical Origins," pp. 9-10.

33. Fore, *Television and Religion*, p. 112. Quentin Schultze makes this argument as well in *Televangelism and American Culture* (Grand Rapids, MI: Baker Book House, 1991).

34. Horsfield, *Religious Television*, p. 27.

35. Ibid., p. 29.

36. J. Thomas Bisset, "Religious Broadcasting: Assessing the State of the Art," *Christianity Today*, December 12, 1980, p. 28. Religious broadcasters began discussing and debating the merits of adding dramatic appeal to their programs even before television. A writer in *Christian Century*, in 1944, said religious radio shows needed "the dramatic, mass appeal which is the genius of radio . . .They must be good radio, using all the successful techniques of professional production." Quoted in J. Harold Ellens, *Models of Religlious Broadcasting* (n.p.: Eerdmans, 1974), p.33.

37. Fore, *Television and Religion*, pp. 113-114.

38. This idea is treated in Todd Gitlin, "Television's Screens: Hegemony in Transition," in M. Apple, ed., *Cultural and Economic Reproduction in Education* (London: Routledge and Kegan Paul, 1982), pp. 202-246.

39. See, for example, Lance Bennett, *News: The Politics of Illusion* (New York & London: Longman, 1983). Bennett argues that mass media simplify issues and social problems through news that has been "personalized, dramatized, fragmented, and normalized" (p.7).

40. Bisset, "Religious Broadcasting," p. 28.

41. Horsfield, *Religious Television*, pp. 19, 54-55; see also Everett Parker, "Old-time Religion on TV—Blessing or Bane?" *Television Quarterly* (Fall 1980): pp. 71-79.

42. See Sandra Sizer, *Gospel Hymns and Social Religion* (Philadelphia: Temple University Press, 1978), pp. 3-6.

43. Horsfield, *Religious Television*, pp. 106-108; and Hadden and Swann, *Prime Time Preachers*, p. 60.

44. George Gerbner, et. al., *Religion and Television* Vol. I (Philadelphia: Annenberg School of Communications, April 1984), p. 3.

45. Horsfield, *Religious Television*, p. 103.

46. Ibid., p. 154.

47. Ibid., p. 117; and Gerbner, *Religion and Television*, Vol. I. p. 3.

48. Horsfield, *Religious Television*, p. 117; "The Christianity Today-Gallup Poll: An Overview," *Christianity Today*, December 21, 1979, pp. 12-19, and William Shupe and Anson Stacey, "Correlates of Support for the Electronic Church, " *Journal for the Scientific Study of Religion* 21 (1984): 291-303.

49. Horsfield, *Religious Television*, p. 117

50. Ibid., p. 119.

51. Rumors of Swaggart's plan to take over PTL, and speculations about Falwell's reasons for doing so, are one sign of the intense competition within the television industry. These accusations, originally made by Bakker and widely circulated by the commercial news media, were persuasive partly because people outside evangelicalism found economic competition to the the most plausible explanation for

Swaggart's attack on Bakker. I believe most media professionals failed to understand the theological basis of Swaggart's actions because they do not take evangelicalism seriously as a legitimate belief system. Two exceptions to this treatment of the issue were "An Unholy War in the TV Pulpits," *U.S. News and World Report*, April 6, 1987, pp. 58-65; and Robert Reinhold, "Pentecostals' Split Exposed by Bakker Affair," *New York Times*, March 3, 1987, pp. 1, 7.

52. Ibid., p. 108.

53. "Surviving the Slump," *Christianity Today*, February 3, 1989, p. 33.

54. Schultze suggests that this was the reason for implementing the study in the first place. The report was produced with the funding of religious broadcasters. Those who gave more than $500 received a final copy of the study; organizations that donated $3000 received access to the computer data tapes. Schultze, "Vindicating the Electronic Church," p. 285.

55. Gerbner et al., *Religion and Television*, Vol. 1, p. 4.

56. Quoted in Bisset, "Religious Broadcasting," p. 31.

6

The Country Preacher and the Christian Broadcaster

The "Jimmy Swaggart Telecast" and Pat Robertson's "700 Club" are narratives about the nature of the universe, about good and evil, and about redemption and damnation. Like the evangelical belief system, these programs address the problems of being and meaning, and the solutions they pose are different. My analysis of these stories attempts to interpret their form and meaning. I am interested in how the programs are constructed so as to elicit identification from their viewers—to win agreement about what is meaningful and what is not. The differences between the programs—thematic, stylistic, strategic—are grounded in the theologies, intentions, and self-conceptions of their stars. Swaggart calls himself a "country preacher," while Robertson identifies himself as a "Christian broadcaster." These self-imposed identities point toward fundamentally different views of television, evangelism, and society. This chapter examines the roles, broadcasting strategies, and the audiences of a country preacher and a religious broadcaster. The aim of my reading of these programs is to discern the structure of appeal for each as they arise from the worldviews that Swaggart and Robertson inhabit and offer to their audiences.

THE PROGRAMS

The usual format of "The Jimmy Swaggart Telecast" is a religious revival service supplemented by fund raising and promotions.[1] The hour-long program opens with the theme song "There is a River," while an announcer relates the various components of the ministry and gives the title and location of this week's crusade. The program cuts to a 3-minute request for funds (by Swaggart, his son Donnie, or his wife Frances), followed by a 1-minute promotion for upcoming crusades, Bible conferences, and other special events. The next six minutes or so are devoted to music—two or three numbers performed by Swaggart and his band and back-up singers. Swaggart sings and plays piano accompaniment for the other performers. The songs range from slow, sentimental ballads about Christ (his suffering, his sacrificial love, and redemptive role) to fast-paced country gospel tunes about the Second Coming, the Rapture, the power of the Holy Spirit, and the Pentecostal tradition. The announcer brackets the sermon from the rest of the program by restating the sermon title. The musical and promotional segments are sometimes reversed, but the sermon always begins approximately 20 minutes into the hour. The televised service is an edited version of Swaggart's live performances and lasts about 20 minutes, concluding with an altar call (12 to 15 minutes long).[2] This section either runs to the end of the hour or is sometimes followed by another short promotional spot.

The "700 Club" is a combined talk-show/news magazine format that originally ran 90 minutes, but is now an hour long, followed in the morning by a half-hour interview program called "Heart to Heart" featuring "700 Club" co-host Sheila Walsh.[3] The show is divided into a series of brief segments, each of which stands on its own, although they are often tied together thematically. The regular cast—host Robertson and co-hosts Sheila Walsh and Ben Kinchlow—give the show continuity, provide the conversational transitions between segments, produce on-set banter, and conduct the live interviews and discussions.[4] Some segments repeat daily—prayer and news reports; interviews are a staple of the program and most shows include one or more pretaped segments (human interest features and salvation stories are common) and appearances by celebrities from the sports or entertainment worlds. Commercial-like promotional spots air approximately on the quarter hour. The show is set in a studio before a live audience; it is broadcast live in major cities and is taped for rerun in smaller markets.

Ellens outlines four "model" formats typically used by religious broadcasters.[5] In the first, television is an extended pulpit and the preacher is modeled after biblical prophets; in the second, the program becomes the site of religious spectacle. The third model uses television as a pedagogical tool, and the fourth employs television as a "leaven" for provoking religious thought. Swaggart emphasizes the pulpit model while adding some elements of spectacle. The music, creative editing, and the passion that flows between Swaggart and his audience make his performance visually appealing and emotionally contagious, but the focus of the program is on his message and preaching. Swaggart relies far less on spectacle than do preachers such as Oral Roberts or Robert Schuller, whose shows use elaborate settings and lavish production values to capture and heighten viewer attention. Swaggart has glamorized the setting of his crusades for television by adding greenery and a large professional band, but the atmosphere remains very similar to that of an old-fashioned camp meeting. The "700 Club" is a combination of pedagogy and spectacle. Prayers for healing, testimonies of miracles, interviews with and performances by celebrities, and slick, pretaped features provide the spectacle. Robertson's social and political analyses, interviews with newsmakers, biblical lessons, news reports, and advice from Christian experts educate the audience on the agenda of the New Christian Right. Differences in the formats of the two programs do not stem from abstract decisions to use a particular broadcasting model, of course. A country preacher must have a pulpit, just as a Christian broadcaster needs a particular kind of forum for presenting an alternative to secular television.

THE PREACHERS

The Country Preacher

Viewers who are born again while watching Swaggart are invited to write for his free booklet, "There's a New Name Written Down In Glory." For Swaggart, "glory" is the essence of what it means to be a Christian; it is an overwhelming, transformative, spiritual experience. "The Holy Ghost will change you miraculously," he tells the audience.[6] Indeed, Swaggart never tires of telling viewers about his own conversion at age nine, and of his transformation through the power of the Holy Spirit. The experience changed Swaggart's life irrevocably; he knew he had been "called" to a special mission.[7] For men such as Swaggart, becoming an evangelist is not an occupational choice, but an ordination by God. Swaggart emphasizes and perpetuates this special status: it is what gives him the power to speak and the right to preach.

Like a majority of television evangelists, Swaggart is a Southerner and a product of a conservative Christian tradition. He is a Pentecostal and was an ordained minister in the Assemblies of God

Church until he was dismissed in 1988. Swaggart's career as a religious communicator did not originate on television, but in the southern revival circuit. At age 19 he began preaching on street corners, and later supplemented his sermons with loudspeakers and mass-produced Bible tracts. Swaggart began broadcasting his "Camp Meeting Hour" on radio in 1969 and launched his first television show in 1972. Swaggart came to broadcasting with a specific purpose—extending his evangelistic reach. This was not his choice, he says, but a directive from God to use the airwaves to carry out the "Great Commission."[8] Swaggart is also an accomplished musician who claims that the Holy Ghost taught him to play piano.[9] His more than 50 gospel albums had sold over 15 million copies in 1985. Swaggart's music, like his theology, has country roots and is wedded to his evangelistic efforts.

In February 1988, when Swaggart confessed to visiting a prostitute, Jimmy Swaggart Ministries employed 1,500 people and included the 7,500-seat Family Worship Center, the Jimmy Swaggart Bible College, extensive foreign mission efforts, a state-of-the-art Teleproduction Center, and two programs with 9.3 million American viewers a month (the Sunday crusade and a 30-minute panel discussion show called "Teachings in the Word" aired on weekdays) which were translated into 13 languages and broadcast to 145 countries. At that time the annual income of the ministry was $141 million.[10]

After his teary confession via national television on February 21, 1988, Swaggart's empire shrank dramatically. At that time his Sunday crusade was viewed in at least 1.96 million homes (this figure from Arbitron does not include cable). A year later that number had decreased to 851,000 homes. Swaggart's revenue from donations had dropped more than 50%; in 1989 he received an estimated $60 million.[11] By October 1991, Swaggart's program had slipped to seventh place among nationally broadcast religious programs.[12] These losses in viewership and income stem not only from viewer disillusionment, but also from the broadcast industry's response to Swaggart's actions. Upon Swaggart's initial confession, officials of the Assemblies of God Louisiana District Presbytery ordered him to stop preaching in person or over the air for three months. Swaggart complied and promised to return to the airwaves May 22, 1988. During this period "The Jimmy Swaggart Telecast" consisted of reruns of earlier crusades. Meanwhile, the national Assemblies of God Executive Presbytery decided that Swaggart should receive a stricter, one-year suspension, particularly since this was the punishment he had demanded for Jim Bakker's sexual misconduct. When Swaggart rejected the harsher penalty, national officials dismissed him from the church. (In so doing they also gave up the $12 million per year that Swaggart had been sending to the church's foreign mission efforts and also they lost a powerful national spokesperson.) Swaggart's dismissal triggered a series of industry reprisals against his ministry. Robertson's Christian Broadcasting Network cancelled both of Swaggart's programs, depriving him of weekly access to 40 million homes. PTL and the Black Entertainment Network followed suit, resulting in the loss of another 30 million homes; his crusade program was later dropped by Turner's Atlanta Superstation as well. Further, the ministry was hit by layoffs, defections by ministers and Bible college students, cancellations by independent TV stations, and a decrease in its local congregation.[13]

Despite these devastating losses, Swaggart did not, as many predicted, fold up his tent. He survived the scandal and its effects, according to Harrell, because he "managed to save the lifeblood of that ministry—and that's TV."[14] After returning to the air as promised, Swaggart began cutting back spending in most areas of the ministry and channeled funds into cross-country preaching tours and television. As Harrell noted: "It seems his strategy is to take to the circuit and rebuild from the bottom up."[15] Because Swaggart's roots are the "bottom"—the country preaching circuit—this was a logical strategy. He is no stranger to poverty or to the sawdust trail and returning to these origins was the best route to revitalizing his career as a preacher. As Harrell said:

> Swaggart can take his talents and go back to the grass roots and rebuild. Many of these people (TV evangelists) are nothing more than media personalities. That's not the case with Swaggart. . . . What the scandal did was force him back to his strengths.[16]

Further, because the religious tradition from which Swaggart springs is based on the notion of inevitable, recurring sin and redemption, his fall, confession, self-mortification, and renewal are persuasive arguments for the validity of the belief system. As Swaggart wrote in May 1988 in his magazine, *The Evangelist:*

> As I have said before: 'God cannot receive glory out of sin, but He can receive glory out of a crucified life.' And when you see Jimmy Swaggart stand behind the pulpit and over television, you will see a man who has crucified the flesh. It has come at a terrible price, but better that price than no price at all.[17]

As with the Bakkers, the fact that Swaggart had sinned, suffered, and sought forgiveness is a point of identification with his followers. It is an admission of human fallibility that binds together preacher and congregation. As Swaggart said, "Some have said to me, 'Brother Swaggart, we could relate to your message; the anointing was on it; however, we were never quite able to relate to you. But now we can relate to you,"[18] Those followers who remained loyal to Swaggart commonly reiterated this sense of identification; witness some comments from crusade attenders in Alabama: "I feel he's a man of God," said a pastor, "All have sinned and fallen short." A woman at the crusade noted, "We're all sinners. I think he's doing a great job."[19] Indeed, Swaggart's response to his fall, in terms of symbolic action, operates as a kind of consolatory, therapeutic rhetoric by dramatizing a strategy for coping with human fallibility.

While Swaggart may have been able to recover from one "fall," a second scandal put enormous stress on his ministry. In October 1991, while accompanied by a prostitute, he was pulled over in California for a traffic violation. The story made national headlines and shortly afterward, Jimmy Swaggart Ministries announced the end of the telecast "for the foreseeable future." Swaggart and his wife Frances resigned from the ministry board, turning it over to their son Donnie and two others. The decision to halt the telecast and sell much of the ministry's broadcasting equipment and undeveloped land was an attempt to salvage the local Family Worship Center and bible college in the face of severe financial problems. A month earlier, a New Orleans jury had awarded $10 million to Marvin Gorman, a Louisiana preacher who had sued Swaggart and the ministry for defamation. Gorman, who had his own local religious television program, had been a key figure in the 1988 allegations about Swaggart's sexual misconduct. The suit charged that Swaggart and others in the ministry had retaliated by accusing Gorman of being a "womanizer"—charges that eventually ruined Gorman's local TV ministry. The announcement that Swaggart was leaving the air followed a new wave of layoffs and resignations at the bible college and the television ministry.[20] As noted earlier, Swaggart did not leave television entirely, but his telecast is now seen primarily on cable and consists of reruns rather than current crusades.

In some ways, Swaggart's downfall is not surprising. In a rigidly dualistic world view—win which salvation and sin, good and evil, spirit and body are mutually exclusive categories—there is no way to reconcile contradictory aspects of self. One is either saved or a sinner, pure or depraved, wholly spiritual or totally enslaved to the flesh. Swaggart's inability to reside only in one side of this dichotomy is a testament to the enormous psychological demands of strict separatist evangelicalism. The following analysis of his preaching and the theological system that guides it attempts to illustrate why this worldview is appealing in spite of, or because of, those demands, and how that appeal is structured within Swaggart's program.

Born in 1935 and raised in Ferriday, Louisiana, Swaggart in many respects has remained a country boy. Although he commanded a multimillion dollar media empire, he is, in his words, a "simple country preacher." Swaggart regularly appeals to his roots in this tradition and describe his televised crusades as "the old sawdust trail, sort of upgraded."[21] In fact, these roots in the "dirt-poor, circuit-riding tradition of Pentecostal evangelism" may make it difficult for preachers such as Swaggart to cope with the power and wealth associated with successful TV ministries. According to Harrell, "Most of these guys [TV evangelists] come from poor unsophisticated backgrounds of Pentecostal preaching, and there's nothing in their background that prepares them for the positions of power they're thrust into.[22]

Swaggart's admission of human weakness is one point of identification between him and his followers, but their consubstantialty had already existed through their mutual inheritance of a distinct tradition of ministry—that of country preaching. To call Swaggart a country preacher is to locate him in a well-established tradition of evangelism with clearly defined techniques and goals. Rosenberg's study of the "chanted" sermons produced by a group of predominantly black "folk preachers" provided me with a framework for examining Swaggart's art.[23] For it is no exaggeration to say that preachers such as Swaggart and the men in Rosenberg's study have developed a mastery over oratory in much the same way that painters, actors, or writers learn to master the materials of their respective arts. The country or folk preacher's art is his performance. Preachers such as Swaggart do not just deliver sermons, they perform them. Rosenberg likens the folk preacher to "an actor strutting on a stage," whose goal is to move the congregation to religious ecstasy.[24] Passion is an essential part of the service because it is through the emotions that a congregation is made ready to "yield" to the Holy Spirit. Members of the congregation also play a vital role in the performance. Their response to the preacher affects his timing, delivery, the direction of the sermon, and the degree of his involvement.

This type of service, which Rosenberg calls "antiphonal," is rooted in the Second Great Awakening. The camp meetings of the early 1800s encouraged people to express their religiosity emotionally and physically—to become ecstatic. Indeed, ecstasy comes from the Greek — which means to stand away from or beside oneself (to be outside of ordinary experience). John Wesley's Methodism taught that spiritual perfection was achieved through the heart rather than the mind; spiritual rebirth was thus not the result of an intellectual decision but of fervent desire. Conversion was an overwhelming emotional experience, accompanied by weeping, moaning, dancing, convulsions (referred to as the "jerks"), and babbling (speaking in tongues). In such circumstances, the preacher could hardly remain a detached, passive observer. Instead, he was a catalyst for the conversion experience and this demanded his own emotional involvement.

The emotionalism of Baptist and Methodist teachings was particularly attractive to poor whites and black slaves in the early 1800s. Because preachers from these denominations were also generally poor and not highly educated, they could more easily identify with oppressed and ignorant social groups. In fact, masters often invited these preachers to minister to slaves because they taught "a religion of consolation."[25] Pentecostalism, with its emphasis on emotion and the display of spiritual gifts, has historically been more attractive to the lower classes. As a belief system, it has also been characterized more by religious behavior than by an elaborate theology. Swaggart stresses Pentecostalism's simple origins and is deeply suspicious of the intellect. A high school dropout himself, Swaggart insists that Pentecostalism's strength is not its theological sophistication but its spiritual fervor. "The Holy Spirit doesn't work with our minds," he tells viewers. "It works with our hearts."[26]

Since the days of camp meetings, the South has been the stronghold of conservative evangelicalism. Many of the major televangelists are southern-born, including Robertson, Roberts, Copeland, Graham, Humbard, Robison, and Crouch. The largest audiences for TV ministries are also located in the South. All of the preachers in Rosenberg's study were born in the South, although many had relocated to southern California after WWII, as had the members of their congregations.[27] The country preacher and the chanted sermon are also largely Southern phenomena; although found predominately in black churches, this style of preaching also occurs in white churches in some rural areas.[28] While there are important distinctions between Swaggart's style and that of the preachers in Rosenberg's study, there are enough similarities to argue that both stem from the same tradition of folk preaching. Further, it is by looking at Swaggart as a country or folk preacher that we can best analyze how he constructs his appeal and practices his art.

The "manuscript preacher" and the "spiritual preacher" are both part of the Protestant tradition.[29] The former relies on a text and on the logical development of narrative to illuminate the meaning of God's word. In this sense, the manuscript preacher employs tools of pedagogy; he teaches rather than preaches. Jerry Falwell is one of the best examples of this style. Falwell reads his sermons from cue cards. He establishes a thesis, outlines the points he will cover (usually no more than three or four), and proceeds to explain each point before reaching a summary statement and conclusion. His sermons resemble a classroom lecture. The manuscript preacher is oriented toward the written word, and his sermon follows the linear development demanded by written language. (It also makes for rather boring television; I find Falwell's services extremely didactic and tedious. The lack of overt religious fervor is also characteristic of strict fundamentalists such as Falwell who reject the dramatic emotionalism of charismatic religion.) The spiritual preacher, on the other hand, may begin with a line of text—usually a passage from the Bible—but he is not bound by a manuscript. Rather, his sermon is oriented to the spoken word; his performance is oral and he exhorts or orates rather than teaches. Both spiritual and manuscript preachers draw on the "text-context" form of preaching that is part of the Protestant tradition. The preacher begins with a quotation from Scripture and then elaborates it by applying the passage to everyday life. Swaggart is a spiritual preacher who uses the text-context format; the titles and themes of his sermons each week originate in the Bible.

Spiritual sermons may be "chanted" or "nonchanted." Through chanting, a preacher "attempts to fit his language into metrically consistent patterns" in order to create an effect on the audience.[30] Swaggart resorts to a form of chanting at key points in his sermon and does so precisely to evoke audience response. (I return to this point in a later chapter.) Most of Swaggart's performance is spiritual, nonchanted preaching. This style of preaching is more like conventional oratory. The syntax is flexible and ideas are developed from sentence to sentence. The language is similar to conversation, which it resembles when put in writing.

Rosenberg contends that most spiritual preachers employ a nonchanted style, particularly when the congregation is middle class and/or white.[31] Because the function of chanting is to bring listeners to religious ecstasy, it creates discomfort for many modern worshipers who are accustomed to staid church services. Swaggart's audience, while primarily white, is largely working or lower-middle class and predominately rural and southern. Such viewers are more familiar with and hospitable to a style of preaching that would seem alien to many middle-and upper-middle-class churchgoers. As Rosenberg notes:

> Contemporary white middle-class churches do not indulge themselves in emotion and seem embarrassed by the 'passion' displayed in other more Fundamentalist churches. . . . American middle-class society, for the most part, is ashamed of public emotion: we do not weep in public, and we do not shout in church.[32]

Jimmy Swaggart does both, and often. For Swaggart, the degree of passion experienced in a religious service is a gauge of the depth of belief.
He regularly denounces the absence of feeling in most churches—an
indication, he says, that the Holy Spirit has abandoned the majority of
American denominations. He often pokes fun at noncharismatic worship with a joke that has become very familiar to his regular viewers:
It seems that a man died during a church service and the paramedics
had to pull everybody out before they could locate the actual
corpse.[33]

Because it is the function of the preacher to ignite the audience's religious passion, it is essential that he too be fueled by the
Spirit. This is a state that cannot be willed. Rather, the spiritual
preacher is "called" to God's work. Nor does the Holy Ghost approach
timidly—it "rolls right over" the believer like a tidal wave.[34] Like the
men in Rosenberg's study, Swaggart considers himself chosen by God
to spread the gospel. Rosenberg says that "this feeling that one is
divinely summoned is important in understanding sermon techniques."[35] Being "called" is the preliminary step toward becoming a
preacher or evangelist. Rosenberg's folk preachers followed a common path to their calling. They began as children internalizing the
materials and techniques of local preachers. They spent a period of
apprenticeship developing a repertoire of oratory skills and sermon
themes. Like Swaggart, these preachers also shared a background in
music, either as professional or amateur singers or as members of a
church choir. Chanted sermons are musical in structure, and it is common for a preacher to break into song during the performance;
Swaggart often slips portions of gospel hymns into his sermons. Entry
into the folk preaching tradition occurs when the preacher has "mastered certain aspects of language and certain rhythms which he knows
are sure to elicit a predictable response."[36]

Swaggart has inarguably mastered the art of eliciting audience
response. At his height he preached to a weekly U.S. audience of 8 million and drew as many as 80,000 to crusades in Latin America.[37]
Swaggart is a powerful and highly skilled orator who employs the
techniques of folk preaching on a scale that would astound the men
who led the camp meetings. What is perhaps most remarkable about
Swaggart is that he has been able to transfer the kind of intimacy and
passion characteristic of nonmediated revivals to a medium that generally replaces dialogue with one-way communication and stresses
observation over interaction. He has accomplished this merger of TV
and country preaching by skillfully exploiting the technical capacities
of television to reconstruct for viewers the experience of participating
in the actual revival.

The folk preacher's performance is almost completely dependent on the intensity of the audience is response. If the audience is "off" (nonresponsive or bored), the preacher's performance suffers. When the congregation is "up," it is actively involved throughout the performance; people hum along in certain sections, sing, shout, and clap to punctuate phrases. The preacher takes his cues from these responses. His timing, rhythm, degree of emotion, and direction of the oratory are all affected by how the congregation receives his words. For this reason, Swaggart's performance must be live. It is difficult to imagine him performing alone in front of a camera, or in the manufactured, orchestrated setting of a TV studio, as Robertson does on the "700 Club."[38] The television audience must be moved to "participate" by identifying with the crusade attendees, because the type of emotional engagement engendered in a live revival cannot be duplicated with absent, physically dispersed listeners.

Spiritual preaching, and chanted sermons in particular, developed because church services can be lengthy and uninspiring affairs. Chanted sermons evolved alongside spirituals and gospel hymns, which were incorporated into 19thcentury revivals to buoy the spirits of participants. Rosenberg calls the chanted sermon "an ideal conflation of the prose sermon and the spiritual," and says that "chanting or singing was first used to liven a potentially dull sermon and to establish a rhythm so as to make the performance as emotionally stimulating as the obviously successful spirituals."[39] Moody was the first preacher to integrate gospel hymns into his urban revivals, and the form of Swaggart's crusades is very similar to Moody's.[40]

Music and chanting were intended to stimulate interest among revival attendees and to instigate their involvement in the service. Retaining audience interest is even more critical in televised religious services. Television cannot bore, because it is too easy for viewers to switch to another program, turn off the set, or become distracted by other activities in the home. Viewers expect to be entertained by television even when they have tuned in to also be informed, uplifted, or educated. This is part of the "media logic" described by Altheide and Snow.[41] Television and radio, they say, employ an "entertainment perspective" to capture and hold viewers' attention. We have come to expect entertainment as an intrinsic part of the medium and we enter into a relationship with television performers on the basis of this expectation. The entertainment perspective works "to establish and make sense of the activities to follow."[42] Being entertained necessarily elicits emotional involvement, even if it is vicarious (e.g., mediated): "A significant measure of entertainment is the degree of spontaneous emotional display among the audience or participants. . . . any performer measures the success of a show by the emotional response of the audience."[43]

Swaggart's program is constructed so as to highlight and make central the degree of emotional exchange between performer and crusade audience with the aim of extending this emotion to viewers at home. Robertson, in contrast, must elicit audience response indirectly; he ascertains viewers' reactions with the aid of phone banks, letters, rating services, and market surveys. The studio audience does not supply immediate emotional feedback other than through cued applause. In fact, it cannot do so within the structure of the program's format, as I argue in the analysis of the "700 Club." Direct audience involvement in Swaggart's crusades is not simply one component of the program—it is the raison d'etre of the performance. An evangelist requires a congregation, and the quality of his preaching is absolutely dependent on how he is received. The country preacher must therefore be highly attuned to the mood and tenor of his audience. He must understand his listeners' "patterns of experience" and intuit their desires if he is to fulfill those desires and create identification. In Rosenberg's words:

> The skillful preacher develops his sermon with a certain care and with the emotions of the audience in mind. This is a test of the preacher's aesthetic sense; his timing—his development of ideas and sentiments—is part of the sermon's structure and it too must please in order to move.[44]

The Christian Broadcaster

In the spectrum of evangelical TV programming, the "700 Club" diverges the most from traditional revivalism, according to Frankl.[45] The show originates in the cultural form of television; it is a standard TV format filled with religious content. The preaching elements of the "700 Club" are subordinated to the demands of the format rather than being the central reason for the broadcast. Nor does Robertson see himself as a TV preacher: "We [at CBN] consider ourselves professional broadcasters. . . . I've never been an evangelist as such. It turned out that the Lord wanted me to buy a television station, but I never was an evangelist."[46] The communications director of Robertson's presidential campaign reiterated this fact during the presidential race: "Pat has been labeled a TV evangelist, but he's not. He hasn't been a pulpit preacher for 25 years. He's a religious broadcaster, a businessman, a newscaster. There is a subtle difference."[47] In fact, this difference is significant, as I will argue.

Robertson is a Southerner, but he is no country boy. Born in

1930, he is the son of a former U.S. senator and was educated at prestigious schools. A former Golden Gloves middleweight fighter, ex-Marine, and graduate of Yale University Law School, Robertson bought his first UHF station in 1960 for $37,000. At the time he had $70 which he called his "seed money."[48] The station went on the air three months later, the first UHF facility in the country to devote more than half its programming to religion. Although he was an ordained Southern Baptist minister until he resigned during his presidential campaign, Robertson operates more like a businessman than a preacher. Indeed, during the campaign Robertson described himself as a "Christian businessman" to distance himself even further from scandal-ridden TV ministers.[49]

Robertson built up his broadcasting empire from its humble beginnings to establish CBN, at one point the nation's fourth largest cable television network. At its peak in the early 1980s, CBN had acquired three more American TV stations in addition to the original station at Virginia Beach, as well as five radio stations and another television station in Lebanon. Robertson also established CBN University in 1978. The fully accredited school offers master's degrees in communications, education, biblical studies, business administration, and public policy. Robertson has said he hopes to make the school the "Christian" equivalent of Notre Dame. In 1977, CBN became the first TV ministry to lease a full-time satellite channel, and by the mid1980s it was feeding its channel to more than 250 stations and hundreds of cable systems across the nation. Many of CBN's broadcast holdings were sold in 1985, because Robertson wanted to concentrate capital investment in program development and in operating the satellite channel, although he held on to the Middle East station. That year CBN raised $233 million.[50] Most of the network's money comes from a hierarchy of donors' clubs and from sympathetic corporations.[51] Although "700 Club" members' donations are an important source of funding, a relatively small percentage of viewers donate the majority of the money.[52]

When CBN first joined Home Box Office and Ted Turner's Atlanta Superstation on RCA's Satcom I satellite, its programming was all religious. By 1981, Robertson had renamed the channel CBN Cable Network and began offering nonreligious programming in the form of older syndicated shows such as "Gentle Ben" and "Father Knows Best;" religious programming was reduced to 25% (including the "700 Club" which was aired three times daily). In 1988, the network was renamed again, this time as the CBN Family Channel. The impetus behind this change was a desire to broaden the audience by attracting viewers who might be adverse to watching religious television. CBN skillfully competed for air time by downplaying its religious orientation (one employee worked full time getting the "religious" tag removed from local TV listings) and by offering its cable service free to cable operators, giving stations subsidies for advertising costs and providing preproduced television and radio spots.[53]

The following year CBN sold the channel as the result of a two-year Internal Revenue Service investigation that initially focused on Robertson's presidential campaign fund-raising activities, and then turned to the relationship between CBN and the Family Channel.[54] CBN appeared to be violating IRS regulations that specify the percentage of funds that a nonprofit organization (such as a TV ministry) can acquire from affiliated for-profit entities (such as the cable channel). At the urging of IRS investigators, the Family Channel was officially disconnected from the TV ministry in December 1989 and recapitalized for $250 million.[55] The Family Channel became a holding company of the newly created International Family Entertainment (IFE). Telecommunications Corporation International of Denver (TCI), one of the country's largest cable enterprises, bought a 13% share of IFE for $40 million; the remainder of the $250 capitalization came from convertible debentures or junk bonds.[56] Pat Robertson was named chairman of the board of IFE; his son Tim was appointed president of IFE and of the Family Channel. The Robertsons also own stock in IFE, but the exact percentage of their share has not been made public.

This transaction solved a number of problems that had been brewing within the TV ministry for some time. Contributed income to CBN had already begun to decline around the time Robertson decided to run for president; his departure from the "700 Club" to conduct the campaign and his subsequent failure to win the GOP nomination further adversely affected donations, as did the highly publicized scandals involving the Bakkers and Swaggart. Meanwhile, the Family Channel's revenues from cable operators and advertisers were increasing, and this money was being used to subsidize the ministry whose cash flow was unstable, because it was tied to donors. It was this transfer of funds that the IRS objected to. The creation of IFE and the infusion of cash from TCI satisfied the government by separating the cable channel and the ministry. It also created a financial cushion so production of the "700 Club" would be less dependent on day-to-day donations from viewers and guaranteed the program a secure time slot and a sizeable audience via the Family Channel. It further enabled the ministry to set up an endowment for its university. CBNU was renamed Regent University in October 1989 and was given $100 million in "seed money" for an endowment—a step that was considered necessary to give the school autonomy from CBN and to enable it to grow and develop greater legitimacy as an academic institution.[57] Pat Robertson is chancellor of the university.

The entire transaction exhibits Robertson's business acumen and foresight—both in terms of the future of religious television and the direction of television generally. According to Butch Maltby, who served for two years as vice president for institutional advancement at CBN (Regent) University (1988—1990), Robertson is painfully aware that most television ministries rely on the same pool of donors; the source of funding is therefore finite. It is a case, Maltby says, of "the same animals going to the same trough." The "brilliance of the strategy" of creating IFE and separating the Family Channel from the CBN ministry is that it permits Robertson to reach new viewers (and potential supporters) and to cushion the "700 Club" from the vagaries of donor fatigue. This is a problem for all religious broadcasters, and other TV ministries are also developing strategies to generate income apart from donations.[58] The deal between IFE and CBN was also carefully structured to guarantee Robertson a strategic market position in television. The terms of the sale stipulate that the "700 Club" will have a place in the Family Channel schedule in perpetuity. It further stipulates that the channel will air only family-style programming and will reject advertising that is not in line with conservative Christian values (e.g., ads for alcohol, sexually explicit ads, public service announcements that go against evangelical values, etc.).

The Family Channel itself is quite a success story. Now part of most basic cable service packages in the United States, the Family Channel is the fifth largest cable channel in the country and can be viewed in 48.5 million homes. The channel receives 70% of its income from advertising and the remainder from cable operators, has been turning a profit since 1984, and sees itself as the chief competitor to the Disney Channel. The Family Channel philosophy is to provide programming "totally devoted to traditional family values," according to Tim Robertson.[59] Besides the "700 Club," which is broadcast twice on weekdays (mornings and evenings), and "Heart to Heart," which follows the morning installment, other religious programming on the channel includes some early morning Bible shows and several Sunday religious programs. Seventy-eight percent of the network's fare is entertainment, carrying on the programming strategy initiated by CBN. The Family Channel offers movies, vintage comedy and drama series, old westerns such as "Bonanza" and "Gunsmoke," as well as 12 original series of its own (e.g., "Zorro," "Bordertown," "The Adventures of the Black Stallion," and "Rin Tin Tin K-9 Cop"). In Fall 1990, the channel committed $100 million to new programming and expanded its primetime line-up from two to seven nights. It also produces programming for children, including "Something Else," a half-hour kids' talk show. In an article entitled "TV's Assault on the Family is No Joke," published in James Dobson's *Focus on the Family* magazine, Tim Robertson suggested that "the trend of the '90s is a new search for values and a new quest for the meaning of life." He said the Family Channel is responding to those needs and providing an alternative for people who are dissatisfied with regular TV fare:. . . "our solution is to provide the very finest in alternative programming, shows that are positive, of high quality, that stress pro-family, Judeo-Christian values."[60]

Since separating from the cable channel, CBN has been concentrating on the other key elements of its ministry: prayer counseling via phone banks, a sophisticated direct-mail operation for maintaining contact with CBN donors which informs them of social and political issues that Robertson feels are important, "Operation Blessing" which handles relief to the needy and mission efforts in the U.S. and abroad and, of course, the flagship "700 Club." The name of the show originated in a 1963 fund-raising telethon when Robertson needed $7,000 to keep his station operating. Calling the telethon the "700 Club," Robertson asked for 700 viewers to pledge a regular monthly donation of $10 to guarantee the station's future existence. Telethons and phone banks quickly became a successful and regular part of the ministry after Robertson discovered that people were willing to watch the telethons, even in the absence of identifiable programming, because they enjoyed hearing the religious testimonies of other viewers. These personal testimonials and faith histories became a regular feature of the "700 Club" and formed the basis of Walsh's "Heart to Heart" interview program.

The "700 Club's" incarnation as a talk show began in 1966; the show then included two co-hosts (originally Jim and Tammy Bakker) and guests (usually evangelical authors and musical artists). Phone banks were retained to receive viewers' calls for counseling and prayer. The program was unusual by commercial broadcasting standards—it was flexible and open-ended and the specific content was determined by hosts and guests being "moved by the spirit." When the spirit was idle, they might simply sign off early. When the "700 Club" was syndicated in the 1970s, it had to adhere to a more predictable format and length. Robertson took over as host, accompanied by Danuta Soderman and Ben Kinchlow, a former Black Muslim. The talk show format continued until 1980 when, relying on market research, the "700 Club" was revamped to its current talk show/news magazine format.[61]

This renovation is part of CBN's general programming direction over the last decade as it moves toward a closer resemblance to the formats and production values of commercial television in order to broaden its appeal. Talk is still an important component of the show, however, and much of its form and substance derives from its adoption of the talk show format. The "700 Club" parallels the format and content of the "Today Show" and "Good Morning America," but does so from a Christian perspective. The show

> competes with network morning news shows for many of the same guest political figures, movie stars, athletes and authors; but whether they represent secular or religious interests, Christian testimony is threaded through every discussion.[62]

Parallels between the "Today Show" and the "700 Club" have less to do with their choice of guests than with the requirements of the format. The talk show format was established in television's early years with Edward R. Murrow's "See It Now." That program inaugurated one of the mainstays of the talk show—the interview with a famous person. The "Today Show" followed this precedent and extended the interviews to celebrities and best-selling authors in order to appeal to its predominately female, morning audience. When "Today" host Dave Garroway was later joined by R. Fred Muggs, a chimpanzee, ratings soared. This set into place a second component of the talk show—an entertaining foil for the host. Many talk programs have followed this comic—straight-man pattern (Johnny Carson and Ed McMahon, Merv Griffin and Arthur Treacher, etc.) as a way of adding humor and generating the on-set patter characteristic of the format. The talk show format relies heavily on the host who acts as the program's emotional and intellectual center. Since Jack Paar's success on the early "Tonight Show," audiences have also learned to appreciate hosts with whom they can identify emotionally. This emotional identification is characteristic of the most successful talk show stars and is part of the intimacy at a distance central to parasocial interaction. The emphasis on celebrity, use of gimmicks or humor, and strong TV personalities are now standard elements of the format: "What passes for information and analysis [in these programs] is almost invariably couched in, or interlaced with, these very elements."[63] The "700 Club" follows this pattern: Robertson's personality dominates and shapes the flow and substance of the show, most episodes include at least one interview with a political figure or a celebrity from the entertainment and sports worlds, and his co-hosts fill the role of the sidekick. Maltby says the function of the "700 Club" co-hosts is "setting up the ball so Pat can spike it."[64]

The talk show and magazine formats, whether Christian or secular, share certain characteristics: they deal with social issues in predictable forms (e.g., panel discussion, interview, report, monologue); they present information in brief segments that are held together by the regular cast, common setting, and thematic organization; their treatment of topics is generally superficial and assumes a short audience attention span; they tend to personalize issues and dramatize the role of individuals; and they generally express the range of permissible viewpoints on an issue through techniques of framing (both technical and ideological).[65] Morning programs such as the "700 Club" generally contain shorter segments than their nighttime counterparts, because viewers are less likely to have 20 minutes of uninterrupted attention in the morning. News is generally presented first on the assumption that it appeals to men, who cannot watch the entire show. The news and public affairs portions of the "700 Club" are always placed at the beginning of the show; later segments focus more on "feminine" concerns such as parenting, marriage, and fashion. Maltby suggests that the "700 Club" has a "bifurcated audience"— those who tune in for the news reports and political analyses and then stop watching, and those who skip these segments in favor of the softer features and faith testimonies. When asked if these two viewing groups were organized along gender lines, Maltby said it was "an interesting question," but one that the show's producers could not definitively answer.[66]

Morning magazines characteristically offer a diverse conglomeration of topics packaged in uniform lengths. This format does not require sustained attention and continually cues viewers when one segment is ending and another is about to begin. Segments on the "700 Club" range from about 6 to 15 minutes; the average piece is 9 minutes, making it easy for regular viewers to tune in and out according to their interests and the demands of other morning activities. Transitions between segments are clearly marked by theme music and applause for viewers' convenience. The placement of the "700 Club" in the evening prime-time lineup on the Family Channel raises interesting questions about how the morning talk show works in a nighttime slot. This evening placement in the broadcast schedule does, however, give Robertson potential access to a different set of viewers with a different mode of attention. For one thing, it permits him to potentially reach more men who would be at work during the morning installment.

Since I first began studying the "700 Club" in 1985, it has undergone significant changes. The combination of the PTL and Swaggart scandals that tarnished all TV ministries through guilt by association, and Robertson's temporary departure to conduct his presidential campaign, dramatically affected viewership and donations. The "700 Club's" Nielsen rating dropped 30% between February 1986 and February 1989 (Arbitron recorded a 53% decrease in audience size, but it does not measure cable viewers). Before July 1987, the program had regulary been among the top-10 rated religious shows; in February 1989, Arbitron ranked it 16th.[67] Maltby said that contributions to the ministry had dropped from $60 million to $50 million per year since the scandals.[68]

While most television ministries have suffered from the scandals, the "700 Club" has been one of the hardest hit. Frankie Arbourjilie, vice president of public affairs at CBN, blamed the decline primarily on temporary Robertson's absence.[69] But there is evidence that Robertson's problems with the "700 Club" are similar to those experienced by all network executives. Between the time Robertson left the program in Spring 1987 and his return in May 1988, the "700 Club" went through a rapid series of changes as producers tried to counteract viewer flight. Tim Robertson initially took over as host—a transfer of responsibilities his father hoped would be permanent. Co-host Danuta Soderman left the show abruptly in Spring 1987 after publishing an autobiography detailing the sinful life she had led prior to finding Christ. Given the widespread perception that moral scandal and TV ministries were synonymous, CBN apparently objected to its employees airing their dirty laundry publicly (especially when Robertson's campaign was underway). Ben Kinchlow, the other long-time co-host, departed in 1988 amid rumors that he did not get along with Tim Robertson and that he was unhappy about being passed over for the host position. Kinchlow appeared for a while on TBN before returning to the "700 Club" this year. In Summer 1987, producers began experimenting with the format hoping to make the show look more contemporary to match the persona of its younger host. Sets, graphics, and music were changed, and a series of different co-hosts were introduced, including CBN regular Scott Ross and former Miss America Terry Meeuwsen. These rapid and apparently erratic changes served to confuse the audience and to adversely affect ratings and donations. Hadden and Shupe attributed the show's slump to a lack of chemistry among the cast that weakened viewers' attachment to the show and their willingness to support the ministry financially.[70]

Robertson's eventual return to the show was an attempt to rescue the "700 Club" from confusion and to woo back its old audience—an imperative task since CBN's future rests on that of its flagship program. Contemplating a return to the show, Robertson said: "I did not realize that my personal presence on the '700 Club' was as important as it is for the audience."[71] As he admitted in August 1988: "For better or worse, the financial health of this ministry revolves around the health of this show. The '700 Club' is the bread and butter of this operation." That month brought the debut of a "revamped and rejuvenated version" of the "700 Club."[72] Changes included new sets, graphics, and theme music, as well as a new co-host, Sheila Walsh, a younger contemporary Christian singer from Scotland whom Robertson hoped would inject some charisma into the program.

Maltby suggests that the choice has been successful. While "initially some older viewers found her hard to understand because of her [Scottish] accent," the audience has since come to view Walsh as a sensitive, caring, religious presence on the show.[73]

The revamped "700 Club" also featured substantive changes: it contained less overt evangelism and more Christian-oriented news, political commentary, lifestyle features, and entertainment. Maltby described the triad of Robertson-Kinchlow-Soderman as "the heyday of the '700 Club'" when the intermeshed roles and personae of the trio provided the kind of chemistry that attracts a devoted audience. He said that many long-time viewers particularly "lamented the loss of Kinchlow."[74] The recent return of Kinchlow suggests that the show's producers are trying to recreate the old chemistry with a Robertson-Kinchlow-Walsh trio. While all this juggling may appear erratic to viewers, Shupe points out that Robertson is merely employing the same strategies as those used by commerical network executives intent on salvaging a flailing show: "He's doing the same thing the other big boys are doing at the other networks . . . he is trying to find a format that works."[75] In fact, the "700 Club's" similarity to commercial television in terms of format and programming strategy are what characterize the show as "religionized" television. Moreover, such substantive changes are further developments in a programming philosophy Robertson has been pursuing for several years—one that I noticed when I first began studying the show in 1985 and that points to the increasing conformance of much religious television to the forms and values of secular culture.

Given this embrace of commercial television's priorities, the role of a Christian broadcaster is quite different than that of a television preacher. As head of CBN and chair of IFE, Robertson has had to concern himself with operating and marketing a network or channel rather than selling one or two programs to independent stations. A Christian broadcaster must pay attention to problems of program flow, market fragmentation, and competition from independent and network programming. Robertson has, of necessity, adopted the operating procedures, market research methods, and programming strategies of his secular competitors. This was the rationale behind adding a lineup of entertainment programs and producing Christian versions of standard commercial TV formats. Besides the "700 Club," CBN at one time produced a soap opera ("Another Life") and a news show, both of which have been discontinued.

In creating its own programs—a talk show, a soap opera, and a news show—CBN replicated standard commercial formats that have been successful in attracting and maintaining audiences. Robertson stresses the importance of adopting the techniques of commercial television and says the biggest mistake made by religious broadcasters is "to superimpose their 'thing' on the media. They should discover what the media are doing and adapt to the media format."[76] The Family Channel is an excellent example of such adaptation. Marketed as a wholesome variation on the standard network fare, the Family Channel is parallel in form to commercial television but more unified in the moral perspective of its content. By embedding the "700 Club" in the regular broadcast schedule, Robertson is strategically positioned to reach viewers who are predisposed to agree with his socio-theological perspective. CBN's strategy, and now that of the Family Channel, is to offer 24-hour broadcasting packaged as an attractive and "moral" alternative to most commercial television. This, in fact, was the reasoning behind the formation of CBN, according to Dabney: "since the media were controlled by secular humanists . . . it was necessary for Christians, at whatever financial sacrifice, to have their own media, and especially their own television network."[77] In other words, evangelicals must develop their own facilities and means of symbolic production to compete with the secular symbol system of commercial television. What CBN and its successor the Family Channel offer is not televangelism, but an "evangelistic thrust" incorporated into the programming strategy.[78] The reruns and new programs portray an America where good and evil are easily distinguished and family and gender roles are clearly defined. The world portrayed is one in which the values espoused in the entertainment programs are reinforced by the values of the "700 Club"—a world, moreover, in which right and wrong are absolute.

CBN's broadcast strategy also incorporates and caters to the entertainment perspective that viewers have come to expect from television. That is, a program must please viewers in order to move them. Robertson openly employs this strategy. In a statement published in *Christianity Today*, he defended the "700 Club's" use of glamour and diversion:"to maintain professional standards in our industry and to be effective in the marketplace, a degree of entertainment and showmanship is sometimes necessary."[79] One religious broadcaster remarked in 1980 that the adoption of diverse formats and the inclusion of drama and entertainment were making Christian television more accessible and would likely lead to larger audiences. He added that such diversity reflected a general trend in evangelical broadcasting—a "drift away from teaching and preaching toward counseling, interpersonal relationships, holistic living, and physical healing." He noted that this change is also related to market imperatives, pointing out that the 1979 Gallup/*Christianity Today* poll showed "a correspondence between these programming trends and the felt needs of the Christian radio and television audience."[80] In this respect, evangelical television comes to mirror its secular counterpart. Both rely on mediated audience feedback (whether through ratings or phone banks) to develop programming strategies and program content. The maintenance of audiences is essential to continued financial support (from advertisers or viewers). Thus, what is aired is that which sells—a sentiment not too different from that of secular network executives; witness a comment by Arnold Becker, a vice president for television research at CBS: "I'm not interested in culture. I'm not interested in pro-social values. I have only one interest. That's whether people watch the program. That's my definition of good, that's my definition of bad."[81] Robertson may defend the diversity of the "700 Club's" content in terms of finding new ways to deliver the Christian message, but the content is also carefully produced and packaged to appeal to a target market. As he says, the program must "be effective in the marketplace."

Besides adopting the entertainment perspective characteristic of secular television, Robertson, like other top TV ministers, has also appropriated commercial televisions's marketing methods. CBN uses conventional rating services such as Arbitron and Nielsen and also commissions its own research. The network was the largest contributor to the Annenberg/Gallup study which provided detailed audience data about participants who gave more than $500. CBN's marketing division and the communication department at CBNU have also conducted audience research.[82] It was the results of such market studies that led to the decision to include news on the "700 Club" and to the switch in the early 1980s from a straight talk show to a magazine format.[83] Besides rating services and market surveys, evangelical broadcasters receive direct feedback through phone banks, mail and donations. These, in turn, affect program strategies.[84] As one religious broadcaster notes, mail becomes a "built-in polling device" so that "unless broadcasters have ironclad formats, their programs begin to focus on those issues and emphases that bring in the mail—and the money."[85]

Changes in the "700 Club" since its inception as a straightforward talk show reflect market demands. The program has become more serious and politicized in the past several years. In the early days, Robertson chatted with an endless stream of Christian authors hawking their books and handed out biblical precepts, social commentary, and miracles in equal measure. He has purposefully downplayed some of the more supernaturalistic elements of the show over the years—a decision based both on his political aspirations and on a change in market strategy. Robertson no longer performs healing or speaks in tongues on the air, according to Dabney, because "it comes on as cornball or zany, and saps the show of the intellectual seriousness he wants it to have."[86] The increasing incidence of personal faith testimonies and growing emphasis on healing in a broad sense are also signs of this market sensitivity. Market research has told producers of the show that viewers are "most interested in things that build their faith," according to Maltby.[87] Robertson and the "700 Club" producers, then, are highly attuned to the relationship between format and ratings, as evidenced in the spate of changes to the program in the last three years. Robertson's description of the show's format and purpose indicates a keen sense of his market and of its growing interest in subjects outside the domain of traditional revivalism:

> Our programming covers a broad spectrum in order to reach a wide variety of human interests. These range from the traditional church worship services and music to Bible teaching, news briefs, contemporary Christian music, discussions of current events, economics, international relations, finance, social conditions, good health, biblical prophecy, principles of Christian living, and so on. All have Christian dimensions for the benefit of our audience.[88]

Changes in the "700 Club's" content reflect the imperatives of operating and expanding an audience-supported program and network. In the early 1980s, CBN was in the process of becoming the nation's fourth-ranking cable network. The organization expanded its programming and made large capital investments in facilities and equipment. The "700 Club" is produced in a $22 million communications center; the state-of-the-art studio where the program is staged "easily outclasses all, save possibly NBC's famed Studio 8."[89] Such expansion requires generous audience support, both in terms of the number of donors and the size of their donations. Traditionally, viewers of evangelical television have been predominantly lower- or working-class older women. Robertson's programming and marketing strategies indicate a desire to extend his reach beyond this traditional viewership. Adding nonreligious programming to attract a general audience to CBN and the Family Channel, adding more public affairs to the "700 Club" and inserting it into the prime-time lineup, and downplaying the sectarian aspects of evangelicalism seem to be part of a plan to develop a wider viewership and a broader base of support. This, in turn, is reinforced by the producers' sense that the "700 Club" is unique among Christian programs, both in its content and in its ability to reach beyond its natural constituency.[90]

According to Frankl and to the Annenberg study, the traditional audience for religious television is most attracted to programs that emphasize the themes of 19thcentury revivalism. Shows that stress politics and social issues and that adopt commercial formats run the risk of alienating this audience in their quest for new viewers. Research indicates that men and younger viewers are more likely "to

be receptive to religious programs that are 'more like secular television.'"[91] Shows such as the "700 Club," then, seem to be trying to redefine religious television and its audience, a move that raises questions
about what constitutes the boundary between secular and religious
programming. Is there a point, for example, at which a program ceases
to be religious and becomes secular? Is religious television defined by
its content or by its form? Frankl contends that whether a show is
more "religious" or more "secular" depends on the degree to which it
has been influenced by the imperatives of television. The "700 Club,"
she says, is most like secular TV compared to other evangelical programs because of its near total appropriation of television's format
strategies and discursive conventions:

> [The show's] preaching component is minimal. It is apparent that
> Robertson's role as a 'preacher' has been changed for television:
> he has become a host. Although he may teach a segment, even
> using chalk and blackboard, the topics are often political or inter-
> national matters. Robertson's presentations are low-key and infor-
> mative, more like Walter Cronkite than Billy Sunday.[92]

Although Robertson certainly encourages conversion on the show,
this message is simply one among many, rather than the central reason for the performance as it is with Swaggart. The prayer segment is
usually two to five minutes long and is bridged to other segments with
the same conversational and musical transitions that hold the entire
package together. Other direct religious messages, as Frankl points
out, "are usually embedded in commercial-like fundraising appeals"
that encourage viewers to become part of the CBN"family."[93]
Swaggart, of course, also appeals for funds, but he does so in terms of
facilitating the Great Commission rather than creating an alternative
to secular television. The primary message of the "700 Club," as
expressed through its format, is as much political as it is religious; it is
a forum for the concerns and aims of the New Christian Right. The line
between politics and religion seems to be blurred even for the program's producers. The log for each "700 Club" episode identifies segments in the following categories: public affairs, religious, sports,
informational, and entertainment (it is impossible to imagine
Swaggart's program being tagged in this way). The log for one show I
watched identified as "religious" an interview with a former U.S.
Marine officer. Although the man testified to having been born again
while serving in Vietnam, the heart of the interview by Robertson
focused on how liberals at home had prevented a clear victory there
and concluded with a discussion on the current "marxist threat" in
Central America.[94]

With its blend of explicit politics, entertainment, and lifestyle features, the "700 Club" not only erodes the boundary between religious and secular television, it also blurs the line between religion and politics. This is not surprising given Robertson's conversionist theological perspective; in a 1982 interview with evangelical theologian Francis Schaeffer, the two men decried the separation of church and state which they saw as the result of humanists' "tyranny" over contemporary American society.[95] The reunification of church and state, moreover, is a central goal of the Christian conservatives. In the worldview espoused by the New Christian Right, and by Robertson as one of its leaders, the traditional evangelical separation between the spiritual and the worldly must be eliminated.

This is a key difference between Swaggart and Robertson; it is what makes the former's crusade program a rejection of contemporary culture and the "700 Club" an accommodation to, even an affirmation of, modern society. The "700 Club" is a television show that comments on social and political affairs from an evangelical perspective. It is not televised religion, but religionized television. Robertson is a TV personality, not a preacher. He manages and gives continuity to a stream of professionally produced political messages and "moral" entertainment packaged for a specific market. The show is conventional television with an alternative message. As Hoover says, the program's "political messages are purveyed in an evangelical and fundamentalist context but within a video setting that is unashamedly secular."[96] By appropriating the conventions of commercial television, CBN implicitly endorses the medium's central role in representing society's values and beliefs and in defining its terms of social discourse. Robertson constructs his story about society using the same language (standard televisual modes of representation) as the "enemy" (the "secular humanists" who control commercial television).

Swaggart, on the other hand, sees television primarily as a tool. He bends to television's imperatives to make his crusade more visually interesting and to solicit the funds that keep him on the air, but the form and substance of the program are dictated by the demands of revivalism. All other uses of television, in Swaggart's view, are manifestations of "the world" and inherently sinful. The "Christian broadcaster" embraces television; it is his profession and his reason to speak. Television is an end in itself, because it permits access to and control over symbolic production. The "business" of the "country preacher" is saving souls, and television is merely a means to this end. He uses the medium to carry out his calling, which comes from God.

THE AUDIENCES

Although the general religious television audience shares certain characteristics—predominately female, over 50, rural, lower income and education—there are significant differences between audiences for particular programs. These differences are not arbitrary; they have to do with the programs' substance and form, and with the speakers' and listeners' patterns of experience. The actual audience of religious programs is fairly fragmented, and those who watch do so for very specific reasons.[97]

According to the Annenberg/Gallup study, Swaggart counts among his viewers the highest number of men (although women are still the majority), the largest percentage of Southerners (nearly half), and one of the biggest proportions of rural dwellers (46%). He also reaches the fewest Catholics of all television preachers and attracts the highest percentage of Protestants. Some 42% of his viewers did not complete high, school and only one in ten attended college (three% graduated). Swaggart's viewers were the most likely to say that religion is very important to them and the most likely to hold evangelical views. The study concludes that Swaggart seemed to have the greatest appeal to traditional, conservative Protestants in the southern Bible belt.[98]

The "700 Club," in contrast, has the lowest number of viewers from rural areas and the fewest with only a grade-school education (29%). One quarter of the audience has some college education and 10% are graduates. The program attracts the largest proportion of viewers between 30 and 50 years old (47%), the highest share in the Midwest (40%), and the highest percentage of married viewers. It also has the greatest number of viewers who belong to and regularly attend a church. The Annenberg study notes that "Pat Robertson . . . appears more successful at capturing a 'churched' audience from 'Middle America'."[99] The "700 Club" continues to attract a significant share of the traditional religious television audience, however. Its viewers are predominately female in all age groups, and the Gallup study reported that more than 70% of its viewers over 50 years old are women.[100] The morning audience for all talk shows, of course, is predominantly female.

In 1985, CBN commissioned Nielsen to survey the audiences for the top 10 religious programs. Two CBN researchers assessed those findings in a study that compares audiences by the total number of viewers per week and month, and by age and gender.[101] The "700 Club" attracted the smallest percentage of male viewers of all 10 programs (22%) and was deemed "best at attracting 'the lady of the house'," presumably because the show airs in the morning when more women are able to watch. Swaggart's crusade, in contrast, attracted the highest number of male viewers (37%) among the top 10 shows.[102] When the audiences are differentiated by age, however, it appears that the "700 Club" was better than Swaggart at appealing to younger viewers of both sexes. Nearly three-quarters of Swaggart's female viewers are 55 or older, while 45% of women who watch Robertson are 25 to 54 years old. These ratios are also true for male viewers; 61% of the "700 Club" male audience is 25 to 54, while 60% of men who watch Swaggart are over 55.[103] These figures support my earlier argument that Robertson is hoping to reach a younger, more educated audience and that the entertainment and political and current affairs content of the "700 Club" is part of that strategy. As the authors of the study note: "Other research done by CBN indicates that the news in the '700 Club' is an attractive feature for younger audiences."[104]

Neither the Nielsen survey nor the Annenberg study gives figures on the occupational and economic status of religious TV viewers. The TV ministries undoubtedly contract their own research in these areas, but because of the intense competition for viewers within the "electronic church," they are not anxious to share their findings with outsiders. Hoover points out, however, that although "700 Club" producers claim that their audience is significantly different from viewers of most religious television, research does not fully support that belief. The Annenberg/Gallup study did find that weekday viewers have a tendency to be members of traditionally Pentecostal or charismatic denominations, to be more conservative theologically, to be more frequent church attenders, to be women or minorities, and to come from the lower classes.[105] But because that study grouped all weekday programs together, it is difficult to know how closely the "700 Club" fits this pattern.

Producers' perceptions of their audience come from a variety of sources, including internal market research. Television ministries also rely on more informal feedback in assessing their viewers and shaping their programming, including comments by people who call for prayer counseling, letters from viewers, responses from CBN employees and, of course, donation levels. A study by Thomas examined the relationship between viewers' socioeconomic class and religious television content; her research is based on the perceptions of the class background of the audience held by program producers and by outside sources. Thomas identified the "700 Club" as being aimed at an "upwardly mobile audience" and Swaggart's show as attracting a "working class" viewership; she found significant variations in the programs' content that corresponded to differences in the social class of the intended audience.[106] (This study is addressed in more detail in the next chapter.)

My research and observations of the "700 Club" and Swaggart's telecast lead me to suggest a determinate relationship between the programs' meaning and form and the "patterns of experience" of their intended audiences. A "country preacher" is more appealing to older, southern, rural dwellers of lower education, because his theology and preaching style are rooted in their history and religious experience. Swaggart's patterns of experience fit those of his followers—he speaks their language. Robertson's appeal is less proscribed by the boundaries of traditional Pentecostalism. As the barriers which both isolated and protected conservative evangelicalism have eroded, its message has increasingly reached people outside its traditional boundaries. Robertson's upbeat, slickly produced gospel of health and prosperity is more attractive to the suburban and urban middle classes. Younger people also appear to feel more at home with the "700 Club," which demands little and promises much, than with Swaggart's message, which refers often to death and counsels people to give up earthly pleasures for eternal joy. Many churchgoers are likely to feel uncomfortable with Swaggart's harangues against apostate Christianity and moribund denominations. Robertson's theology is supportive of church membership, because churches are one of the New Christian Right's most important organizing tools.

While it is tempting to see the distinctions between these audiences simply as market fragmentation, to do so is to forget the role of meaning in the speaker-listener relationship. The appeal of the "700 Club" and Swaggart's crusade is not just a matter of fitting market imperatives to audience characteristics. The programs appeal to specific viewers in particular historical circumstances, because they hold meaning for those viewers. And that meaning is always a complex, interactive creation. The "voice without" can speak to the "voice within" only if it has something to say to people's experiences, beliefs, and values. Robertson's and Swaggart's audiences are dissimilar, because the stories these men tell, and the histories they appeal to, are different.

NOTES TO CHAPTER 6

1. Swaggart's crusade is aired on Sunday on independent and/or cable stations. In larger markets, the program may be broadcast several times during the day. In Seattle, for example, when I first began watching Swaggart, the crusade aired three times in the morning and once in the evening; since the scandals, the show is much scarcer in

most TV markets.

2. Typically, the program consisted of his crusades in the United States or foreign countries, or occasionally a broadcast of services at his own church (the Family Worship Center) in Baton Rouge; the format in this case is similar to the crusades. Periodically, the program consisted of a fund-raising telethon to raise money for the ministry's international missionary efforts which center on Swaggert's telecast.

3. Channel 13, KCPQ-TV, in Seattle broadcasts a 60-minute version; my original analysis was based on this format; today, the show is only produced in an hour-long version.

4. During my initial study of the "700 Club," Robertson was accompanied by Danuta Soderman and Ben Kinchlow. The show has undergone several cast and set changes since Spring 1987. My original study is based primarily on programs that Robertson hosted.

5. J. Harold Ellens, *Models of Religious Broadcasting* (Grand Rapids, MI: Eerdmans, 1974).

6. "Jimmy Swaggart," Channel 13, KCPQ-TV, Seattle-Tacoma, April 26, 1987.

7. Swaggart's autobiography is filled with references to this calling. See Jimmy Swaggart with Robert Paul Lamb, *To Cross a River* (n.p.: Logos Internaltional, 1977).

8. The "Great Commission" to save the world for Christ comes from Matthew 28: 18-20: "Go forth therefore and make all nations my disciples; baptize men everywhere in the name of the Father and the Son and the Holy Spirit, and teach them to observe all that I have commanded you." Preachers such as Swaggart believe television is a tool for saturating the globe with the Christian message and is thus a fulfillment of the Great Commission. Swaggart says he initially resisted going into radio and television and did so only because God directed him to become a media evangelist. See *To Cross a River*, pp. 184, 210.

9. Swaggart, *To Cross A River,* p. 35.

10. Richard Ostling, "Power, Glory—and Politics," *Time*, February 17, 1986, p. 67; and Lewis J. Lord, "An Unholy War in the TV Pulpits," *U.S. News and World Report,* April 6, 1987, p. 64; Gustav Niebuhr, "TV Evangelists Rebound From Viewer Erosion," *Atlanta Journal*, May 1, 1989, pp. 6-8; Peter Applebome, "Swaggart's Troubles Show Tension of Passsion and Power in TV Evangelism," *New York Times*, February 28, 1988, p. A30.

11. G. Niebuhr, "TV Evangelists Rebound," p.6.

12. Susan Finch, "Swaggart Ministries Going Off the Air," (New Orleans) *Times-Picayune*, October 26, 1991, pp.A1,9.

13. Mike Dunne, "Swaggart to Oversee Troubled Empire Upon Return to Pulpit," *Baton Rouge Morning Advocate*, May 22, 1988, pp. 7-8.

14. G. Niebuhr, "TV Evangelists Rebound," p. 6.

15. Greg Garrison, "After The Fall," *Birmingham News*, May 7, 1989, p.10.

16. Ibid.

17. Dunne, "Swaggart to Oversee," p.7.

18. Ibid.

19. Garrison, "After The Fall," p. 7.

20. Finch, "Swaggart Ministries Going Off the Air."

21. "TV's Unhloly Row," *Time*, April 6, 1987, p. 63.

22. Applebome, "Swagart's Troubles," p. 30.

23. Bruce Rosenberg, *The Art of the American Folk Preacher* (New York: Oxford University Press, 1970.)

24. Ibid., p. 12-13.

25. Ibid., p. 14-15.

26. "Jimmy Swaggart," October 16, 1986.

27. Postwar migration spread conservative evangelicalism to other parts of the country. While the "Bible Belt" still exists, its boundaries are less clear that they were in the 1920's and 30's. Social mobility is simultaneously religious mobility. As evangelicalism moved to new geographical and social territories, the historical barriers protecting it from the forces of modernization weakened.

28. Rosenberg, *American Folk Preacher*, p. 10.

29. Ibid.

30. Ibid., p. 10.

31. Ibid., pp. 10-11.

32. Ibid., p.45.

33. "Jimmy Swaggart," April 16, 1987.

34. Ibid.

35. Rosenberg, *American Folk Preacher*, p. 23.

36. Ibid., p. 25.

37. Richard Ostling, "Offering the Hope of Heaven," *Time*, March 16, 1987, p. 69.

38. Swaggart's early television program, however, was set in a TV studio. Shot in Nashville in the studio used for "Hee Haw," Swaggart's first program was 30 minutes long. It included 10 to 15 minutes of country gospel music, a 10 minute Bible lesson, and five to 10 minutes of promotion for his crusades and albums. His teaching program, "Studies in the Word," used a pretaped format that did not require interaction with a live audience. Swaggart, *To Cross a River*, p. 217.

39. Rosenberg, *American Folk Preacher*, p. 17.

40. See Sandra Sizer, *Gospel Hymns and Social Religion* (Philadelphia, PA: Temple University Press, 1978), p. 114, for a description of Moody's revivals.

41. David L. Altheide and Robert P. Snow, *Media Logic* (Beverly Hills, CA: Sage, 1979).

42. Ibid., p. 22.

43. Ibid., p. 21.

44. Rosenberg, *American Folk Preacher*, p. 42.

45. Frankl, *Televangelism*, p. 117.

46. Kenneth R. Clark, "The $70 miracle named CBN," *Chicago Tribune*, July 26, 1985, Sect. 5, p. 3.

47. Quoted in Lord, "Unholy War in the TV Pulpits," p. 64.

48. Robertson, like several television preachers including Jim Bakker and Paul Crouch, received initial funding from The Full Gospel Businessman's Fellowship International. The FGBMFI, a Pentecostal organization of business and military men, began in 1952. For more information on this group, see Larry Kickam, "Holy Spirit or Holy Spook?" *Covert Action Information Bulletin*, 27 (Spring 1987): pp. 15-17.

49. Lamar Graham, "700 Club," *Norfolk Virginian-Pilot*, August 2, 1988, p. 9.

50. Stewart Hoover, *Mass Media Religion* (Newbury Park, CA: Sage, 1988), pp. 73-79.

51. Sara Diamond, "Preacher Pat for Prez," *Mother Jones*, January, 1986, p. 8; Ostling, "Power, Glory—and Politics," pp. 62, 67.

52. Hoover, *Mass Media Religion*, p. 89. Hoover notes that "special or major donors (4% of all donors) contribute 50% of CBN's yearly budget."

53. Pat Aufderheide, "The Next Voice You Hear," *Progressive*, September 29, 1985, p. 36. In brochures distributed by cable companies, CBN is labeled "inspirational."

54. April Witt, "Robertson Likely to Rejoin CBN," *Norfolk Virginian-Pilot*, May 11, 1988, p. 11.

55. Interview with Butch Maltby, former vice president of Institutional Advancement for CBN University, November 30, 1990.

56. Tele-Communications Inc. is also involved in the new interfaith cable networt, VISN. The network received a two-year loan from TCI to help meet its $6 million in operation costs each year. The willingness of cable operators such as TCI to support VISN may reflect the cable industry's desire to improve its public image and head off regulation by Congress. See Larry Witham, "Churches Promote Religious Network for Cable TV," *Washington Times*, March 16, 1990, pp. 10-11.

57. Maltby, interview with author.

58. Randy Frame, "Surviving the Slump," p. 3.

59. Daniel B. Wood, "Family Channel Focuses on the Inoffensive," *Christian Science Monitor*, February 9, 1990, p. 11.

60. Joseph Farah, "TV's Assault on the Family is No Joke," *Focus on the Family*, November 1990, p. 11.

61. This history is drawn from Hoover, *Mass Media Religion*, pp. 74-77.

62. K. Clark, "The $70 Miracle," p. 30.

63. Elayne Rapping, *The Looking-Glass World of Non-Fiction TV* (Boston: South End Press, 1987), p. 121.

64. Maltby, interview with author.

65. Rapping, *Looking-Glass World*, p. 120.

66. Maltby, interview with author.

67. Marjorie Mayfield, "For CBN, The Worst May Be Over," *Norfolk Virginian-Pilot*, March 5, 1989, p. 7; Tim Fitzpatrick, "Money Keeps Pouring In To Televangelists, Expert Says," *Salt Lake Tribune*, October 28, 1989, p. 11.

68. Maltby, interview with author.

69. Mayfield, "Worst May Be Over," p. 7.

70. Graham, "700 Club," p. 10.

71. Witt, "Robertson Likely to Rejoin CBN," p. 11.

72. Graham, "700 Club," pp. 9, 11.

73. Maltby, interview with author.

74. Maltby, interview with author.

75. Ibid., p. 10.

76. Quentin Schultze, "The Mythos of the Electronic Church," *Critical Studies in Mass Communication* 4 (1987): p. 256, quoted from P. M. Rice, "Interview with Pat Robertson," *Your Church*, May/June 1979, pp. 5-15.

77. Dick Dabney, "God's Own Network," *Harper*, August 1980, p. 36.

78. K. Clark, "$70 Miracle," p. 3.

79. J. Thomas Bisset, "Religious Broadcasting: Assessing the State of Art," *Christianity Today*, December 12, 1980, p. 31.

80. Ibid., p. 29.

81. Quoted in Todd Gitlin, *Inside Prime Time* (New York: Pantheon, 1983, 1985), p. 31.

82. See David W. Clark and Paul H. Virts, "Religious Television Audience: A New Development in Measuring Audience Size," paper presented at the Center for the Scientific Study of Religion, Savannah, GA, October 25, 1985.

83. Razell Frankl, *Televangelism* (Carbondale: Southern Illinois University Press, 1987), p. 82.

84. Hoover notes that "700 Club" producers rely on audience feedback via the phone banks and letters to gauge the impact of programming decisions. See *Mass Media Religion*, pp. 80-81.

85. Bisset, "Religious Broadcasting," p. 29.

86. Dabney, "God's Own Network," p. 47; this perception is also shared by some CBN employees according to one of my informants.

87. Maltby, interview with author.

88. Quoted in Bisset, "Religious Broadcasting," p. 31.

89. K. Clark, "$70 Miracle," p. 3.

90. Hoover, *Mass Media Religion*, p. 91.

91. Frankl, *Televangelism*, p. 126.

92. Ibid., pp. 91-92.

93. Ibid., p. 12.

94. Log for program 043-87, February 12, 1987.

95. "700 Club," August 31, 1990; rebroadcast of a program originally aired in February 1982.

96. Hoover, *Mass Media Religion*, p. 77.

97. Peter Horsfield, *Religious Television* (New York: Longman, 1984), p. 111; George Gerbner et al., *Religion and Television* (Philadelphia: Annenberg School of Communications, April 1984), pp. 10-13.

98. Gerbner et al., *Religion and Television*, pp. 63-64; Horsfield, *Religious Television*, p. 112.

99. Gerbner et al., *Religion and Television*, pp. 63-64.

100. Jeffrey Hadden and Charles E. Swann, *Prime Time Preachers* (Reading, MA: Addison Wesley, 1981), p. 62.

101. Clark and Virts, "Religious Television Audience."

102. Ibid., p. 20.

103. Ibid., p. 30, Table 2.

104. Ibid., p. 21.

105. Hoover, *Mass Media Religion*, pp. 91-95.

106. Sari Thomas, "The Route to Redemption," *Journal of Communication* 35 (Winter 1980): pp. 111-122; I discuss these findings more fully in a later chapter.

7

Dualist vs. Conversionist Theology: Politics, Prosperity, and the Problem of the Self

Although Swaggart and Robertson both belong to the charismatic Pentecostal tradition, their conceptions of Christianity differ in important ways. Robertson is grounded in a conversionist perspective, preaches a health and wealth gospel, encourages political activism among his viewers, and devotes much of his program to lifestyle features and advice on practical and psychological problems. The explicitly political slant of the "700 Club" reflects Robertson's heavy involvement in the New Christian Right. Swaggart holds a dualist perspective, denounces the gospel of health and prosperity, discourages political action in and material engagement with "the world," and disdains psychology (both Christian and secular) as a capitulation to modernism. While Swaggart is scornful of "secular humanism" and comments on the evils of communism, abortion, homosexuality, and so on, he has kept a distance from the New Christian Right (he did, however, belatedly endorse Robertson's decision to seek the 1988 presidential nomination).[1]

SEPARATION AND ACCOMMODATION

Key differences in the themes of the two programs are grounded in the belief systems and worldviews of their stars; these differences are connected as well to their respective audiences. Swaggart attempts to maintain the dualist opposition between Christianity and "the world"; Robertson tries to overcome that opposition through the transformation of the world to fit his theology. Both positions are part of evangelicalism's history—they constitute two strategies of negotiating the insider/outsider paradox that Marsden identifies. The growth of the New Christian Right's influence in the past decade indicates that Robertson's position has been gaining strength among many evangelicals. The trend in religious programming toward material and psychological concerns also signals structural and theological changes within the evangelical belief system.

The themes of Swaggart's crusade parallel the message of 19th-century revivalism: individualized piety, the inevitability of sin, the need to be spiritually reborn, the mandate to spread the Good News, and the separation of worldly and spiritual concerns. In addition to these stock themes is Swaggart's constant renunciation of false belief systems. The only path to salvation is to be born again into the charismatic tradition—to become a "spirit-filled," "Bible-believing," "tongues-talking" Christian. In this sense Swaggart's theology is highly monopolistic, excluding many professed Christians from the ranks of the chosen. Swaggart's crusades revolve around this limited set of themes that are enhanced and amplified through various rhetorical strategies. The themes of the "700 Club" echo the ideological positions of the New Christian Right: the program stresses public over private religiosity, political engagement rather than separation from the world, and social transformation which follows from individual salvation. Robertson's theology is integrative rather than divisive, and this stems from the imperatives of creating and sustaining conservative evangelicalism as a social movement.

As a leading member of the NCR, Robertson is involved in organizing his viewers around the theme of what Frankl calls "cultural fundamentalism."[2] He is attempting to unify rather than divide conservative evangelicals, and does so by downplaying theological differences and casting social problems in moral terms. The "700 Club" does not criticize particular denominations or draw lines between charismatic and noncharismatic evangelicalism. Robertson's discussions of theology are confined to generalizations and stress only those beliefs and practices that are widely agreed upon (e.g., biblical literalism, the need for a personal relationship with Jesus, the imperative of being born again, etc.). According to Gerard Straub, who produced the "700 Club" for almost three years, Robertson and most TV preachers "offer bare fundamentals of faith and ignore complex theological issues that will either bore the audience or provide them with opportunities for disagreement."[3]

Hoover's research supports this claim. CBN and the "700 Club" strive to be "as broadly palatable as possible" and part of this goal involves toning down and homogenizing the theological stand of prayer counselors. As one staff member of the counseling center told Hoover, "CBN tries to be a balanced ministry." That means, says Hoover, avoiding "sectarian and particularist beliefs" and "petty disagreements" that might divide the conservative Christian community.[4] The major themes of the "700 Club" revolve around broad moral tenets: the sanctity of the family, the twin threats of secularism and communism, the erosion of traditional values, the faltering of America's redeemer role, and the healing power of embracing Christ. These are issues that most conservative Christians can agree upon. The program brings viewers together around such issues, while avoiding theological or ecclesiastical points of dissension. Hoover found that his CBN sources freely admitted to a "careful process of 'watering down' of the most unique and potentially controversial elements of the Pentecostal roots of that program, so as not to offend the large, public and heterogeneous audience they see to be their target."[5] Such moderation, he adds, "leads to a religious 'universalism' of a kind, where a wide variety of religions and religious viewpoints are tolerated by the program and by its audience."[6]

Swaggart's theology is far more divisive, and adherence to a strict definition of proper Christian belief is a central part of his preaching. Although he criticizes secularism, Catholicism, Judaism, Hinduism, and so on, his most strident attacks are often directed at "apostate Christians."[7] Because Swaggart insists that to be saved one must be a charismatic Christian blessed with the gifts of the Holy Spirit, all other forms of evangelicalism are apostasy. He regularly chastises churches and preachers who fail to teach this "full gospel" message. Fundamentalists, Southern Baptists, and even his own former denomination have earned Swaggart's scorn on occasion. His critique of the prosperity gospel and Christian psychology are indirect slaps at a number of prominent televangelists, including Robertson. Swaggart's condemnation of the PTL and Oral Roberts are typical of his refusal to minimize theological differences. His preaching and writing also abounds with denunciations of religious TV programming that subordinates God's word to "Hollywood-style entertainment."[8] Swaggart can afford to be confrontational, because he is not in the business of building a political movement. In fact, he highlights divisions between the "truly saved" and the rest of humanity so as to create a consubstantiality on the basis of this special election.

The religious universalism of the "700 Club" is related to Robertson's prominent role in the coalition of the Christian and political right wings. As Diamond argues,

by taking an ambiguous position on key theological issues,
Robertson, more than any other born-again leader, has successful-
ly smoothed out conflicts that kept fundamentalists and pentecostals divided and generally apathetic about politics prior to the
1980s.[9]

A founding member of the Religious Roundtable and one of the spon-
sors of the 1980 Washington for Jesus rally, Robertson belongs to several right-wing organizations devoted to foreign and domestic political
issues. His latest political project is the Christian Coalition, created in
1989 out of the ashes of his failed presidential campaign. Registered
with the Internal Revenue Service as a "social welfare organization,"
the Coalition is a tax-exempt organization that raised (and spent) $5
million in 1991 and expects to spend twice that in 1992, organizing
grass roots support for "pro-family" issues and politicians.[10] The New
Christian Right political agenda guided that of Robertson's television
ministry throughout the 1980s. CBN provided money to former
Guatemalan president Efrain Rios Montt for counterinsurgency measures, was one of the largest private donors to the Nicaraguan *contras*,
and encouraged "700 Club" members to lobby Congress for aid to the
Salvadoran government. In one program, Robertson applauded the
"charisma" of Roberto D'Abuisson, leader of El Salvador's fascist
ARENA party and the man who reportedly ordered the assassination
of Archbishop Oscar Romero.[11] Robertson formed the Freedom
Council in 1981 to organize his presidential campaign at the state
level. The council was conceived as an educational organization to
teach evangelicals about the workings of party politics. Operating
through local churches, the Freedom Council trained preachers and
organized voter registration drives before being dissolved in 1986
after an IRS investigation.[12] Conason suggests that the Christian
Coalition may eventually face a similar investigation, because its activities appear to contradict its tax-exempt status which prohibits direct
involvement in partisan politics; in the meantime, the Coalition is
mounting a nationwide campaign devoted to "turning out the
Christian vote in 1992."[13]

The programming of the "700 Club" reflects this political agenda. During 1986 and 1987, the show promoted mandatory school
prayer and the teaching of creationism, lobbied for the SDI defense
system, supported the South African government,[14] defended the
Nicaraguan "freedom fighters," criticized sex education in public
schools, backed Reagan in the Iran-*Contra* scandal, argued that the
U.S. lost in Vietnam because of negative press coverage at home,
denounced arms negotiations with the Soviet Union, attacked Planned
Parenthood, linked AIDS to the "sin" of homosexuality, and accused

secular humanists of destroying the nation's moral fiber. Hoover's study of the "700 Club" found a similarly conservative agenda:

> The program has opposed abortion, and has favored prayer in the schools, capital punishment, banking reform, a strong defense policy, censorship of 'pornographic' and violent media, and has opposed the women's movement on some key issues including the Equal Rights Amendment, and urged a more isolationist foreign policy.[15]

While the newest version of the "700 Club" features different sets, graphics, music, and co-host, and includes lifestyle features and salvation stories, its general themes are still consistent with what Frankl calls "cultural fundamentalism" and what Wacker terms "Christian Civilization."[16] This is the same political ideology held by orthodox Protestants in the late 19th century, according to Marsden: "Free enterprise economics, success-oriented competitive individualism, opposition to expansion of the federal government, extreme fear of socialism, conspiracy theories of history, flag-waving patriotism, and imperialism all confirm this connection."[17] Frankl claims that superpatriotism, ultra-conservative economic policies, and traditional sexual and family values are "the major themes of cultural fundamentalism as an ideology of a social movement."[18] This ideology unites the Christian and political right wings. Although Swaggart is certainly conservative, his message centers on individual salvation and personal piety. Robertson adds to these concerns an extensive focus on social and political issues. In this respect, Swaggart's worldview is constituted outside the boundaries of the New Christian Right. As Frankl argues, the messages of the "electonic church" fall into two dominant categories: "popular religion" and "cultural fundamentalism."[19] Swaggart preaches the former, Robertson the latter.

The Gospel of Health and Wealth

An important part of the "700 Club" worldview is the theme of material success. Robertson's theology is built on what he calls the "Kingdom Principles." This is the scriptural adage—"you reap what you sow"—updated. Put crudely, every investment in the Lord is returned with dividends. Robertson has defined it as "giving and getting in equal measure. . . . We do it. It works. You *give* to be obedient to God and *getting* is a natural consequence."[20] The Kingdom Principles receive frequent mention on the program and support fund-raising telethons which assert that giving to the "700 Club" is one of the surest routes to God's blessings. This is what Robertson calls the "principle of reciprocity" whereby God "intended for his people to be on the top, not on the bottom."[21] In one show he cited the example of a man whose income increased five-fold after giving to CBN. Soderman added that the principle of reciprocity "is sort of like a spiritual bank account."[22] The cast encourages viewers to "give out of your need" in order to reap heavenly returns. In one episode, for example, Kinchlow told Robertson about a woman (on a fixed income and in poor health) who decided to send her entire disability check to the "700 Club." Kinchlow explained that three days later she received an unexpected check for $3,000. "Praise God," Robertson replied. "Let's give God a hand. . . . You there at home, if you want miracles, just step out in faith on the Kingdom Principles, and see what God is willing to do for you."[23]

The health and wealth gospel—or giving to get—is a popular theme in much of contemporary televangelism. This message is partly pragmatic, given TV ministries' dependence on audience support. But it is also more than that. In our society we expect something for our money—even appeals for charitable donations are made more attractive by their being tax deductible. This is related to the historical development of capitalism whereby all value has come to be equated with exchange value. That is, the value of something is determined by its price. TV preachers incorporate this logic into their appeals for funds. Last week's donations are worth so many souls brought to Jesus. Swaggart's fund-raising appeals are usually supported with footage of people surging toward the altar or viewers in foreign countries engrossed in his telecast.[24] The health and wealth gospel portrays the value of donations not only in terms of anonymous souls saved, but also in terms of personal rewards for the donor. The "700 Club" depicts people who have reaped material benefits for their support of the show's mission. The old "Word of Knowledge" segment often included examples of "financial healing." In one show Robertson referred to a man whose need for $100,000 would be met in three days "through the miraculous power of the Holy Spirit."[25] In another, Soderman prayed that a viewer would receive the $27,500 he needed to start up a business.[26] Promotional spots also proclaim this message. In one spot, a "700 Club" member testified that after he sent money to CBN, God had shown him how to be "prosperous, financially and spiritually."[27]

Guests also reinforce the message that being a Christian brings material blessings. A middle-aged black woman from Philadelphia, adorned in expensive jewelry and furs, testified that God had told her to save her money and "go into real estate." She had amassed a fortune by obeying God's word, and coincidentally had been a long-time believer in the Kingdom Principles.[28] Celebrities from the sports and entertainment fields reveal how becoming a Christian reinvigorated their careers and brought them greater fame and success.[29] Such Christian "stars" circulate among several religious programs (e.g., Rosie Greer, Dean Jones, Roy Rogers, and Pat Boone; Dale Evans and Efrem Zimbalist, Jr. even have their own shows on TBN). The testimony of these celebrities invariably backs up the tenets of the health and wealth gospel. The message—that poverty and failure are the fruits of un-Christian living—is reinforced by the lavish furnishings of the sets and expensive attire of the performers. There is an intriguing irony in this success theology: The overwhelming majority of audience members for these programs are neither wealthy nor glamorous. As Dabney notes: "Most of these people, presumably, are living ordinary lives. But the Christian celebrities tell them that ordinary life is contemptible, and that there is a magical way out."[30]

The health and wealth appeal, as manifested in Robertson's Kingdom Principles, plays on the ideology of the American Dream. It offers a picture of those who have made the dream come true and promises viewers that they too can enter this charmed circle. But, like everything in modern society, the dream has a price. In fact, if it had no monetary value, the dream would be worthless. The "700 Club" quite openly attaches a price to viewers' desires. Inside CBN headquarters stands a pillar which houses a microfilm containing the "Seven Lifetime Prayer Requests" of hundreds of viewers. Before the pillar was sealed, viewers who sent in $100 or more could get their seven requests added to the microfilm so they would be "surrounded by prayer" 24 hours a day. Implicit in this fund-raising scheme was the notion that the requests would likely be answered. Kinchlow reported in one show, for example, how a woman with an ingrown toenail who had sent in her money and prayers, had three of her requests answered within the week and her toenail "miraculously healed." "Praise God," Robertson responded. "You know you can't outgive God."[31]

This financial success philosophy is not unique to Christian television. Rags to riches stories, nighttime soap operas about the ultra-wealthy, and voyeuristic programs such as "Lifestyles of the Rich and Famous" are stock fare on commercial television. Market surveys and ratings indicate that these programs are attractive to a significant number of viewers. While it is simplistic to say that television merely gives people what they want, it is true that the *intended* audience of a program significantly shapes the show's content. Thomas' content analysis of 23 top-rated religious programs concluded that the class background of the intended audience influenced how key themes were treated. Those programs aimed at an "upwardly mobile" audience, including the "700 Club," addressed economic and material themes quite differently than did those shows created for a "working-middle" or "working class" audience (the latter includes Swaggart's show). Thomas found that programs aimed at an upwardly mobile audience tended to encourage the pursuit of material success at a much higher rate than did shows intended for working class viewers.

In the episodes studied, the upwardly mobile programs never identified money as a source of evil, occasionally conceded that money would not buy happiness, and most often suggested that wealth could bring contentment if it was properly used. (One of the proper uses, of course, is giving to TV ministries.) Working class programs offered quite a different perspective on money. They emphasized that money does not bring happiness, or that it is the root of evil or sin, in about equal proportions, and they rarely suggested that wealth is positive, even when put to good use.

Upwardly mobile programs also scored higher on the number of prayers for "tangible" outcomes (e.g., material goods and events), while prayers in the working class shows were most often "spiritual" petitions (e.g., related to metaphysical outcomes).[32] The study also found significant differences in the degree to which the two types of programs encouraged worldly accomplishment and involvement in social and political activities outside the church. Upwardly mobile programs rated higher in both categories; the working class shows stressed personal piety over worldly accomplishment and generally counseled listeners to remain aloof from the world.[33] Thomas proposes that the messages of the two types of programs correspond to the social conditions and expectations of their viewers:

> It is socially functional to present the poor with teachings that stress the ultimate worthlessness, indeed baneful or dangerous character, of material wealth and its quest. . . . [and] as the 'social ladder' is 'ascended,' it appears to be more acceptable to begin promoting the merits of worldly achievement and acquisition alongside more traditional Christian teachings.[34]

Further, the messages of these two types of programs are consistent with the therapeutic rhetorics of consolation and compensation.

Political Activism vs. a Politics of Passivity

Thomas's findings support my observations of the "700 Club" and Swaggart's crusade. Not only does the former promote a connection between material success and Christian living, it also strongly encour ages viewers to engage in the social and political causes of the New Christian Right. After a favorable CBN news report on the SDI system, for example, Robertson advised viewers to call or write their congressional representatives.[35] CBN was also one of the key plaintiffs in the Alabama court case concerning the use of "secular humanist" educational materials and set up a special fund (titled "Humanism Cases") for further legal fights over public school curricula. The "700 Club" has aired numerous segments on this subject and has encouraged its viewers to examine reading materials in their local schools.[36] When CBN reported on Human and Health Services' employee Joanne Gasper's decision to cut federal funding for Planned Parenthood because it offered abortions, Robertson urged viewers to call the White House on her behalf.[37] The show has also encouraged its audience to oppose sex education in public schools and to review material offered to teenagers regarding contraception and protection from AIDS. When Phylis Schlafly appeared on the program to promote her Eagle Forum's efforts on this issue, Robertson applauded her statement that the correct Christian stand on teenage sexuality is abstinence. He also urged viewers to support Schlafly's organization. The inclusive nature of the NCR permits Robertson to join forces with Schlafly, a right-wing Catholic. Swaggart's exclusive theology would prohibit his supporting a "non-Christian" such as Schlafly.[38]

The overtly political content of the "700 Club," and its propensity for counseling viewers to engage in political and social issues, places it firmly within the agenda of the New Christian Right. The program is actively involved in constructing an ultraconservative story about the nature of society and about evangelicals' role within it. The "700 Club" enthusiastically supported the Reagan administration, and Reagan himself twice appeared on the show. In his second appearance, Robertson joked with the then-president that they should swap jobs.[39] According to Frankl, Robertson and other TV ministers who fund raise for moral and political goals are "reversing 'The Great Reversal'" and carving out a sphere of influence in the political arena. The messages of Robertson's program "strongly support and reinforce the moral positions of the New Christian Right—from family issues to aggressive political actions in Latin America."[40]

Robertson's failure to win the Republican nomination not only affected the "700 Club," but was also a setback for his larger political project. Gerbner speculates that viewers outside the "hard-core" religious audience, who had been drawn to the show for its news and political commentary, may have been turned off by Robertson's "rather hard-nosed, basic fundamentalist ideas" expressed in the campaign. On the other hand, pentecostal viewers who initally supported Robertson's candidacy may have been upset by his efforts to distance

himself from faith healing, apocalyptic visions, and other manifestations of charismatic Christianity. Alley also suggests that Robertson
may have lost status in the minds of viewers who saw him as "close to
the centers of power" through his association with the Reagan administration; "[Robertson's] days of heady relationshps with all the big
shots in Washington are gone," says Alley.[41] Further, because
Robertson and many of his supporters genuinely believed his candidacy was ordained by God, his loss was a severe disillusionment—one
that Maltby says was strong enough to turn some viewers away from
the "700 Club."[42]

Robertson has not abandoned his political interests or aspirations, however. He has merely redirected his efforts. After the campaign he announced plans to form a new political action committee,
Americans for the Republic, which would provide funds and training
for conservative Christians who wished to get involved in politics.
Robertson said the new PAC would give him "a vehicle for continued
political visibility." The Christian Coalition, an ostensible "non-politi-
cal" organization, plays a complementary role in the development of
his national political influence. His decision to return as "700 Club"
host reflects political motivations as well. After ruling out seeking the
governor's seat in Virginia, Robertson explained:

> It would be very difficult to do as much good for this nation in the
> governor's mansion in Richmond as I could as a private citizen
> with the national constituency I have right now, coupled with pos-
> sibly some television, which gives a much larger platform to talk
> about issues.[43]

Whether Robertson has decided to permanently abandon his pursuit
of political office remains open to speculation. He has predicted "a
Christian in the White House by the year 2000," but may be referring
to Vice President Dan Quayle, a member of a right-wing Presbyterian
sect and a favorite of the Christian Coalition.[44]

Robertson's books are another important forum for dissemi-
nating his views. He described a recent book, *The New Millennium*, as
a "Christian megatrends" during promotional appearances on a number of secular news and talk shows in Fall 1990. These appearances on
television outside the "700 Club" not only expose his ideas to viewers
beyond his natural constituency and help legitimate Robertson as a
national political figure, they also provide him with occasions to do
what he loves most—to expound on his social and political visions.
Schultze has suggested that if Robertson were free to do exactly as he
pleases with the "700 Club," it would be primarily a conservative

Christian version of the "MacNeil/Lehrer News Hour." But because the show depends on viewer support and the desires of its market, much of the program focuses on personal problems and faith testimonies.[45] Maltby concurred with this assessment and said that Robertson satisfies his "public affairs orientation" through alternative outlets; besides appearances on secular programs, Robertson is involved in Christian radio. He is a frequent guest on WNTR, a conservative station in Washington, D C, and also does political commentary through Broadcast Equities, the for-profit radio arm of IFE.[46]

Swaggart addresses politics much less directly. He condemns homosexuality, abortion, humanism, and communism often, but does so in terms of sin, and he is equally harsh toward all belief systems different from charismatic Christianity. The solution to these problems, moreover, is not political and social, but spiritual and individual. Those who are born again and filled with the Spirit have greater resistance to such sins because these activities will no longer be attractive. The ills of society—abortion, teenage pregancy, drugs, divorce, homosexuality—cannot be blamed on Washington or the education system, which Swaggart says are merely symptoms of the disease. Nor can these problems be solved by laws or force. Rather, "they can only be changed by a change of heart." This change of heart, accepting Jesus personally, is the only action "that can be effected for good in your life. He is the answer."[47] The thrust of Swaggart's evangelism is to save souls, not to change the political complexion of society. Swaggart actually became less overtly political in his American broadcasts in order not to offend viewers and thus endanger his program's standing with independent stations.[48]

This is not to say that Swaggart is apolitical, since every worldview contains a politics. But Swaggart's theology contains an implicit political passivity through its emphasis on disengagement from "the world" and is therefore deeply conservative by virtue of tacitly endorsing the social status quo. This is one reason Swaggart has been welcomed by Latin American dictators such as Chile's Augusto Pinochet. In keeping with the highly individualistic character of Protestantism generally, and with orthodox Protestants' hostility to the liberal social gospel, Swaggart's theology stresses individual rather than social salvation. Such a theology is highly compatible with political regimes who fear any organized social opposition. Swaggart's role in Latin America, then, is akin to that of antebellum preachers in the American South who offered slaves a religion of consolation that did not threaten their masters' power. Thus, Swaggart's theology does have important political implications, particularly in Latin America where he has preached extensively.[49]

Eschewing overt political activism is more than a programming strategy, however—it is related to Swaggart's separatist theology. It is difficult to maintain a separation from "the world" while engaging in political lobbying and organizing around social issues. Moreover, joining political causes runs counter to the individuated conception of religion that informs Swaggart's worldview. Swaggart's premillennialist roots also work against the idea that Christians should engage in politics. Although Robertson and Swaggart both hold a premillennial eschatology, their views of the end of the world are different. Robertson is a "post-tribulationist" who believes that Christians will live through the seven-year tribulation. The Kingdom of God will emerge gradually as Christians take over world leadership and a last great revival sweeps the planet. Swaggart is a "pretribulationist," believing that charismatic Christians will be "raptured" before the agonies of the tribulation and will thus have no earthly role in the creation of the Kingdom.[50] From Swaggart's perspective, the outcome of history is predetermined and the vast majority of the human race is already damned to an eternal hell. The *only* action that can alter this fate is being born again. Swaggart constantly asserts that "good works" are impotent when it comes to eternal salvation; it follows from this logic that explicitly political or social activities outside of bringing people to Christ are largely futile.[51] The key is to accept Jesus and this entails rejecting "the world." Swaggart's evangelicalism is decidedly otherworldly and largely incompatible with the goals of the Christian Right in America. He is not trying to change this world, but prepare people for the next one. As Swaggart tells listeners, "You're a citizen not of this world but of another world."[52] In this respect, Swaggart is firmly grounded in an earlier form of evangelicalism; he carries on the tradition of the Great Reversal and Dwight Moody's grand "rescue mission."

REJECTING THE "SPIRIT OF THE WORLD": SWAGGART'S ANTI-MODERNISM

Swaggart's separatist theology extends beyond politics to all areas of popular culture. Forsaking the things of this world means rejecting cultural and leisure activities that distract people from their devotion to God and seduce them to embrace modernism. Swaggart denounces all music that is not religious or, more specifically, that is not the "old-time gospel music" he performs. Many of the songs in the crusade, in fact, take up this theme.[53] Swaggart is also a vehement critic of "Christian rock" which he considers satanic.[54] Activities categorized as questionable, if not openly sinful, include attending movies, sports events and rock concerts, watching television (he has specifically mentioned HBO, the academy awards, sports channels, and glamorized religious programs; the exception is his own telecast), dancing, drinking, listening to secular records, and going to "honky tonks." He has also condemned smoking and suggested that "good women" wear skirts rather than pants. A good Christian, according to Swaggart, will not desire these diversions: "They simply have no bearing," he says.[55] By counseling people to avoid popular culture, Swaggart is attempting to maintain the historical boundary that has protected evangelicalism from contamination by modernism. This is true as well of his contention that worshipers should abandon churches that do not preach the "full gospel message" of the Holy Spirit. Swaggart's theology demands more of followers than does Robertson's. To forego the pleasures of modern society—the fruits of consumer culture—is a genuine sacrifice, and one that requires constant effort and vigilance. As Swaggart acknowledges, the amenities of this world are seductive: "There is a certain amount of pleasure in making millions dishonestly, in being the sex goddess of a nation," he says, "but it is short lived. The pleasures come to an end."[56]

The strict practices demanded by this belief system place its adherents in direct, constant tension with the world around them. Swaggart's followers must eschew the "spirit of the world" which he says "is (regretably) almost everything that is considered 'fun,' 'exciting,' and 'with it'—within the context of the sordid package presented daily to a media hungry world."[57] As Swaggart tells viewers, the pleasures and problems of the world "have nothing to do with you."[58] Christians experience tension in their choice of separation, he explains, because they are "going against the prevailing currents of the world."[59] In this sense, Swaggart preaches a dualist version of Christianity that is anti-modern and anti-materialistic. He insists that Christianity exists outside of the boundaries of the institutional church and is also fundamentally at odds with material accumulation. As Swaggart remarked in one program: "We preachers make a mistake when we tell you that if you come to Jesus it will all be honey and roses, or tell you you're going to get rich. We prostitute the Word and the promises of God when we say that."[60] Wealth, in Swaggart's view, is part of "the world" and in no way related to salvation. In fact, riches and material success lead people away from God, as Swaggart's frequent stories about his cousin, Jerry Lee Lewis, attest. These anecdotes are parables of the spiritual poverty that necessarily accompanies worldly prosperity.[61]

Swaggart's asceticism is full of contradictions, of course, given his $1.1 million estate, his $5,000 Rolex (donated by a supporter), and his expensive attire. He does not preach the primitive communism of the early Christian communities, nor demand vows of poverty as have Christian mystics.[62] His critique of materialism is far more individualistic and conservative than is contemporary liberation theology's criticism of economic inequality and social exploitation. The kinship between Swaggart's beliefs and these other theologies has to do with their taking an oppositional stance toward the larger society and with their emphasis on spiritual transcendence. They propose that satisfaction (the coincidence of being and meaning) does not come from *things* (or institutions), but from *communion* (with God or with others in a relationship mediated by God). Swaggart's communion occurs in relationship with Christ and the Holy Spirit; as he often says, "Christianity is not a religion. It's a relationship with Jesus Christ."[63] Swaggart proposes a challenge of sorts to contemporary society. His theology is a negation of modernism. Progress, enlightenment, and material accumulation have failed to fill humanity's deepest desire— the desire for cosmic connection and for an "ultimate relevance of being." Swaggart condemns modern society, because it has robbed human life of meaning, and he offers a story of the world that restores premodern significance and transcendence.

SUFFERING AFFLICTION:
DUALIST VS. CONVERSIONIST RESPONSES

Robertson offers a less confrontational story. The message of the "700 Club" is culturally accommodating, built on a worldview that assimilates, revises, and renames, rather than rejects, modern values. Robertson's "transformation" occurs within existing institutions and social relationships; according to Straub,

> Pat Robertson sells a 'salvation' that will transform the viewers' life, and a flood of benefits will flow from heaven following salvation: Restored health, healed relationships, career success, monetary rewards, and an improved lifestyle can all be yours if you just say 'yes' to Jesus.[64]

The message of the "700 Club" has striking parallels to the promises of the New Age and human potential movements. There is no place in Robertson's salvific schema (nor in New Age philosophies or pop psychology) for human suffering. The truly saved Christian is healed, enriched, and satisfied, as is the New Ager and the "self-actualized" individual. It follows, then, that poverty, illness, sorrow, and loss are self-inflicted failures—punishments for rejecting the proper path.

Swaggart's theology, in contrast, makes suffering central. Humanity suffers *because* it is human. Evil and bafflement are inevitable fruits of the fall. Human existence, in Swaggart's view, is a travail of sorrow that is inescapable in this life. "Man is nothing," he tells his viewers. "You think you're something. Jesus said you're blind and miserable and naked." In fact, Christians must choose suffering if they are to achieve union with God: "You must choose to suffer afflic-tion," he says. "That's not pretty, is it?"[65] Further, salvation occurs not because we are good or deserving, but because we accept our worth-lessness. "You've got to shout: 'I'm no good. I can't save myself. I'm rotten. I'm filth'," he tells followers.[66] Thus, evil is a human product; Auschwitz, he says, is not of God, but of the world.[67] The sinner attains heaven only because God is merciful. The route to salvation lies in perpetually confessing one's fundamental baseness and peti-tioning God for mercy. The path to heaven, then, is arduous—a contin-ual struggle to transcend worldly evil and human weakness. In this respect, Swaggart's message is framed as a rhetoric of consolation in the face of inevitable human corruption.

This is not to say that Robertson and the "700 Club" do not address suffering. Much of the program is devoted to healing of one sort or another. From its earliest days, when distraught viewers called in their pledges and prayer requests and Robertson healed people on the air, the "700 Club" has recognized the human desire for delivery from misery. In fact, the show's success stems from strategically turn-ing these practices into a means of enhancing ratings and donations. In the early 1980s, extensive market research by CBN revealed that the subject of most concern to regular contributors was healing—that is, people tuned in not so much to receive Robertson's political analyses as to find solutions to their daily travails. "700 Club" executives subse-quently organized the show's content around the theme of God's heal-ing power—a theme that lent itself to a wide variety of topics from divorce to the fight against communism. Interviews, political commen-tary, promotional spots, and telethons could all be adapted to the con-cept of spiritual, psychological, financial, or political healing. The result of this programming decision was a dramatic increase in view-ers and contributions.

The way that suffering and relief from it are incorporated into the "700 Club" reflects Robertson's conversionist theology, the demands of the segmented talk show format, and the imperatives of CBN's marketing goals. Unlike Swaggart, who believes suffering is the lot of a fallen humanity, Robertson sees misery as a temporary state to be overcome through personal and social action. Indeed, it is Christians' duty to deliver themselves from suffering by finding and following God's plan for their lives. It is a rare episode of the "700 Club" that does not include a segment about someone who was in need of healing and found it, often through the intervention of the ministry. Further, the path to such health is as accessible as the television knob. Being born again and finding God's will for one's life "is so easy," Robertson tells his viewers. In one show, former co-host Soderman offered a "Freedom Pack" with simple fixes for "those heavy things that are going down."[68] The "700 Club" offers painless solutions to a painful existence; it promises a rapid, transformative cure similar to that proffered in TV advertisements.

The constraints of the talk show format also work to simplify any problem so it can be contained within the logic of the segmented format. The program offers simple solutions and easy-to-follow guidelines to happiness, success, and salvation; serious issues are juxtaposed with lighthearted ones, and both receive the standard 9-minute treatment demanded by the magazine format. For example, during an segment featuring a Christian marriage counselor, a viewer called in to confess that her husband was physically abusing her and asked for advice. As the woman sobbed on the phone, Robertson suggested that she offer her husband "redemptive love" and quickly moved on to a question from the studio audience.[69] As Straub points out, "the complexities of television production and the nature of the medium do not permit an in-depth analysis of any problem, and the television preachers understand the importance of the 30-second solution."[70] Promotional spots are slickly produced, short "commercials" that sell the idea that happiness, health, and success are available to the devout believer. In the teaching segments, Robertson will step up to a blackboard and "within minutes chalk out a quick plan for salvation."[71] Deeply entrenched social problems are individualized, and analysis is replaced by simplified guidelines. Such simple, formulaic solutions are standard in the talk show format in which

> Experts tell you how to make any crisis as smooth and painless as possible. Recovering from traumas as diverse as a child's bedwetting or a nervous breakdown are handled in two to three minute segments in which experts give us five simple rules or steps.[72]

Although the notion of God's healing power is an important part of the evangelical tradition, its prominence in the "700 Club" is as much a marketing decision as a theological one. In the last year, there has been a noticeable increase in the amount of time per program devoted to the theme of miraculous healing. Maltby points out that some members of CBN's "inner circle" genuinely believe that the world is on the brink of its "last days." Because premillennial theology predicts an increase in miraculous events as the Second Coming draws near, the increased emphasis on miracles in the program is a reflection of that prophesy.[73] But this development may also be interpreted as a sign that CBN executives are attempting to revive ratings and previous donations levels by returning to a program strategy that worked well in the past. On one level, then, this change in content suggests that the show is returning to more theological, less political concerns—going back to Robertson's roots in charismatic Pentecostalism. But at another level, it is also a continuation of the ministry's ongoing strategy of fitting program content to market demands—a case of "giving to get" in reverse. As some critics of the health and wealth gospel suggest, the practice of "giving viewers what they want" necessarily "distorts the historic Christian message." According to Schultze, evangelical programs that are "driven by the desires of the market rather than the content of the message" must downplay the more demanding aspects of Christianity. The historic Christian gospel, he says, is "not nearly so flashy and interesting" as the televised version; it "calls for faith and perseverance" while both consumer society and the "electronic church" emphasize instant gratification and miraculous transformation.[74]

The decision to emphasize healing and to devote much of the "700 Club" to the daily struggles of its viewers reflects more than a marketing strategy, however. It indicates the extent to which subjectivization has penetrated evangelicalism. Much of the content of the program is devoted to the myriad struggles facing Christians in the modern world. Lifestyle and self-help segments are a staple part of the show. Experts tell viewers how to cope with divorce, depression, unplanned pregnancy, obesity, and addiction. Robertson, of course, is the prominent expert on the "700 Club"; his opinions and advice permeate the program and are offered as well in his magazine, *The Flame*, and in his many books. In his *Answers to 200 of Life's Most Probing Questions*, Robertson explains everything from depression and divorce to the mystery of the trinity and whether there will be pets in heaven.[75] Guests disclose how they coped with unfaithful partners, overcame their homosexuality, dealt with the discovery that they are terminally ill, and came to terms with unhappy childhoods. At times an entire program is devoted to a particular crisis or problem (I have seen death, obesity, smoking, teenage sexuality, and broken families treated in this way); in such cases the multisegment format is maintained by breaking down the problem into news reports, testimonies, interviews, audience questions, pretaped "salvation stories," and so on. Promotional spots often show a family or individual undergoing some kind of crisis; meanwhile, the announcer suggests that viewers call a prayer counselor or send for a free booklet that answers their problem. The theme of the "700 Club" telethon in 1987, entitled "Lives in Crisis," revolved around examples of individuals and families who had been "healed" with help from the CBN ministry. The 1990 telethon, "Seven Days Ablaze," was similarly organized around viewers' desire for healing; during the month preceeding the telethon, viewers were encouraged to send in their requests for healing of all kinds. The solutions to these dilemmas are posed in spiritual terms— you can weather emotional storms with God's help—but implicit in the message is that living a proper Christian lifestyle will prevent many of these crises.

THE PROBLEM OF THE SELF:
TWO THERAPEUTIC STRATEGIES

Differences between Swaggart's and Robertson's treatment of suffering reflect conflicting attitudes toward the problem of the self within conservative evangelicalism. The prevalence of the health and wealth gospel in evangelical television and the proliferation of Christian self-help literature and counseling services are signs of evangelicalism's general accommodation to the subjectivizing pressures of modernization and to the widespread "therapeutic ethos" in contemporary America.[76] Even Swaggart's former denomination, the Assemblies of God, which has historically eschewed capitulation to contemporary culture, has recently created counseling centers and a rehabilitation program for wayward ministers.[77] These developments are an implicit acknowledgment of the modern problem of the self, and thus a concession to modernism which has rendered the self a puzzle to be solved in the first place.[78]

   Hunter characterizes this response to subjectivization as a "psychological Christo-centrism" whereby emotional health derives from establishing a harmonious relationship with Jesus.[79] The large volume of Christian advice and self-help literature published in the last decade, the development of Christian therapy and a Christian approach to sexuality, and the stream of experts who tell viewers how to solve their problems in an appropriately Christian manner are bound together by a common theme.[80] Christian psychology offers promises of gladness, joy, victory, and satisfaction, all of which naturally flow from correct Christian living. As Hunter points out, the message—that "if one is spiritual, one is happy and contented"—requires "public and subjective denial of inner suffering, dread, and boredom as essential features of human existence."[81]

By offering advice on a variety of psychological and emotional dilemmas, the "700 Club" poses Christian answers to the problem of the self. Just as the program is a secular format with Christian content inserted, its psychological perspective is an appropriation of the terms and forms of secular psychology and the human potential movement "filled" with Christian solutions.[82] In this sense, the ministry is part of what Davis calls the "subject industry" in contemporary society. The subject industry is "the manufacture, through the media, of popular conceptions of subjectivity and the therapies and programs of 'self-help' whereby these notions are disseminated and inculcated."[83] The "700 Club," then, acknowledges and accommodates the process of subjectivization—or the modern preoccupation with the self. It does not ask viewers to question the historical process by which the self has become a problem, but merely to find Christian ways to adjust to it. This version of evangelicalism stands in opposition to the ascetic tradition of Christianity. As Hunter notes: "The spiritual exercises of self-discipline and self-denial are hardly conceivable in a situation where that which is to be denied and disciplined is under near-constant examination."[84]

Swaggart takes quite a different approach to subjectivization. He identifies the problem of the self as a product of "the world" and advises followers to solve the problem by rejecting its importance. As he said in one telecast, self-consciousness itself is sin—a sign that people have elevated themselves above God. "You've got to get rid of self-consciousness," he asserts, and "get full of God-consciousness."[85] In fact, concern with the self is the original sin; Adam and Eve were cast out of paradise (or communion with the sacred) because they shifted their attention from God to themselves: "Man's greatest sin is that his every thought is not on God," Swaggart says.[86] Preoccupation with one's emotional and practical problems is a manifestation of this sin, because it elevates the self over the creator. As Swaggart tells viewers, the problem is not that human beings are plagued with an inferiority complex, but that they have a "superiority complex." This sense of superiority—the self's obsession with mastering the world—is also characteristic of Satan, he argues. Swaggart's hostility toward psychology stems from his disdain for the self. "You still have self," he tells listeners. "That's the hardest problem the Holy Spirit has. God hates it [self]."[87]

Psychology is sinful—a product of secularization—because it attempts to find human reasons for and solutions to people's problems. In Swaggart's worldview, there is only one source of suffering and that is sin—the state of separation from God. For Swaggart, obsession with the self is a manifestation of this gulf. One does not join God by thinking about "my hairdo" or "my car," Swaggart insists, but by thinking of nothing but the Lord "When I go to bed at night, when I get up in the morning, my eyes are on God. I think of Him every minute of the day."[88] The struggle between good and evil, joy and sorrow, cannot be decided through the actions of human beings, but through the victory of God over Satan. The way out, then, is to align oneself with God and receive eternal life, or with Satan and suffer eternal hell. It is this all-important decision that determines the outcome of an individual life, and it is the *only* choice that really matters. If you choose God, you also choose joy, which Swaggart differentiates from happiness. Non-Christians are "happy," he concedes, but happiness is a "roller coaster ride," short-lived and humanly made. Christians have "joy" which is eternal and God-given.[89] While Christians must sacrifice worldly happiness, they are also freed from the pain of temporality—they will live forever. Swaggart's mission is intensely single-minded; he is there to beckon, scold, and exhort people to choose God. He is a conductor on the train to eternity.

What this means, I propose, is that Swaggart *does* address the question of the self in terms of the fundamental "problem of meaning"—human suffering, bafflement, and evil. Swaggart's belief system acknowledges and solves these dilemmas by relegating them to "the world" and seeking to transcend them. Believers are freed from the problem of the self by renouncing this world and turning their sights on the next. This religious perspective, then, also bows, albeit indirectly, to the modern problem of the self. The process of modernization that has produced the individual "subject" has simultaneously dispelled earlier systems of meaning. As we have lost our connection to older signifying systems that gave us an identity—and specifically from religious beliefs that explained both our lives and our death—we have come face to face with our mortality. The modern problem of the self demands that we create a meaning not only for our existence, but also for its inevitable end. Swaggart's theology offers answers to both existential problems: It tells people why they live and promises them they will not die. By denouncing the problem of the self, Swaggart offers a way out—a line of flight—or in Merton's terms, "a flight into faith."[90] The irony of this path is that in fleeing from mortality, believers must actually seek their death. There is, in Swaggart's theology, a profound longing for the end of earthly existence. "I'm so tired of this life," he weeps. "I'm so tired of man's pitiful ways."[91] Swaggart is not just fearless in the face of Armageddon, he yearns for it, because the apocalypse will justify his beliefs and his life's work. The end will provide the ultimate legitimation of his existence, flooding his being with meaning.[92]

In a world that increasingly denies or relativizes all significance, this totalizing answer to the problems of being and meaning is undoubtedly attractive to those people who are still capable of a deep belief in eternal life. Swaggart's solution to the problem of the self—rejecting the world—is aimed at people for whom the world is already a struggle. Swaggart's message is persuasive to those whose patterns of experience coincide with his assessment that the modern world is sinful and empty. Suffering, confusion, and wickedness will cease only in union with God, and most particularly at the point when the believer "wakes up in the arms of Jesus" after death.[93]

Robertson, on the other hand, is not tired of this life; he is merely weary of its being run by godless humanists. The "700 Club" does not counsel viewers to reject the world, but to work within culture to change it—to restore "Christian Civilization" by transforming society so that it conforms to their beliefs. The program asserts that becoming a Christian will bring happiness, success, and influence in *this* life. It is a conversionist stance that offers compensation for evangelicals' displacement from the center of society. Robertson's message, then, is directed at people who do not feel themselves quite so alienated from society; it speaks to insiders rather than outsiders. His listeners are either members of the middle and upper-middle classes, or those who aspire to these positions—people who have reaped some rewards from the existing social structure and who would like to reap even more. This audience is not interested in forgoing the material and cultural benefits of society; it wants a theology that supports and legitimates its social position and aspirations. The story told by the "700 Club" and by the New Christian Right is affirmative. The enemy is not the inherently sinful "self"; it is non-Christians who have undermined the proper functioning of society by separating public and private morality.

The goal of the New Christian Right, and of its leaders such as Robertson, is not to reject the world, but to control its guiding metaphors. As Heinz says, "the contest over the meaning and course of the American story is a contest over whose sacred canopy shall prevail."[94] The sacred canopies erected by Swaggart and Robertson are, ultimately, incompatible. The New Christian Right is engaged in a quest to gain control over society; its cohesion as a social movement is enhanced by referring to religious symbols that make that struggle sacred. Swaggart does not seek to control society but to transcend it. He wants to shed the mortal skin that binds him to the things of the world. Swaggart cannot envision a "moral majority," because he believes most people are incapable of choosing the arduous path to God. He is the man with a lifeboat who saves as many as he can, but who knows the world is still a sinking ship.

NOTES TO CHAPTER 7

1. See Fred Barnes, "Rarin' to Go," *New Republic*, September 29, 1986, pp. 14-15; Dudley Clendinen, "Robertson's Camp Hopes to Capture Vast TV Evangelical Vote in Nation," *New York Times*, September 30, 1986, p. B4.

2. Razelle Frankl, *Televangelism* (Carbondale: Southern Illinois University Press, 1987), pp. 114-115.

3. Gerard Straub, *Salvation for Sale: An Insider's View of Pat Robertson's Ministry* (Buffalo, NY: Prometheus, 1986), p. 293.

4. Stewart Hoover, *Mass Media Religion* (Newbury Park, CA: Sage, 1989), pp. 84, 85.

5. Steward M. Hoover, "Television Myth and Ritual: The Role of Substantive Meaning and Spatiality,' unpublished paper, March 6, 1987, p. 9.

6. Ibid., p. 16.

7. In a fund-raising special, for example, Swaggart called apostate Christians one of the biggest threats to world evangelization efforts. "Jimmy Swaggart," June 7, 1987. More recently, he argued that when God comes to "separate the wheat from the chaff," an event that is very near according to Swaggart, many people who see themselves as Christian will not be among the elect. "Jimmy Swaggart," September 23, 1990.

8. See, for example, Jimmy Swaggart, "The Spirit of the World," *The Evangelist*, September 19887, pp. 16-21. It should be noted that since the scandal, Swaggart has been more humble, less strident in his attacks on other beliefs. He now often prefaces a negative judgment with "I'm not meaning to be too critical but . . ."

9. Sara Diamond, "Pat on the Head," *Nation*, February 13, 1988, p. 208.

10. Joe Conason, "The Religious Right's Quiet Revival," *Nation*, April 27, 1992, p. 534.

11. Ibid.; also see the *Covert Action Information Bulletin*, "Special Issue on the Religious Right," No. 27, Spring 1987, for more information on Robertson's political activities.

12. This grass roots organizing strategy was a key factor in Robertson's victory in Michigan's precinct delegate contest in 1986. He acquired more delegates than Rep. Jack Kemp and stayed even with Vice President George Bush. See "Television Preacher Turns into an Important Player in GOP Presidential Race," *Seattle Times*, June 10, 1986, p. A3; Pat Aufderheide, "The Next Voice You Hear," *Progressive*, September 29, 1985, pp. 34-37; Larry Kickham, "Holy Spirit Holy Spook?," *Covert Action Information Bulletin* 27 (Spring 1981): pp. 4-5.

13. Conason, "Quiet Revival," pp. 555, 559.

14. Sara Diamond notes that the "700 Club" has "habitually characterized the African National Congress as a band of Soviet inspired
killers and tried to persuade viewers to oppose economic sanctions
against the apartheid regime." A CBN reporter also characterized
South Africa as "a very progressive country." "Pat on the Head," p.
207.

15. Hoover, *Mass Media Religion*, p. 77.

16. For example, in shows aired during August and September
1990, the program questioned the blockade of Iraq on economic
grounds, decried public funding of "anti-Christian" art, and attacked
one of its favorite enemies, the American Civil Liberties Union.

17. George Marsden, "The Gospel of Wealth, the Social Gospel and
the Salavation of Souls in Nineteenth-century America," *Fides et
Historia*, Spring 1973, p. 18.

18. Frankl, *Televangelism*, p. 115.

19. Ibid., p. 127.

20. KCPQ-TV, Channel 13, Seattle-Tacoma, "700 Club," February 13,
1987.

21. Ibid., February 12, 1987.

22. Ibid., February 13, 1987. Robertson came up with this method
of fund raising early in his broadcasting career. See Pat Robertson
with Jamie Buckingham, *Shout It From The Housetops* (Plainfield, NJ:
Logos International, 1972), p. 162.

23. Dick Dabney, "God's Own Network," *Harper's*, August 1980, p.
45.

34. Swaggart's fund raising specials place great emphasis on the
fruits of worldwide evangelistic efforts; see, for example, his telecast
episode entitled "Partners in the Harvest," March 15, 1987.

25. Dabney, "God's Own Network," p. 40.

26. "700 Club," February 11, 1987.

27. Ibid., February 27, 1987.

28. Ibid., February 13, 1987.

29. Dion is one of the many stars whose turn to Christ prefigured a
career comeback. He delivered his testimony and lip-synched his latest hit on the "700 Club," February 24, 1987.

30. Dabney, "God's Own Network," p. 45.

31. Ibid., p. 46.

32. Sari Thomas, "The Route to Redemption: Religion and Social
Class," *Journal of Communication* 35 (Winter 1985): pp. 115, 117-118.

33. Ibid., pp. 115-116, 118.

34. Ibid., p. 119.

35. "700 Club," February 16, 1986.

36. Ibid., March 18, 23, and 24, 1987.

37. Ibid., February 12, 1987.

38. Ibid., February 27, 1987.

39. Sara Diamond, "Preacher Pat for Prez?" *Mother Jones*, January 1986, p. 9.

40. Frankl, *Televangelism*, p. 117.

41. Marjorie Mayfield, "For CBN, the Worst May Be Over," *Norfolk Virginian-Pilot*, May 11, 1988, p. 11.

42. Butch Maltby, interview with author, November 30, 1990.

43. April Witt, "Robertson Likely to Return to CBN," *Norfolk Virginian-Pilot*, May 11, 1988, p. 11.

44. Conason, "Quiet Revival," p. 553

45. Quentin Schultze, interview with the author, September 5, 1990.

46. Maltby, interview with author.

47. "Jimmy Swaggart Telecast," February 1, 22, 1987; November 23, 1986.

48. Frankl argues that Swaggart, like Schuller and Humbard, purposefully avoids controversial issues so as not to alienate viewers, *Televangelism*, p. 98. I would say that Swaggart enjoys controversy as long as it is theological in nature. He has become more careful about making politically or socially charged statements because of the threat of losing airtime. Swaggart got into trouble in 1984 over statements about Mother Teresa and the Holocaust; stations in Boston and Atlanta (including WANX, owned by CBN), dropped the show for its persistent attacks on Catholicism. A Miami station also threatened to cancel his telecast. Swaggart, typically, blamed the secular media for misrepresenting him. See Steve Chaple, "Whole Lotta Savin' Going On," *Mother Jones*, July/August 1986, p. 45, and "Swaggart's One-Edged Sword," *Newsweek*, January 9, 1984, p. 65.

49. For a discussion of Swaggart's work in Latin America, see David Stoll, *Is Latin America Turning Protestant? The Politics of Evangelical Growth* (Berkeley: University of California Press, 1990), and Dennis A. Smith, "The Gospel According to the United States: Evangelical Broadcasting in Central America," in Quentin Schultze, ed., *American Evangelicals and the Mass Media* (Grand Rapids: Academie Books, 1990), pp. 289-305.

50. Kickham, "Holy Spirit or Holy Spook?" p. 6. Diamond makes this point as well in "Pat on the Head," as does David Harrell in *Pat Robertson: A Personal, Political and Religious Portrait* (New York: Harper & Row, 1988).

51. "Jimmy Swaggart," July 16, 1987.

52. Ibid., April 5, 1987.

53. "Old Camp Meeting Time" is an example of this genre: "I like the old meeting, preaching, praying, shouting, singing . . . I like the old-

time worship of the Lord." Ibid., June 14, 1987.

54. Ibid., July 27, 1987.

55. Ibid., April 12, 1987. Readers will note with irony Swaggart's own undoing by "the world"—his inability to practice what he preached. This is not because he did not believe in his own theology, but because he could not live up to its rigid demands.

56. Ibid., May 24, 1987.

57. Jimmy Swaggart, "The Spirit of the World," p. 16.

58. "Jimmy Swaggart," January 11, 1987.

59. Ibid., May 24, 1987.

60. Ibid.

61. Ibid.; see also Jimmy Swaggart with Robert Paul Lamb, *To Cross a River* (n.p.: Logos International, 1977), p. 159.

62. Swaggart sees no contradiction in rejecting the world and living in comfort. His house, he says, was built "at cost. It only has two bedrooms. It is nice. It's above the normal house. I don't want to apear to be something I'm not." In Steve Chapple, "Whole Lotta Savin' Going On," *Mother Jones*, July/August 1985, p. 44; see also Michelle Mayron, "O, Brother," *Spin*, December 1986, p. 59.

63. "Jimmy Swaggart Telecast," February 22, 1987.

64. Straub, *Salvation for Sale*, p. 60.

65. "Jimmy Swaggart Telecast," May 24, 1987.

66. Mayron, "O, Brother," p. 62.

67. "Jimmy Swaggart Telecast," April 19, 1987.

68. "700 Club," July 8, 1985.

69. "700 Club," April 4, 1990

70. Straub, *Salvation for Sale*, p. 293.

71. Ibid.

72. Elayne Rapping, *The Looking Glass World of Non-Fiction TV* (Boston: South End Press, 1987), p. 134.

73. Maltby, interview with author.

74. Quentin Schultze, "Balance or Bias? Must TV Distort the Gospel?" *Christianity Today*, March 18, 1988, p. 31.

75. Ibid., July 8, 1985.

76. See Robert Bellah et al., *Habits of the Heart* (Berkeley: University of California, 1985); T. Jackson Lears, "From Salvation to Self-Realization: Advertising and the Therapeutic Roots of the Consumer Culture, 1880-1930," in R. W. Fox and T. J. Lears (eds.), *The Culture of Consumption: Critical Essays in American History*, 1880-1980 (New York: Pantheon, 1983), pp. 3-38; and Eva Illouz, "Reasons Within Passion: Love in Women's Magazines," *Critical Studies in Mass Communication* 8 (1991): 231-248.

77. Edith Blumhofer, "Swaggart and the Pentecostal Ethos," *Christian Century*, April 6, 1989, p. 334.

78. James D. Hunter "Subjectivization and the New Evangelical Theodicy," *Journal for the Scientific Study of Religion,* 20(1) (1982): pp. 39-47. Sweet makes a similar argument in "The 1960s."

79. Hunter, "Subjectivization," p. 42

80. For a discussion of how some Christian conservatives have incorporated elements of the "sexual revolution" into their belief system, see Barbara Ehrenreich, Elizabeth Hess, and Gloria Jacobs, "Unbuckling the Bible Belt," *Mother Jones,* July/August 1986, pp. 46-51, 78. The "700 Club" also takes a more modern attitude toward sex. Although insisting that sex should occur only between married couples, Kinchlow remarked that God can show Christians "how to use His tool for our mutual benefit and pleasure." "700 Club," February 27, 1987.

81. Hunter, *American Evangelicalism,* p. 98.

82. This approach has created controversy within evangelicalism. David Hunt's *The Seduction of Christianity* (Eugene, OR: Harvest House, 1985) accuses Robertson and other preachers of advocating the techniques of the "New Age Movements." Hunt's book generated a good deal of outrage among evangelicals; it was the subject of heated debate on an episode of TBN's "Praise the Lord," and Swaggart has quoted Hunt extensively in his televised sermons. Hunt wrote a second book with the same theme, *Beyond Seduction: A Return to Biblical Christianity* (Eugene, OR: Harvest House, 1987). His ideas spurred a response from Gary DeMar and Peter Leithart, *The Reduction of Theology: Dave Hunt's Theology of Cultural Surrender* (Ft. Worth: Dominion Press, 1988). Swaggart has taken positions similar to Hunt's in his ministry magazine. See *The Evangelist,* September, 1986.

83. Walter Davis, *Inwardness and Existence* (Madison: University of Wisconsin Press, 1989), p. 180.

84. Hunter, "Subjectivization," p. 46.

85. "Jimmy Swaggart Telecast," April 12, 1987.

86. Ibid.

87. Ibid., April 19, 1987.

88. Ibid., April 12, 1987.

89. Ibid., April 26, 1987.

90. Robert Merton with Marjorie Fiske and Alberta Curtis, *Mass Persuasion* (Westport, CT: Greenwood Press, 1946), p. 143

91. " Jimmy Swaggart Telecast," April 26, 1987.

92. This longing for an end to his suffering takes on a new significance in light of Swaggart's sexual obsession and the torment that undoubtedly accompanies it. Since the scandal, there is a new nervous quality to Swaggart's preaching. He frequently refers to his "enemies" and "critics" without specifically mentioning the incidents that ignited the criticism; this is keeping with his stance that true

Christians are always persecuted by an ungodly world. But he also seems very close to the edge during his sermons—the tears come more often, and in inappropriate places, and he falters in his train of thought more frequently.

93. Ibid., June 14, 1987. Many songs in the crusade treat this theme; for example, "Heaven's Jubilee," which says "some glad morning we shall see/Jesus in the air coming after you and me" "Jimmy Swaggart," May 24, 1987.

94. Donald Heinz, "The Struggle to Redefine America," in R. Liebman and R. Wuthnow, eds., *The New Christian Right* (New York: Aldine, 1983), p. 144.

8

The Appeal of Form: Performance, Address, Setting

If, as Burke argues, winning listeners' consent to one's form is to achieve a degree of mastery over them, Swaggart and Robertson must select and employ forms of communication appropriate to both their messages and their audiences.[1] Through devices and strategies of form, the two men draw on their listeners' patterns of experience, appeal to their desires, and thus prepare them to yield to the content. It is at this level that symbolic form can be powerful and satisfying. The following two chapters address the characteristic forms used by a country preacher and a religious broadcaster. Chapter 8 analyzes performance styles, modes of address, and the settings of the programs; Chapter 9 examines the role of ritual in the shows, the rhetorical strategies, and the use of televisual framing techniques.

The forms of the programs embody the historical responses of evangelical Protestantism to modernization, and these responses are reflected in the theological, cultural, and political differences between Swaggart and Robertson. Swaggart's form—that of a country preacher—seeks immediate and passionate engagement from the audience. Swaggart exhorts and preaches; his listeners' relationship is that of communicants; the purpose of the communication is worship (or an act expressing reverence to a divine power exhibited in creed and ritual). Although the crusade is pretaped and edited, its appeal depends on the spontaneity and immediacy of the original live performance. Robertson's form—that of a religious television host—creates a mediated but congenial "friendship" with the audience. He informs,

177

explains, and teaches; his listeners' connection is that of "television audience" or "700 Club" partners; the purpose of the communication is to instruct, inspire, and entertain. While the "700 Club" is aired live, its "spontaneity" is preprogrammed into the format to produce an orderly flow of information, entertainment, and promotion.

PERFORMANCE STYLE

Swaggart's style can be compared to that of a stage actor. Because he performs for huge crowds, his mannerisms and gestures are highly exaggerated and dramatic so as to convey his message and emotional state to those at the periphery of the auditorium or arena. He must project himself outward and appear as if he is speaking personally to each member of the audience. One observer pointed out that Swaggart's stage manner (e.g., gestures, stance, use of microphone) resembles that of a rock musician.[2] Indeed, Swaggart often refers to the fact that he plays and sings for God, rather than for the "world" like his cousin Jerry Lee Lewis. If it were not for his "infilling" of the Holy Ghost, he says, he would not be preaching but "in some bar playing 'My Cheatin' Heart'."[3] Swaggart also employs a wide range of roles on stage; he acts out the parts of various characters in his anecdotes and biblical stories. Now he is the risen Lazarus, waddling across the stage in his winding cloth; now he is an alcoholic on his knees praying for God's forgiveness. By adopting these roles—performing his parables—Swaggart breathes life into religious doctrine and proves the timeliness (and timelessness) of Scripture. He also entertains the audience; it is much more engaging to witness a story than to simply be told it. This style of performing is highly visual—an important component of televisual discourse. Swaggart is rarely depicted as a talking head for extended periods; instead we observe the whole man, waving his arms, strutting, dancing, crawling on his knees, mopping his brow, pacing across the platform, holding the Bible aloft as he exhorts the audience.

Robertson's style is tailored to, indeed created by, television. The intimate conversational setting of the TV studio and the proximity of the camera (most shots are close up or mid-range) require a performance style compatible with such settings. Robertson, the cast, and guests are nearly always seated (he does occasionally stand at a blackboard during Bible teaching or history lesson segments), and their gestures are compact. In this setting, performers must convey thoughts and emotions through facial and hand gestures. The live segments consist primarily of people seated in a half circle so they can look at each other and at the cameras with an economy of movement. This is standard in the talk show format; the emphasis is on conversation, and the camera highlights this interaction by switching from speaker to speaker. We never see the cast stand except during transitions when they move to another portion of the set or when a co-host takes audience questions. The goal is to recreate the relaxed atmosphere of a conversation with friends. Robertson's manner is calm, friendly, and authoritative. He does not raise his voice even when he obviously strongly agrees or disagrees with a guest. Instead, he relies on the breadth of his knowledge, which viewers have seen demonstrated in the past, to make his points. These are backed up with statistics, examples, and biblical references. The philosophy of the "700 Club" mirrors Robertson's style. He says he believes in a "vigorous discussion of issues," but does not "try to force [his] views on people."[4] The show is presented in "as simple and as direct a style as appropriate . . . we are ourselves in a relaxed and straightforward relationship with our guests."[5]

Robertson's style and his authority as a speaker derive from his "anchorperson" role. As Masterman notes, "anchor persons tell us through their control of a programme's discourse—their linking, framing, commenting upon and placement of each item—how the program's other discourses are to be read."[6] We tend to identify with the anchorperson, and thus to accept his or her interpretation of the message, through our repeated exposure to television's discursive conventions; such conventions include anchorpersons' "structural dominance within the show," their "direct eye contact with the audience," and their "long-standing familiarity."[7] In the "700 Club," Robertson acts as the facilitator for the smooth flow of images and ideas on the program; he comes across as congenial, even-tempered, stable, and firmly in control—not only of the show, but also of the world outside the studio. His image and style can best be described as paternal. Robertson portrays the kind of fatherly authority associated with TV figures such as Walter Cronkite and Robert Young. Viewers feel safe in such hands—a security that develops over time as they come to know and trust his persona.

THE USE OF VOICE[8]

Swaggart's use of voice is an integral part of his performance. Modern amplification has given Swaggart an advantage over 19thcentury revivalists. He does not have to shout to be heard by the throng and this enables him to employ a much greater range of voices. He can, and does, slide from a shout to a whisper to make his points and to portray his cast of characters. Such techniques give Swaggart a great deal of control over the audience. Listeners are hushed when he drops to a stage whisper, are excited and boisterous when he shouts out God's praises or rails against the sins of modern society, are moved to tears when he is overcome by the Spirit, are exalted when he speaks in tongues. This use of voice is theatrical and is associated with live stage performances.

Robertson's voice is a product of television. It is the voice of a TV moderator or news announcer: even, dispassionate, modulated, cordial. The range of voices permitted a TV host is quite narrow compared to Swaggart's wide repertoire. Indeed, Robertson has only one voice—he approves or disagrees within the same restricted range of sound and we must rely on his facial gestures and our past knowledge of the program to determine his feelings about a subject. Because the talk show format uses an intimate camera, the viewer is able to make such fine distinctions, which would be impossible for the audience at Swaggart's crusades. The conventions of the format—the proximity of the camera, the small set, the conversational voice—contribute to the creation of a comfortable familiarity that characterizes the parasocial interaction that develops between the TV personality and audience.

MODE OF ADDRESS

Communication or address, Burke says, can be compared to courtship.[9] A speaker "courts" an audience with specific intentions, using a language and form of address designed to evoke a desired identification. The mode of address employed in a particular setting tells us something about those intentions and about the quality of the speaker/listener relationship. People petition superiors, for example, discuss, argue, and agree with equals, and exhort, cajole, scold, or instruct inferiors.[10] Duncan argues that it is "the relation between speaker and audience that determines motivation because it determines how we address each other and thus how we affect each other."[11] Form and substance are therefore intimately connected within the structure of appeal because how an address is staged determines what can be said.

An important element of the rhetorical power that Swaggart and Robertson exhibit resides in their being privileged speakers. As an evangelist, Swaggart has been called by God to exhort sinners and bring them into the fold. This special status permits him to speak with the urgency and authority of a biblical prophet. Listeners submit to his threats and exhortations because of that authority; they accept forms of address they would likely reject in other circumstances. Swaggart must continually recreate his right to speak by pointing to his status as a "God-called evangelist."[12] In the crusades he tells congregants that he does not scold them because he enjoys it, but because God has ordered him to convey the harsh truth about humanity's precarious position. Swaggart insists that he is only a messenger—just a "poor country preacher"—while reminding listeners that ordained messengers have special access to God.[13] He refers often to his conversations with the Creator and noted in one program that he will be permitted to spend a few minutes with Christ at the Second Coming.[14]

Swaggart constructs his status as privileged speaker through self-address. He refers to himself frequently in the third person, a device that removes him from the intimate realm of I-you dialogue. At the altar call he urges people to "come to Brother Swaggart," and during the sermon often asks himself rhetorical questions in third person form (e.g., "What do you mean by that, preacher?"). This device separates the man from his role, thereby creating the sense that Jimmy Swaggart as evangelist inhabits a realm outside the activities of ordinary men and women. When Swaggart stands in the center of an overflowing Chilean national stadium and thunders, "Hear me. Hear me," he is speaking not as a man, but as a vessel of the Word.[15] When he suddenly interrupts a sermon and remarks, "My Lord, that's good preaching," he becomes Swaggart the man observing Swaggart the preacher.[16]

As Rosenberg notes, a preacher's sense that he is divinely summoned is important to understanding his sermon techniques.[17] Much of Swaggart's power as an orator rests on creating this distinction between himself as evangelist and his listeners as those who need salvation. He cannot get too close to his audience—become too intimate—or this privilege will dissipate. For Swaggart to conduct us toward salvation, the audience must be must believe he is more familiar with the route than they. He must also be more intimate with God than with his listeners. Swaggart's charisma derives from his ability to evoke such confidence in his viewers; it is enhanced by connecting his purpose to already powerful religious symbolism. By tapping into a reservoir of sacred symbols, a charismatic leader "evokes a deep response from the public by touching the symbolic dimensions of consciousness in such a way that responding to such a leader makes meaning, recovers identity, and revitalizes roots."[18] Robertson's charisma is based on the pseudo-intimacy created in parasocial interaction. His privilege as a speaker stems from the authority held by media personalities (e.g., news anchors and talk show hosts). For Robertson to be persuasive, he must balance intimacy and authority by constructing an image of benevolent paternalism. The "700 Club" produces this intimate authority by mixing its modes of address; it speaks to viewers sometimes as inferiors and sometimes as equals. In the Bible lesson segments, Robertson instructs people directly; in his commentaries he analyzes and sums up complex political issues with a paternal finality that assumes viewers are generally ignorant on such topics. He advises listeners to get involved in particular issues and contact political representatives with the same fatherly assurance. The style of instruction on the "700 Club" differs from Swaggart's technique. Swaggart commands his listeners with an address that is urgent and passionate; Robertson coaches his audience to accept certain positions by resorting to reason. After a CBN news report lays out the "facts" of a particular issue, Robertson often urges viewers to call the White House or contact their congressional representatives.[19] He does not tell them what position to take, however, but only suggests they make their views known. He is well aware, of course, that the program has already framed the issue in a way that makes the "Christian" perspective obvious and assumes most viewers will make the right choice.[20] By leaving the final decision to viewers, Robertson appears to treat them as equals; his persuasion is backed up by evidence rather than by emotion.

The "700 Club" also appeals to reason by featuring nonevangelical guests. Robertson has been host, for example, to Joan Mondale, the Rev. Jesse Jackson, communications scholar George Gerbner, and a representative of the tobacco industry. By exposing viewers to contending viewpoints, the program employs the strategy of secular news and public affairs shows; it presents "both sides" of an issue so that audience members may decide for themselves. Swaggart is not so ecumenical. Non-Christian viewpoints are used mainly as rhetorical devices to reiterate the truth of Swaggart's perspective—they are contrasted to the charismatic Christian worldview and used as indexes of the world's moral dilapidation. The only choice offered to viewers of Swaggart's program is that of redemption or damnation. Further, salvation for Swaggart is not attained by making up one's mind but by listening to one's heart.

The intimacy created by the "700 Club" also appeals to the heart—not through the passionate, almost erotic emotionality of Swaggart's performance, however, but via the warm congeniality of the "700 Club" "family." As LeSage points out, the "maternal" set of most morning talk shows creates an emotional identification for viewers who are invited to share in the personal experiences of the performers.[21] This air of intimacy is enhanced by the fabricated familial relations of the "700 Club" cast. In an earlier incarnation of the show, this familiarity was particularly striking. Former co-host Soderman came across like a mother or older sister; she deferred to Robertson who played the wise but kindly father, and teased Kinchlow who portrayed the slow, good-natured brother. The current co-host, Sheila Walsh, performs a daughterly role in relation to Robertson's wise father persona. The cast members, as "family," reveal their own fears and hopes, draw out the inner concerns of their guests, and repeatedly express love and caring for their audience. They thus invite the viewer to become part of the program's extended family. Indeed, as one of the show's promotional songs says, the "700 Club" is "so much more than a TV show; we're a family that's getting together."[22] The success of the show depends on maintaining this delicate balance of authority and intimacy. Viewers must respect the performers and trust them, both emotionally and intellectually. LeSage argues that the Christian talk show is particularly "effective television," because it so skillfully blends paternalistic authority with maternal emotionality.[23]

It is this blending that makes the "700 Club" appealing to its primarily female audience. Women viewers are invited to identify with co-host Walsh, an identification that provides satisfaction on several levels. Walsh's persona is that of an attractive, articulate, conventionally feminine woman who is successful in her work and in her marriage; she is comfortable deferring to Robertson in traditionally male areas of politics and economics, but is granted authority in traditionally female spheres of interpersonal relationships and emotional concerns. The relationship between Walsh and Robertson supports patriarchy by presenting the polarization of gender roles and identities as natural and God-given. The inevitable tensions that this gender polarity (and inequality) produces in real relationships are absent in the coupling of Walsh and Robertson. Further, their personae are constructed so as to portray this polarity as equally beneficial to both men and women. Part of the appeal of this TV "family," in fact, is the way in which it banishes gender conflict and does so by representating Robertson and Walsh as ideal parents whose relationship is not marred by this tension. Robertson is the good father who never abuses his paternal authority, who never exposes the fist inside the velvet glove. Walsh is the good mother who is perpetually available and nurturing, who is never resentful or angry about her subordinate position and thus will not direct that resentment at her children (the viewers). While the program frequently addresses the many problems of actual marriages, the solutions are framed in terms of reestablishing the "natural" balance of gender roles that God has ordained for men and women. Thus, the program acknowledges the difficulties experienced in contemporary marriages and provides an explanation that is also a solution to them. The relationship between Walsh and Robertson embodies that solution because it offers viewers a model of the proper Christian male and female roles.

Upon reflecting on my own responses to the "700 Club" I realized that I was most emotionally engaged during segments where
Soderman, and later Walsh, explored the private travails of guests.
These interviews focused on a variety of problems, but in each case
Walsh or Soderman played a therapeutic role by creating a safe environment for the guests to expose some deep inner pain or lack in their
lives—a lack that was validated by the female co-host and that was
ultimately healed by embracing Jesus. The appeal of these segments, I
suggest, resides in identifying with the interviewee and thus vicariously receiving support and validation for one's own suffering from these
unconditionally loving "mothers" (who are simultaneously united with
the unconditionally loving Father). This is the maternal appeal of the
"700 Club." While male viewers no doubt respond to such nurturance
as well, women may be more susceptible to it because they so rarely
receive this kind of comfort in their own lives, since it is they who are
responsible for providing this nurturance to others (primarily their
male partners and children).

The gender dimensions of Swaggart's appeal operate quite differently, as I discovered in analyzing my response to the program and
live crusade. As a woman, and therefore as a social subject historically
relegated to the category of "other" within Western culture's central
dichotomizing schema—culture vs. nature, mind vs. body, reason vs.
emotion, male vs. female—I found myself responding to the mystery,
sensuality, and passion that are central to Swaggart's theology and
rhetorical appeal. One of feminism's key criticisms of patriarchy concerns the devaluation of the "feminine," which is typically defined
along precisely these lines: Women are mysterious, tied to nature
through their bodies' capacity to bear children, and ruled by their
emotions and their bodies. They are, in short, less civilized than men.
Because these aspects of experience are devalued culturally, their
appearance in the public discourse of television is both unusual and
appealing in the way that all telling of "secrets" can be. It is a public
performance, by a male, of qualities that are generally assumed to be
private and female. For there is, in Swaggart's performance, a decidedly "feminine" quality that is at odds with the highly patriarchal structure of the belief system he professes. I believe that part of Swaggart's
appeal for female crusade attenders and viewers is the fact that he
acknowledges and validates, through his performance, some of the
important aspects of women's experience. The appeal for men is similar in that Swaggart's performance, and the context of the crusade,
offers them a model and a site for expressing feminine parts of themselves that in most situations must be repressed if their masculinity is
not to be called into question. For both genders, then, Swaggart's crusades offer a place to experience parts of oneself that have been

devalued or sealed off; it offers an occasion for transcending and healing the internalized polarities of mind/body, reason/emotion,
male/female, public/private, thus reunifying the divided self.[24]

Duncan identifies five types of address that speakers use to
court listeners: the general public is addressed as "they"; community
guardians as "we"; friends and confidants as "you"; the self as "me";
and the ideal or ultimate source of order as "it."[25] It is through their
terms of address that Swaggart and Robertson construct particular
types of community and a vision of who belongs and who does not.
Swaggart's "they"—those outside the elect—is far broader than is
Robertson's. Swaggart excludes "apostate Christians" (e.g., noncharismatic evangelicals), while Robertson speaks to all who accept the
tenets of "cultural fundamentalism." "They," for Swaggart, includes
everyone who has not been born again and filled with the Holy Spirit.
For Robertson, "they" refers primarily to secular humanists and non-
Christians. Both men, however, require a "they" in order to produce
"enjoinment in the moral arena." Robertson needs secular humanism
as the antagonist to conservative Christianity; Swaggart needs the
unsaved to justify his calling. If there is no "them" there can be no
"us," and the terms of belonging become meaningless.

"We" refers to the guardians of the community. Swaggart's
"we" comprises the small minority of born again, charismatic
Pentecostal Christians whose task it is to lead humanity to God and
effect salvation at the level of the individual. As Swaggart says, these
chosen few are "reflections of His light. He reflects off of us to a dark-
ened world that desperately needs enlightenment."[26] Robertson's "we"
refers to the custodians of morality who are called to enforce public
morals at a social and political level. Straub relates seeing a "700 Club"
guest issue a call for "militant believers" and then join Robertson in
praying for a national revival: "What America needs, they believe, is the
total eradication of immorality and evil," and this will occur only when
conservative Christians have gained control of the public domain.[27]

Swaggart's chief mode of address is "you"—the term used to
speak to friends and confidants. He employs this direct address 30, 40,
even 50 times during a program (e.g., "You are a fallen creature;" "I'm
going to say something that will bother you;" "You need a redeemer,"
etc.). He also speaks to the TV audience in this way; at several points
in a program Swaggart is shown looking directly into the camera and
prefacing a remark with "You there by television . . ." Although direct
address establishes intimacy, it is not, in Swaggart's oratory, the intimacy of equals. Rather, Swaggart speaks directly to his listeners,
because his status as divine messenger gives him special access to
their souls. As an evangelist, he has the right to exhort, chastise, and
warn people in the most intimate terms. This direct address has

another important effect: It bypasses (or attempts to) the mediating role of television and obscures the fact that the actual crusade is also staged to generate material for the televised version. Further, direct address, with its dialogic qualities, is essential to the art of country preaching. By speaking directly to individual listeners, Swaggart tries to retain the intimacy of a live service in which preacher and congregants are interactive and interdependent. Such intimacy is crucial to Swaggart's strategy of appeal. The type of consubstantiality he hopes to create depends on getting listeners to participate in the "dialogue"— to feel that they, as individuals, are the "you" to whom he speaks.

The passion of Swaggart's performance is related to his liberal use of this form of address. Duncan notes that "in address to other individuals we enter into the most profound experience in communication."[28] Swaggart's passion is not just a theatrical device—it issues from his relationship to his audience. If, as Duncan says, "The self is born in dialogue with others," then breakdown in dialogue threatens to annihilate the self—it puts the speaker at risk.[29] Swaggart's rhetorical power and his emotional appeal stem from this risk. Because his success as a preacher is ultimately dependent on his audience's response, Swaggart makes himself highly vulnerable on stage. In Duncan's words, "address to a significant other is a moment of commitment, and thus a moment of anxiety, and, if failure occurs, a moment of anguish."[30] There is something extremely compelling about witnessing a performer flirt with this potential anguish; it permits us to experience vicariously the vulnerability that always arises in interpersonal relationships.

Rosenberg observed occasions when a preacher "lost" his audience and experienced a breakdown in dialogue. In such cases, the preacher also lost his timing, flailed about trying to recapture the narrative thread, or resorted to formulas to reestablish connection with the congregation.[31] Swaggart occasionally loses his audience by digressing too long and far from the topic or by inadequately stimulating listeners' emotions early in the sermon.[32] At such moments, "dialogue" breaks down and Swaggart finds himself "alone" on the stage. From my observations, Swaggart is usually aware when the audience has strayed. He draws people back into the conversation by resorting to stylistic and substantive devices that have proven effective in the past (e.g., themes of sanctification and redemption delivered through predictable rhetorical formulas).

To avoid moments of anguish, the country preacher uses stock phrases throughout the sermon as a barometer of the audience's involvement. A "refrain" formula functions as a stall to buy the preacher time to compose his next lines. The "stimulant" piques listeners' interest and elicits their verbal or gestural response.[33]

Swaggart's stimulant reminds congregants of the sacred nature of the occasion: "Glory,Glory," "Hallelujah," "Glory to God." His refrain is designed to maintain contact or dialogue and consists of variations on the question "Do you hear me?" (e.g., "Can you hear me?", "You get me?" "You understand?" "Do you hear what I'm saying?"). Swaggart's refrain also exhibits his vulnerablity. If the audience does not hear him, the dialogue is ended. He can no longer speak and his being is called into question. As Duncan puts it: "We cannot become selves until we are understood and until we know we are understood.[34]

The "700 Club" does not present occasions for this kind of risk and failure, either on the part of the cast or the audience. Robertson, his co-hosts, and guests speak primarily to each other; their communication has been preplanned to avoid the redundancies, mistakes, and long pauses typical of ordinary conversation. Robertson is coached in advance on his guests' background, opinions, and expertise to avoid moments of anguish in dialogue.[35] When the performers do address the audience (in the studio or at home), they are not dependent on eliciting a response (except for cued applause). There is no chance for a failure of dialogue between speaker and audience, because the latter is not offered an opportunity to speak. Questions from the studio and home audience are selected beforehand, and questioners are coached by a co-host in order to regulate the sequence and length of each query.

At certain times Robertson and the cast do speak directly to the audience—primarily when asking viewers to contact CBN (to become partners, request prayer, give testimony, solicit information and products, or donate money). During the prayer segment viewers are personally invited to pray with the cast and to call a prayer counselor to bear witness to their conversion or to receive additional prayer. Transitional segments advise viewers of upcoming features and ask them to stay tuned. Promotional spots urge people to support CBN or send for literature. Robertson often speaks directly to viewers following a report on a particular social or political issue, and also addresses the audience during Bible teaching segments. These appeals to listeners, however, are less passionate and personal than is Swaggart's address to his audience. Robertson's address is more formal; he speaks to "Ladies and Gentlemen" rather than to an individual "you." Often viewers know they are being spoken to directly only because a performer looks straight into the camera or issues general directives (e.g., "stay tuned," "coming up next," etc.).

Even when the "700 Club" cast members do address listeners directly, their performance is not dependent on immediate feedback. They are not vulnerable in the way that Swaggart is during a sermon. That is, Robertson and his co-hosts are never in danger of being alone on the stage. The "700 Club" is constructed in such a way that the audience is not an integral, essential part of the performance. The "you" to whom Robertson speaks is abstract and physically dispersed; he speaks to a TV audience rather than to a congregation. His address is similar to that of secular news programs and talk shows. Such programs speak to an anonymous audience—one that is constructed in the minds of producers, hosts, and news anchors—and which can "respond" only through the impersonal mediation of rating services and market research. Phone banks and mail personalize this feedback somewhat on the "700 Club," but the response is delayed and is quite different from the immediate, spontaneous interaction of Swaggart's crusades. Swaggart's audience is not coached to respond by floor directors or televisual cues, but by the strength of his performance.

The formats of the programs also contribute to differences in their mode of address. Swaggart attempts to hold viewers for 40 to 45 minutes with the power of his oratory. The sermon and altar call are presented without interruption and are meant to be consumed without breaks. Swaggart conducts a religious service to which congregants are expected to devote their total attention. That is, they are expected to worship. There is no time out in the sermon for trips to the kitchen and bathroom. The "700 Club" does not necessarily expect 60 minutes of uninterrupted attention. The show diversifies its messages (in form and substance) on the assumption that people will tune in and out during the hour. It strives to capture attention in 6- to 10-minute increments, cueing viewers on pending items of interest. The kind of emotional engagement demanded by Swaggart's sermon would be difficult, if not impossible, to produce in ten minutes. The mode of address and the way it is staged on the "700 Club" belong to television. Swaggart's form of address, and the space in which it is enacted, are properties of religious ritual—a point I return to in the next chapter. A religious ritual and a television performance take place in very different settings; the setting of an address, moreover, determines not only what can be said, but how it is communicated.

THE SETTING OF COMMUNICATION

The setting of an urban revival calls forth a very different type of communication than does that of the TV studio. I characterize this difference as ecstatic versus congenial communication. This is not to say that Robertson does not move people, but that the "700 Club" studio audience cannot be brought to religious ecstasy, because it would interfere with the smooth flow of the program. The studio audience is certainly an important component of the talk show format—it gives viewers a point of identification and enhances the "live" aspect of the program. For the most part, however, the talk show studio audience functions like a part of the set, and for much of the program it is simply absent. The audience disappears during the pretaped and off-set segments of the "700 Club" and is invisible and silent during many of the on-set portions of the show (e.g., interviews with guests). Audience response is regulated through the conventions and technical requirements of the format.

The audience is integrated into the program flow, applauding on cue during transitions between segments and appearing as a part of the set when the camera pans back to frame the cast. During the prayer segment, the audience becomes more visible; the camera shows us people immersed in prayer and occasionally lingers on the faces of particularly fervent petitioners. This participation is silent and passive, however. Audience members do not speak, call out or raise their hands heavenward. To do so would interrupt the performance of Robertson, his co-hosts, and guests. In this way the cast retains complete control over communication on the set. Speech flows one way—from those with the authority to speak to those who must listen. Audience members are granted the power of speech in only one context—when questions are taken from the floor. These segments are also regulated. A member of the cast (usually a co-host, indicating the privileged position of Robertson) controls the microphone, selects questions, and steps away when the allotted time is up.

The role of the audience, then, is carefully controlled according to the constraints and conventions of the format. The program must fit into a 60-minute slot with each segment having a standard length. The format does not allow for spontaneity or unsolicited audience responses. Swaggart, on the other hand, is not bound by such strict time constraints because his performances are not broadcast live. While the crusades have a definite structure (music, pitches for money, and acknowledgments of local congregations run about 60 to 75 minutes; sermon and altar calls last an hour), he may shorten or lengthen any part of the service to fit the specific context and the mood of the audience. The finished product, of course, has to fit into a 60-minute format, but this is a problem to be solved by the program's editors, not by Swaggart. This flexibility is essential to the structure of Swaggart's appeal. The success of a spiritual sermon is totally dependent on evoking responses from the congregation. The preacher must have the flexibility to gauge the temperament of the audience, to play on listeners' feelings, and to vary his delivery according to the strength of their responses. Swaggart is no doubt confident in his ability to move an audience, but he probably cannot guarantee they will be sufficiently open to the Spirit in the 20 to 30 minutes that a televised sermon runs.

A live broadcast would place enormous pressure on Swaggart to produce the appropriate response in a very short time. It would also dramatically shorten the time devoted to music and congregational singing. In the live crusade, group singing and musical performances take up nearly half of the revival and are extremely important devices for warming up the audience. This use of sacred music, which originates in Moody's revivals, is a standard part of evangelical services. One of my informants said hymns are used in church services and revivals as part of the devotional process; they are an integral element of worship.[36] Music is particularly important in Swaggart's crusades. An accomplished performer, Swaggart also appreciates the emotional power of music. The crusade I attended included seven musical numbers (fast-paced country gospel songs, traditional hymns, sentimental ballads, and sing-alongs). In several instances Swaggart called for one or more encores when the audience seemed particularly involved in a song. The power of group singing is quite overwhelming for participants, and Swaggart encourages crusade attenders to immerse themselves in the performance in this manner. At the Vancouver, B.C. crusade I attended, he called for the audience to repeat one refrain of "Amazing Grace" four times, explaining, "I've never heard it sung quite like this."[37] A live broadcast such as the "700 Club" does not permit this kind of spontaneous interaction between performer and audience because the program must move along according to schedule.

The point of the crusade is to move participants to religious ecstasy. To achieve this response, Swaggart needs a setting that permits him the greatest amount of flexibility and spontaneity. The conventions of television, as an industry and an institutionalized discourse, are relatively inflexible and programmatic. Content must conform to the demand of format, program flow, and time restrictions. In most live TV programming, spontaneity is incorporated into the format as one more element of the show. The on-set patter between "700 Club" cast members is a planned part of the program flow. An allotted amount of time is devoted to banter and jokes, and this too must contribute to the overall flow of the show. Each segment is set up to lead to the next, and no extraneous material enters the discourse. Robertson may relate a personal anecdote to Walsh or Kinchlow, but the tale is designed to set up an introduction to the next segment. In this way, dialogue among the cast is a functional part of the format, serving as a bridge between program components. Even that section of the show that appears to be the most spontaneous—the prayer segment—is subordinated to format requirements. If Robertson runs over the time allotted for prayer, the "700 Club" theme music comes up in the background as a cue to wrap up and move on. In the "700 Club," then, format dominates the substance, as opposed to Swaggart's program where substance precedes and determines the format.

This is not to say that Swaggart makes no concessions to the demands of television. At certain points during a live crusade he addresses the TV audience even though the event is not being televised at that moment. He is already anticipating the point when the crusade will be transformed into television. For the most part, however, Swaggart conducts the revival for those in attendance because without their engagement, the event cannot become television. This also permits him more room for failure; unsuccessful crusades or dull or redundant moments during a sermon wind up on the floor of the cutting room. Robertson has less leeway for failure, especially in the live portions of the show. A boring guest or one who resists the host's direction jeopardizes both the flow of the program and the maintenance of audience attention. This is one reason why the "700 Club" relies heavily on pretaped material that can be edited beforehand for maximum effect and integrated into the show's ideological perspective.

The possibility of failure is also minimized through program planning. At any given time, three weeks of the "700 Club" are in some stage of development. The producer holds a formatting conference each week to establish future themes, select guests, plan features and testimonies, and write formats.[38] The disjuncture between the seamless, regulated flow of images and ideas usually presented on the "700 Club," and the unplanned flow of spontaneous speech, was apparent when Swaggart appeared live (via satellite) on the program. He had been invited to respond to Jim Bakker's allegations that Swaggart wanted to take over the PTL. The "700 Club" had initially tried to downplay Bakker's resignation and act as a mediator among the various antagonists in the PTL drama. Swaggart, typically, rejected these conciliatory efforts and during the interview said Bakker had sinned, that the PTL's Heritage USA was a circus, and that Oral Roberts was a laughing stock. Kinchlow, who conducted the interview, grew noticeably silent and uncomfortable and finally managed to cut Swaggart off. Although Kinchlow promised that Bakker would appear the next day to answer Swaggart's charges, the ex-head of the PTL never materialized, and the show's hosts mentioned neither Bakker nor the scandal. At this point, apparently, Robertson decided to minimize CBN's connection with the "holy wars" and return to the safety of the show's normal format and content.[39]

When I began watching the "700 Club" it employed a "living room" setting patterned after commercial talk shows. This type of setting is intended to create an informal atmosphere—to give viewers the feeling that they are observing friends interact "at home." Thus, the cast not only comes into our homes via television, but we, as viewers, are transported into theirs. By mimicking the landscapes of our own private conversations, talk show sets help create a context for the parasocial interaction between performers and audience. Other Christian talk shows follow this pattern: like the PTL show, TBN's "Praise the Lord" also takes place in a living room set—lavish, overdecorated spaces where the hosts and their guests chat, exhort, pray, and ask for money. The "700 Club" living room set, however, was more tastefully appointed and its cast's attire less ostentatious; it connoted "old rich" compared to the nouveau riche excesses of the PTL and TBN. The living room set creates an atmosphere of familiarity, while maintaining authority for its discourse. LeSage points out that the price the furnishing these "rooms" are out of reach for most viewers. The women who make up the majority of Robertson's audience generally can acquire the lifestyle associated with these surroundings only through the success of their fathers and husbands. In this sense, LeSage says, "the set is patriarchal."[40] But because the living room does represent "home," it encourages a type of discourse associated with a women's sphere—stories that emphasize the personal and emotional. The role of the female co-host is to draw out these experiences for the benefit of the audience. Like Soderman before her, Walsh usually takes over in segments about the family, asking very intimate questions that would seem inappropriate coming from a man. At such moments, Lesage says, the set "becomes the site for a deeply personal 'sharing'." The living room set in Christian television, she argues, combines a "patriarchal cultural legitimacy" and a "'motherly' emotional appeal" that "facilitates the New Right's ability to interpret the public sphere for its viewers."[41]

The revamped "700 Club" has done away with the living room set; Robertson and his co-hosts now inhabit a set very similar to that of Ted Koppel's "Nightline." The cast and guests sit in sleek leather chairs surrounded by semi-darkness; behind them are banks of TV monitors similar to the backdrops in many news programs. Off to one side of the set the prayer counselors and phone banks are ensconced in a glassed-in booth that is visible behind the cast from certain camera angles. This kind of setting also mimics commercial television, though this time in terms of the professional expertise associated with news and public affairs programs. The maternal emotionality of the "700 Club" is still a very important component of the show's appeal, however, and is supplied by Walsh who is a model of the "good listener." Her own program, "Heart to Heart," takes place in a living room set, reinforcing the connections among home, family, and "sharing."

The setting associated with talk shows is highly conducive to the creation of a parasocial interaction between performers and audiences. Programs such as the "700 Club" promote this relationship by establishing a sense of intimacy that extends to the viewing audience. TV personalities such as Robertson become familiar figures through repeated visits to their comfortable surroundings (where both performer and viewer are at home), and through the performers' predictable behavior. A central feature of the talk show is "the attempt . . . to duplicate the gestures, conversational style, and milieu of an informal face-to-face gathering."[42] The setting is homey, transitions are facilitated with jokes and anecdotes; the cast acts like a family, and guests are treated like close friends. The program also attempts to "blur the line which divides [the performers] and the show, as a formal performance, from the audience both in the studio and at home."[43] Robertson and his co-hosts address one another by first names, reveal personal information about themselves, and adopt stereotypical identities that make them familiar to viewers over time. The regular viewer develops a sense of who these people are and how they can be expected to behave in a given situation. Devoted audience members eventually come to feel themselves a part of "the family;" the language of the show comes to hold a special meaning for them—one that is lost on the casual viewer.

The talk show format also blurs the line between performer and audience by incorporating controlled feedback (e.g., questions from the floor and by telephone). Telephone banks heighten the feeling of direct interaction with the cast members who tell viewers repeatedly: "We're here because we care about you;" "We want to hear from you;" "Call and tell us what you think." Such programming techniques cultivate a sense of intimacy that can be effectively exploited to raise money. These devices, of course, are not restricted to the "700 Club," but are characteristic of the whole genre of personality programs that originate in commercial broadcasting. The values stressed in these programs—"sociability, easy affability, friendship, and close contact"—are techniques by which the shows build and maintain audience loyalty and are an important part of the "700 Club's" structure of appeal.[44]

NOTES TO CHAPTER 8

1. In Burke's words: "A yielding to the form prepares for assent to the matter identified with it." Kenneth Burke, *Rhetoric of Motives* (Berkeley: University of California Press, 1969), p. 58.

2. I owe this observation to Alison Hearn.

3. "Jimmy Swaggart," November 30, 1986. For an insightful essay on the relationship of Swaggart and Lewis, and their different paths as performers, see Nick Tosches, "Pentecostals in Heat," *Village Voice*, May 12, 1987, pp. 75, 82-84; and Steve Chapple, "Whole Lotta Savin' Going On," Mother Jones, July/August, 1985.

4. Kenneth Clark, "The $70 Miracle Named CBN," *Chicago Tribune*, July 26, 1985, p. 3.

5. J. Thomas Bisset, "Religious Broadcasting: Assessing the State of the Art," *Christianity Today*, December 12, 1980, p. 31.

6. Len Masterman, *Teaching the Media* (London: Comedia, 1985), p. 166.

7. Ibid.

8. I am indebted to Hildegard Westerkamp for bringing this important aspect of performance to my attention.

9. Burke makes this analogy in *Rhetoric of Motives*, pp. 208-212.

10. Hugh Dalziel Duncan, *Communication and Social Order* (New York: Bedminster Press, 1962), p. 289.

11. Ibid., p. 290.

12. "Jimmy Swaggart," July 26, 1987.

13. Ibid., February 22, 1987.

14. Ibid., May 24, 1987.

15. Ibid., May 3, 1987.

16. Ibid., April 26, 1987.

17. Bruce Rosenberg, *The Art of the American Folk Preacher* (New York: Oxford University Press, 1970), p. 23.

18. Donald Heinz, "The Struggle to Redefine America," in R. Liebman and R. Wuthnow, eds., *The New Christian Right* (New York: Aldine, 1983), p. 144. Burke also notes the rhetorical power inherent in adapting religious symbolism to secular arguments. His analysis of Hitler's *Mein Kampf* argues that Hitler "provided a non-economic interpretation of economic ills" by applying (and thus corrupting) religious patterns of thought and language to political ideology. Burke claims that "the patterns of Hitler's thought are a bastardization or caricatured version of religious thought." See "The Rhetoric of Hitler's Battle" in Burke, *Philosophy of Literary Form* (Baton Rouge: Louisiana State University Press, 1967), pp. 191-220.

19. The "700 Club" regularly displays the White House information number so viewers can contact the president on specific issues. The dispute over federal funding of Planned Parenthood was handled this way, "700 Club" February 12, 1987.

20. This is a safe assumption; in a call-in poll regarding the SDI defense system, more than 96% of respondents were favorable. Ibid., February 16, 1987.

21. Julia LeSage, "Why Christian Television is Good TV," *The Independent*, May 1987, p. 16.

22. "700 Club," February 27, 1987.

23. LeSage, "Christian Television," p. 16.

24. My conception of gender polarization and the process of engenderment is drawn from the work of Nancy Chodorow; see *The Reproduction of Mothering: Psychoanalysis and the Sociology of Gender* (Berkeley: University of California Press, 1978.).

25. Duncan, *Communication and Social Order*. p. 292.

26. "Jimmy Swaggart," October 26, 1986.

27. Gerard Straub, *Salvation for Sale* (Bufffalo, NY: Prometheus, 1986), p. 293.

28. Duncan, *Communication and Social Order*, p. 297.

29. Ibid.

30. Ibid., p. 298.

31. Rosenberg, *American Folk Preacher*, pp. 35, 42.

32. Obviously this will occur more often in the live crusades than in the televised versions because editors can remove such lapses to heighten the impact of the broadcast sermon. But, because the program originates in the live sermon, most of which is spontaneously composed, some digressions are inevitable.

33. Rosenberg, *American Folk Preacher*, pp. 54-55.

34. Duncan, *Communication and Social Order*, p. 298.

35. Straub says Robertson is primed for each guest with fact sheets that include short biographies, quotes from books the guests have written, and possible questions to raise during the interview. Straub, *Salvation for Sale*, pp. 280-281.

36. Conversations with Susan Peck Sullivan.

37. Jimmy Swaggart Crusade, Vancouver, B.C., May 30, 1987. Rosenberg says the presermon singing is a good gauge of the congregation's emotional state: 'If the people are 'high,' the songs will be sung energetically and many of the verses will be repeated." (Rosenberg, *American Folk Preacher*, p. 43). The preacher, of course, may help stimulate the audience's involvement in the singing, as Swaggart did.

38. During his tenure as producer, Straub kept an ongoing file of program themes and potential guests. A sampling of the themes he proposed reflect the cultural fundamentalism, Christian self-help, and NCR politics characteristic of the "700 Club": e.g. "The Working Woman," "WIll the Russians Stop at Afghanistan?" "Israel on Center Stage" (this topic was treated in March 1987), "Don't Worry. Teaching and ministry on why Christians can live free from anxiety," and "One Nation Under God. Looks at the moral drift in America." Straub, *Salvation for Sale*, pp. 273-275.

39. "700 Club" March 24, 1987. CBN's connection with Jim Bakker goes back to the 1960's when Jim and Tammy were part of Robertson's organization. In fact, Jim Bakker was the first host of the

"700" Club" and the first religious broadcaster to discover that crying on the air significantly increased viewer donations. See Pat Robertson with Jamie Buckingham, *Shout It From The Housetops* (Plainfield, NJ: Logos International, 1972).

40. LeSage, "Christian Television," p. 16.

41. Ibid.

42. Donald Horton and R. Richard Wohl, "Mass Communication and Para-Social Interaction," in J. Combs and M. Mansfield, eds., *Drama In Life* (New York: Hastings House, 1976), p. 214.

43. Ibid., p. 215.

44. Ibid., p. 215..

9

The Appeal of Form: Ritual, Rhetoric, and Televisual Framing

TELEVISED RITUAL AND TELEVISION AS RITUAL

Goethals defines ritual as the active participation of individuals who together construct extraordinary space and time. Ritual space is "specifically ordered for communion and interaction," just as ritual time is an ordered structure with a clear beginning, middle, and end.[1] Active participation is crucial within a ritual if it is to "provide an immediate, direct sense of involvement with the sacred, confirming the world view, indeed the very being, of the participant."[2] More important, ritual must be understood as a technique of transcendence; it has to do with the realm of the sacred. Wilson says ritual is "the symbolic enactment of relationships between man [and woman] and what is conceived of as transcendental reality." Through ritual, human beings "express . . . what moves them most" in conventionalized forms that reveal participants' deepest values and beliefs.[3] Blasi suggests that a ritual's persuasive power has to do with its ability "to call to mind, recapitulate, or bring into a background presence a collective epic, a salvation history, or some other contextual significance."[4]

Swaggart's crusades fulfill all of these conditions. His performances draw on the history and salvific schema of charismatic evangelicalism, are conducted within the conventions of a religious revival,
require active participation by the congregants, are set within sacred
space (the auditorium transformed into church), and take place inside
sacred time (beginning: gospel music; middle: sermon; end: altar call).
The predictability of the form is essential to the enactment of the ritual. Congregants and viewers enter into this form knowing what to
expect from Swaggart and from themselves. Roles and purposes are
clearly defined. Swaggart will exhort them to change their lives and
accept Jesus, and if they are sufficiently "open," their hearts will
"yield" and their souls will be filled with the Spirit. The music, particularly group singing, encourages congregants to participate physically;
it provides an occasion to become one "body." In our culture, opportunities to express ourselves in immediate communion with others in
this way are very rare. The crusade exists to create a place for activities that are out of context in most public settings—weeping, moaning,
singing aloud, speaking a divine language. It validates and sacralizes
these experiences, creating an identification between preacher and
worshipers. As Goethals says, "For those who genuinely participate,
rituals offer occasions for identity and renewal."[5]

The "700 Club" does not create sustained sacred time and
space, nor does it permit full participation by its audience. The program has a clear beginning, middle, and end, but its content is internally fragmented, and the overtly religious elements are dispersed
throughout the show. The "Word of Knowledge" segment is the only
one that fulfills some of the requirements of ritual, but it is extremely
brief and its placement in the program is unpredictable. Audience
involvement is highly regulated and mediated. The audience is not
part of the performance; the cast and guests enact their belief in front
of viewers, not with them. Further, because the "700 Club" is largely a
secular format with religious content inserted, its ability to construct
a relationship between viewers and "transcendental reality" is limited.
The experience of watching the "700 Club" has more in common with
viewing other TV programs than with attending a religious service.
The program can be called a ritual only in the restricted sense that
television viewing itself has become a ritualized activity in modern
society (e.g., to say one watches a program "religiously" means that it
is a significant, habitual activity).

To define the term ritual in this way, however, is to strip it of
its sacred dimensions. It also indicates the erosion of religious significance in modern life generally. Thus, any activity may be said to be a
ritual—shopping, attending a rock concert, mall cruising, watching the
Super Bowl. Goethals suggests that as television has become the cen-

tral medium of communication in our society, it has taken over the church's traditional function of producing common myths and integrating the individual into the social whole—it has become the "new religion." One of the dangers of TV-as-religion is that it tends to "trivialize myths and ritual, reducing them to a kind of ornate emptiness."[6] I believe that the "700 Club" has trivialized the sacred by subordinating it to the talk show format. Participation is regulated and minimized, prayer is desacralized by making it conform to imperatives of program flow, and sacred time and space are fragmented.

THE RHETORIC OF CHRISTIAN TELEVISION

Religious rhetoric persuades through authoritative proclamation rather than by rational argument. Listeners are moved by religious rhetoric when they feel the terms of their belief system have been faithfully represented by speakers who hold the necessary authority to deliver divine messages. I am concerned here with the rhetorical strategies that Swaggart's crusade and the "700 Club" use to appeal to viewers and to convince those viewers that Swaggart and Robertson are legitimate vessels of the Word.

Because both preaching and television are oral forms of communication, their intersection in televangelism is highly compatible.[7] Oral discourse is necessarily redundant; it must employ simple themes and uncomplicated language to insure maximum listener comprehension.[8] Because of constraints on listener comprehension, oral communication relies heavily on methods of amplification. Basic themes are amplified through elaboration, paraphrase, and simple repetition. Television has adopted some of the amplifying techniques of oratory and informal speech, as well as devised methods specific to the medium. Television mixes sound and image to convey and reinforce its messages. Because television was originally conceived as radio with pictures, visual elements are generally subordinated to aural information. Silence, even momentary, is extremely rare on television, and viewers count on spoken narrative, music, and sound effects to explain the stream of images that fill the screen. Further, the quality of the visual image on television is relatively poor, so sound must convey information that cannot be communicated visually.[9] TV news programs, talk shows, and televised sermons are particularly dependent on speech, because the visual environment of these programs is redundant. Graphics, film clips, and written overlays add visual interest and enhance or repeat the narrative, but are usually not crucial to comprehension, because the speaker provides the essential information. The combination of sight and sound, then, reduces ambiguity which is a chief concern in a "disposable" medium such as television.

The redundancy of the image is one form of televisual amplification. Serial programming, standardized formats, and conventional techniques of framing also contribute to the predictability and "readability" of television. Live oratory has its own methods of amplification: rhythm, formulaic speech patterns, repetition, and use of culturally embedded myths and fables. The "700 Club" uses techniques of amplification drawn from television; Swaggart employs those of oratory. In oral communication, both mediated and direct, speakers develop their subjects by repeating basic ideas in different words and contexts to illustrate what they mean and also to relate that meaning to the experience of the audience.[10] Because the experience of the audience of a talk show differs from that of a revival audience, so must the methods used to appeal to them.

Repetition in the "700 Club" is both substantial and formal. The show repeats and elaborates the basic themes of cultural fundamentalism in its news reports, interviews, pretaped inserts, commentary, and teaching segments. The regularity of the program—its correspondence to the patterns of the work week—promote habitual exposure so that the show becomes a normal part of the viewer's morning activities. Predictability is also built into the format. The opening credits, theme music, and unchanging set constitute a secure, familiar environment. The cast, whom viewers have come to know over time, greets the audience like old family friends. Certain segments are standard components of every show ("Word of Knowledge," news reports, interviews). The length of the segments are also predictable; viewers come to expect a "commercial" break at regular intervals and can time their morning activities by the show's rhythm. The program also builds repetition thematically. Shows are planned around themes with each segment approaching a subject from a different angle or manner of treatment. For example, the day after the "Amerika" mini-series began, the theme of the "700 Club" was the Soviet threat. The program opened with a news report on the SDI system, led into Robertson interviewing a "sovietologist" from Johns Hopkins University's Foreign Policy Institute on the plan's chances for passage in Congress, was followed by Soderman and Robertson discussing the first "Amerika" installment (with clips from the film), and wrapped up with an interview with a Soviet emigre to the U.S.[11] Sometimes a theme will be repeated over several episodes, as was the case in the week-long series broadcast live from Israel in March 1987.

Regular viewers become familiar with Robertson's theological views and with the "700 Club" format. They know certain themes and segments will recur and this is true even when they miss several episodes. Repetition is important in the process of building audience loyalty and establishing a parasocial relationship between viewers and performers. The show's producers are aware of the importance of this cumulative familiarity, and thus attributed the decline of viewers and donations over the last two years to the program's internal changes, rather than to the TV preacher scandals.

Repetition in Swaggart's program is integrated into his preaching style and in the recurrence of key theological themes. His amplification techniques originate in traditional oratory and are intended to evoke an immediate, visible response from the audience. Rhetorical style, one of an orator's persuasive tools, is determined by the speaker's intentions. "Plain style" is used to teach, "middle style" to please, and "grand style" to move an audience.[12] Robertson rarely uses grand-style rhetoric because this type of speech, for the most part, is incompatible with the conventions of most standard television formats. Robertson employs plain style to inform and instruct and middle style to entertain his viewers; even when he exhorts the audience he does so in a way that does not conflict with the relaxed, informal atmosphere of the show. Swaggart, on the other hand, transgresses the conventions of commercial television and does so by resorting to grand-style oratory. He is able to depart from established TV conventions, precisely because his crusade is constructed as a site of worship, not as entertainment.

A speaker's style includes the selection of words (lexicon) and their arrangement (syntax) to create varying effects on listeners. Metaphors are particularly compelling rhetorical devices because they employ familiar words in new ways, thus making "strange" that which is familiar (or sacralizing the mundane). Sacred language is characteristically metaphorical or imagistic.[13] The New Testament and traditional gospel hymns are rich in metaphors. Over time, these metaphors have become part of a special language that helps constitute membership in the evangelical community. They are devices for establishing terms of belonging that have acquired their resonance historically.[14] Spiritual preachers exploit this rich metaphorical tradition in their sermons, and Swaggart is no exception. As Swaggart's followers come to recognize his stock of metaphors, they also become "consubstantial" with him through the sharing of a sacred vocabulary. Swaggart constantly recycles his repertoire of metaphors, building on the basic themes of the Pentecostal belief system. The lifelessness of noncharismatic churches, the cleansing power of Christ's resurrection, and the nourishing effect of the Holy Ghost are repeated and amplified in new contexts with slightly different wording.

"Hot" is an appropriate metaphor for Swaggart's style: It connotes passion and interaction and is abrasive rather than soothing. Swaggart uses the metaphor of heat to distinguish spiritual fervor from passive acceptance of doctrine. This metaphor originates in Scripture: At the Pentecost, the Holy Spirit descended on the apostles as tongues of flame. Swaggart describes noncharismatic churches as "cold," "dry," "empty," and "dead." These adjectives also describe his own emotional state when he needs an infusion of the Holy Ghost, which he describes as if it were a drug and he an addict: "I'm so hooked on it I've got to have it about every other day."[15] Swaggart's metaphors, like his theology, are based on dichotomies: hot/cold, dead/reborn, empty/full, dry/wet.[16] To be "full" of the Spirit is to be alive, passionate, warm, washed, sanctified. To be "empty" is to be dead, dried up, cold, and removed from God. The Pentecostal-Holiness tradition describes sanctification as an "infilling of the Spirit." Swaggart speaks of the saved as "spirit-filled Christians," and in one program referred to himself as "nine-tenths soul" to indicate an experience of spiritual saturation.[17]

One of my evangelical informants suggested that Swaggart appeals to viewers who want to be "fed the Word of God"—a phrase that echoes Swaggart's references to "hungry hearts" and "spiritual thirst."[18] God's grace is "wet"—it is the "water of life" that cleanses and refreshes the soul. Swaggart frequently uses a river metaphor to refer to both the Holy Spirit and to Christ's blood; the river "gets in your life and starts to flow," it "flows out of your innermost being."[19] He also speaks of "being bathed in the blood of Jesus." The hymn most closely associated with the modern charismatic movement, "There Is A River," is also the theme song of Swaggart's program. The show opens with a long shot of a waterfall as the song plays in the background. This hymn, which was a top-selling record for Swaggart in 1972, is used often during the altar call. Water and rivers, of course, are traditional Christian metaphors for the salvific ritual of baptism.

Swaggart also amplifies his message by manipulating the arrangement of sounds and words to produce an effect on listeners. A common figure of speech, one that Swaggart uses liberally, is anaphora. Anaphora is a form of repetition in which one or more words are used to begin a series of sentences or clauses. The beatitudes are an example of anaphoric construction in the Bible. Kennedy likens the effect of anaphora to "a series of hammer blows in which the repetition of the word both connects and reinforces the successive thoughts."[20] Rosenberg found this type of repetition to be abundant in the sermons of folk preachers; such formulaic construction, he says, is typical in oral composition because it serves as an aid to memory.[21]

Because spiritual preachers such as Swaggart do not work from a text, but compose their sermons spontaneously, they depend on mnemonic linguistic devices, formulaic syntatical structures, and rhythmic delivery. The following excerpt from a crusade in Alabama illustrates Swaggart's use of repetition, formula and rhythm. The title of this sermon, "They Shall Be As Gods," addresses the temptation of worldly possessions and power. Just prior to the passage below, Swaggart had denounced the "fleeting" value of wealth, beauty, and fame which, he argued, belong to Satan's arsenal of temptations. He then contrasts these temporal promises of "the world" and Satan with the eternal character of God's promises (I have italicized those words that received vocal stress):

> God's given me everything he's ever promised me,
> and *more* besides
> and he's *heaped* it up
> and *pressed* it down
> and *shaken* it together
> and it runs over
> and my cup *overflows*.
> (short pause)
> and the *Lord* is my shepherd
> and I *shall* not want
> He *leadeth* me beside the still waters
> He *restoreth* my soul
> He *preparest* a table before me in the presence of my enemies
> My cup runneth *over*.
> (slightly longer pause)
> Hallelujah.
> I'm not talkin' about *dried beans*.
> I'm talkin' about eternal *life*
> I'm talkin' about joy *unspeakable* and *full* of glory
> I'm talkin' about *power* from on high
> I'm talkin' about eternal *life*.
> (long pause)
> Hallelujah.[22]

The entire utterance is unified by the theme of fullness or abundance, which is also a metaphor for being filled with the spirit of God. Swaggart begins by referring to his own spiritual blessings and draws on biblical language and images to flesh out the theme of abundant grace. The first stanza is based on Luke 6:38, evoking its image of a vessel for measuring grain filled to the brim and overflowing.[23] The overflowing vessel then reminds Swaggart of the 23rd Psalm, which also contains an image of a cup running over. He joins both texts, adapting them to his theme of abundant grace and eternal life.

Swaggart amplifies his message both thematically and structurally, and it is his skill at both that makes his preaching powerful. In the first stanza, the word "and" introduces every line and also acts as a predictable oral bridge to the next phrase. This basic construction is also repeated as Swaggart creates rhythmic continuity by stressing the verb in each phrase. He punctuates the stanza by artificially drawing out the last syllable (e.g., "over-flo—ws"). After a brief pause for breath, he launches into the second stanza, connecting it to the first by starting the next two lines with "and." This stanza comes from the 23rd Psalm, which Swaggart and his audience know by heart and which has its own poetic meter. The next three lines begin with "He" and are parallel, both in their use of the archaic verb form and in the fact that the verbs receive spoken stress. In fact, Swaggart changes one line drawn from the psalm ("you prepared a table before me . . .") from second to third person so that it does parallel the preceding lines. The final line of the stanza repeats the idea in the last line of the preceding verse. Like "overflows," "o-ver" is also dramatically lengthened to conform to the meter. This stanza repeats the image of an overflowing cup, just as the final stanza reiterates the theme of fullness and eternal life. Swaggart pauses again for breath before the last stanza and inserts a stimulant ("Hallelujah") to further prod listeners to respond.

The last set exhibits the most dramatic use of anaphora. It begins with a negative statement ("I'm not talkin' about . . .") and switches to a series of parallel positive assertions ("I'm talkin' about . . .") that draw on central sacred symbols (e.g., eternal life, unspeakable joy, God's power). Swaggart further emphasizes these symbols through the placement of stress. The second and fifth lines are identical, hammering home the central message of Swaggart's charismatic theology—the victory over death. After the third set Swaggart pauses again, waiting for the applause and shouts to die down. In a different, much more subdued voice, he punctuates the entire passage with "Hallelujah." Johnson says that skilled preachers often use this final device—"breaking off suddenly at the highest point of intensity and dropping into the monotone of ordinary speech"—to create an effect on the audience.[24]

Passages such as these illustrate Swaggart's art—his mastery over both substance and form—and thus over his audience. Throughout the entire passage, which lasts little more than a minute, the crusade audience has been responding verbally and bodily—

shouting, applauding, and urging him on. Swaggart speaks his lines with his whole body, pacing back and forth with the microphone in one hand and a Bible in the other. By the second stanza, he is prancing across the stage, feeding off the energy of the crowd and of his own preaching. The "hammer blows" of this type of oratory create an aural effect that is very difficult to experience or fully appreciate on paper. It must be heard and heard in the context of religious ritual. As Johnson says, the old-time preacher who had mastered the art of intoning a sermon, who had properly developed his gestures, tempo, and voice, "had the power to sweep his hearers before him; and so himself was often swept away."[25]

Because linguistic devices such as anaphora are used to evoke a response from listeners, their placement in the sermon is a gauge of a preacher's control over timing. Swaggart uses anaphora when he wants to elicit maximum emotional response from the audience. A Swaggart sermon follows a fairly regular pattern, which might be imagined as a sine wave that increases in frequency and proportion as the sermon progresses. He builds momentum and anticipation by pacing the use of repetition. The rhythm created through this rhetorical strategy is not accidental. In fact, rhythm is "the architecture of the sermon," according to Rosenberg:

> In an effective sermon it is always necessary to gradually increase the rhythm so as to inspire the congregation and to build toward an emotional and spiritual peak through the rhythm, whether that peak be at the end of the sermon, or near its middle.[26]

Swaggart's sermons peak near the end, but he takes care to work his listeners toward that pinnacle throughout the service. He stimulates the audience with anaphoric moments, each calculated to move listeners closer to the point of "yielding." The placement of these peaks is a matter of timing, or the ability to pace and sustain rhythm.

Swaggart's mastery over rhythm and timing is most apparent at moments of anaphora, which have their own rhythm. Indeed, I have never seen this linguistic device fail to arouse an audience and even found myself waiting for these peaks. I assume that his regular viewers (and crusade attenders) wait for these moments as well, because it gives them the opportunity to engage emotionally and physically in the dialogue. Listeners respond to this rhetorical technique by clapping, shouting, standing, raising their arms, weeping, and speaking in tongues. It is at such points that Swaggart becomes most physically involved in his preaching: He struts across the stage in a high-stepping gait, shakes the Bible in the air, casts his eyes heavenward. This is when Swaggart comes closest to a chanted form of preaching. Each anaphoric phrase is punctuated by a groan (e.g., "heaped it up-uh," "pressed it down-uh," etc.), and words are often extended to maintain metrical unity. These utterances have a musical quality; Swaggart will often slip into song during chanted portions of the sermon. The hammer blows have a cadence and beat that speak to the emotions of the listeners who "speak" back with their bodies.

Burke has also noted the sensuous appeal of rhythmic communication:

> The appeal of form as exemplified in rhythm enjoys a special advantage in that rhythm is more closely allied with 'bodily' processes. Systole and diastole, alternation of the feet in walking, inhalation and exhalation, up and down, in and out, back and forth, such are the types of distinctly motor experiences 'tapped' by rhythm.[27]

The speaker who is able to exploit this relationship between language and corporeality, Burke says, has an added mastery over her or his audience:

> A rhythm is a promise which the poet makes to the reader—and in proportion as the reader comes to rely on this promise, he falls into a state of general surrender which makes him more likely to accept without resistance the rest of the poet's material.[28]

These moments of surrender are the points of communion in Swaggart's oratory—when his courtship of the audience has been successful. They are also moments of communion with God, or with transcendental reality. Swaggart often breaks into tongues—enters into dialogue with the miraculous—following a chanted section of a sermon. One of the preachers in Rosenberg's study explained that during the chanted verses of a sermon, he feels that the Spirit has taken him over completely—that he is "being fed by God."[29] Compare this experience to Swaggart's metaphor of "getting full" of the Holy Ghost.

Metaphorical language is associative, poetic, and imagistic. It is more emotional and physical than rational, lending itself naturally to sensuous, rhythmic delivery. Metaphors give mundane experience new meaning—they make the ordinary mysterious. In contrast, the discourse associated with news analysis, public affairs reports, and interviews strives for a minimum of ambiguity; it demystifies the unknown. Statements are supported with evidence and develop toward logical conclusions. If Dan Rather or Tom Brokaw were to lace their reports with allusions, metaphors, and rhythmic delivery, listeners would question their authority (if not their sanity). The language of the "700 Club" alternates between this formal, rational discourse of public affairs shows and the familiar, conversational speech of talk programs. Robertson avoids the passionate, poetic terrain of the country preacher because it would jeopardize his legitimacy as a host and professional broadcaster. The "700 Club" audience does not expect to be swept away, brought to its feet, or transported outside itself (to experience ecstasy), but to be informed, entertained, and reassured. Robertson may serve up old-time religion, but he does so in a language and style befitting a politician or newscaster. He urges viewers to choose conservative Christianity over secularism and to subscribe to his health and wealth theology by appealing to their reason and their self-interest, not to their subterranean passions.[30]

Robertson's style is anecdotal and congenial, rather than metaphorical and ecstatic. His speech, appropriate to a talk show or a press conference, would be out of place in a religious service, just as Swaggart's oratory would be ludicrous in a talk show setting. Sacred language is distinctive by virtue of being extraordinary. It is immediate, spontaneous, metaphorical, urgent. It makes the familiar mysterious and points to a reality outside ordinary time and space. Swaggart's language is sacred. Robertson's is not. The rhetoric of the "700 Club" is firmly entrenched in "the world;" it speaks the language of television news and entertainment, which is why the prayer segments of the show seem so unsettling, almost profane. "Piety," says Burke, is "the sense of what properly goes with what"—a knowledge that "reveals the sources of one's own being." In this sense, the prayers on the "700 Club" are impious; appeals to the sacred do not "go with" the rational discourse and slick entertainment of a TV talk show. Nor do petitions for "financial healing" fit well with Christ's teachings. To talk of a "spiritual bank account" is to marry terms that do not properly fit together.[31]

THE PROGRAM FRAME

Media production is a process of framing—selecting and organizing substantial and formal elements to create a particular set of meanings for an audience. Framing is both an ideological and technical process that invests a message with what Hall calls a "preferred reading."[32] The television frame fuses textual, visual, and aural elements to produce a rendering of "what is." When we watch these programs, we understand Swaggart to be an evangelist and Robertson to be a Christian TV host, because their identities have been constructed for us through an elaborate set of professional, aesthetic, and technical conventions. These conventions, moreover, are historically created; this is part of the historical appeal of cultural forms.

Producers of Swaggart's crusade must portray him as an evangelist and assemble the program in a way that reproduces the spontaneous emotionality of a preacher exhorting his flock. Camera perspectives are used to create a sense of dialogue or interaction between Swaggart and the audience.[33] Two stationary cameras sit about 10 rows back near the center of the main floor. They are trained on the stage to capture shots of Swaggart, the band, and assorted dignitaries seated at each end of the platform. Another camera, atop a mobile stand, circulates through the aisles in the front section of the auditorium for close-ups of people listening and responding to the performance. This camera also zooms in on worshipers during the altar call. A portable mini-camera operator travels up and down the aisles, kneels on the floor below the platform, follows penitents to the altar, and sometimes stands unobtrusively on stage behind the performers. Another stationary camera perches high above the audience at the rear or side of the arena and produces the wide shots of the auditorium that convey the immensity of the crowd; these images are often used for program transitions and as background for written material on the screen.

Editors assemble the final product by splicing together images from these various perspectives. The goal is to create for viewers a sense of the emotional exchange between Swaggart and his musical entourage and the revival audience. This is accomplished by skillful editing. Audience shots are carefully interwoven with images of Swaggart and the other performers. Individuals are shown nodding in agreement to his assertions, laughing at his jokes, listening in dismay as he recounts the sins of society, and weeping when moved by the music or preaching. Camera operators are especially alert to signs of strong emotion. Shots of people sobbing or rapt in prayer are staples of the program. Wide-angle shots are used at moments when Swaggart elicits a particularly strong response—when he brings listeners to their feet and gets them to "give God a clap offering." The end product is a back and forth motion between speaker and listeners that resembles dialogue. It is realistic—appears to convey the revival as it happened—but it is not real. The shot of the young couple holding hands and murmuring assent to Swaggart's defense of marital fidelity is a technical device. It is part of the frame and not necessarily a representation of simultaneous events. This is one of the illusions created by television—that what we see is exactly what took place. Swaggart's remarks to the TV audience during a crusade are part of this illusion. It seems to home viewers that they are watching the crusade in progress rather than a manipulated reconstruction of an event that took place weeks or months earlier.

Just as timing is a key element in the preacher's art, the pacing of images is central to the televised spiritual sermon. As the sermon proceeds and Swaggart warms to his subject, the number of audience shots increases. At peak moments, when he resorts to anaphora, tongues, and chanting, shots of the congregation are more frequent. This technique encourages viewers to vicariously participate in the interaction between Swaggart and the crusade audience. We are moved not only by Swaggart's performance, but also by his ability to move others like us. Shots that frame Swaggart and the audience together contribute to this perception. These images portray him as evangelist—the anointed prophet delivering God's message to the world. In Swaggart's words, he represents "a voice in the wilderness."[34]

Images of the audience are important in another respect: by witnessing others who have abandoned themselves to ecstasy, viewers are encouraged to plunge into the same river of passion, to yield to the Spirit and throw off the reserve that characterizes their daily activities. In our society, there are few occasions, public or private, for expressing this type of enthusiasm, in the original sense of the word, which meant to be possessed by God. Hyde suggests that enthusiasm—the "in-dwelling of the spirit" in Pentecostal terms—is experienced in the flesh. These physical expressions of feeling and belief are at odds with the disembodied intellect exalted by rationalism. Modernism, grounded in the superiority of reason, expects religion to also be rational; it thus ostracizes or ridicules belief systems that refuse to bow to the intellect. Charismatics have been treated as "denizens of the zoo," partly because they exhibit their belief corporeally and sensuously (e.g., healing, shaking, babbling, etc.). To the charismatic Christian, however, knowledge is not deduced with the mind, it is revealed through the emotions or body. As Hyde says, the "enthusiast waits for a *sensation* of truth."[35]

Swaggart's performances are framed so as to emphasize the sensual aspect of the enactment of belief. The camera lingers on his hands as he plays the piano, pans in on him as he sweats, shouts, dances, and weeps, and seeks out believers who have been swept away by the performance. Swaggart exhorts his listeners to give themselves over to this enthusiasm, while recognizing that modern society looks askance at such overt religious emotion. In fact, he relishes this outsider identification: "You there by television say 'You're too emotional, Jimmy Swaggart; you're a fanatic.' And I say you're right. I'm a hundred percent, bonafide fanatic for Jesus Christ."[36] It is Swaggart's goal as a preacher, and the producers' goal for the program, to effect in viewers a "fanatical," physical expression of belief. Swaggart knows he has achieved this effect when he has moved listeners' bodies. The edited program tries to capture this physical passion and to generate similar enthusiasm among viewers. Camera and editing techniques are employed with this effect in mind. They are, in other words, motivated techniques.

Because Swaggart conceives of television as a tool to amplify his message, technique is subordinated to substance. The tool must remain as inconspicuous as possible. While the crusade audience is aware of the elaborate technology recording their experience, the TV audience knows it only indirectly.[37] Home viewers rarely see the cameras or the bank of monitors that flank Swaggart. It is important that we at home feel the revival to be as spontaneous and unmediated as possible because we are already removed from the event itself. Swaggart draws us into the crusade by looking straight into the camera and addressing us directly and aggressively: "Listen to me by television. Leave the knob alone. Listen to me by television."[38] Swaggart's sermon, then, is framed so as to render the technology nearly invisible; viewers are asked to temporarily suspend the knowledge that their relationship with Swaggart is mediated. We are invited to forget we are viewers and pretend we are congregants.

Robertson's program, in contrast, highlights and makes central the medium of television. Rather than being a means of transmission, television is the occasion and site of the gathering. We understand Robertson to be a television host because he is framed in a setting appropriate to that persona. His authority derives, in large part, from this setting. As TV viewers, we have come to accept the authority of the TV host or commentator. We may disagree with their message, but we rarely challenge their right to speak. On the "700 Club," camera and editing techniques enhance rather than conceal the fact that the program is mediated. The studio audience is well aware that the performance takes place in order to be broadcast. Most of the time Robertson, the cast, and guests do not look at the studio audience but at each other or at the cameras. The performance is not staged for those in the studio, but for viewers at home.[39] The home audience is also continually reminded that it is watching a televised performance. Transition shots generally frame the set and one of the floor cameras. The studio audience is often shown as the foreground to this frame, a standard technique of the talk show format. Commercial breaks and regulated applause, cued to transitions, are further reminders that we are watching a talk show, not participating in a religious service. Camera techniques also contribute to the experience of the "700 Club" as television. The program's three mobile cameras produce mainly mid-range shots and close-ups. Viewers understand these images to be part of the informal, conversational setting of the talk show. The cast and guests participate in these conventions; they are attuned to the camera, which links them to the viewing audience. The split-second lag between a camera change and a speaker's focus reminds viewers of the technology that mediates their relationship to the performers.

In the talk show format, then, the technology of television controls the relationship between speaker and listener. The "700 Club" exists to be televised, and its very form would be impossible without television's historically developed techniques and conventions. The crusade form exists prior to television, even though it has been adapted in important ways to the demands of the medium. There is no way to hide the technology in the framing of the "700 Club," because the format demands that it be made central. Indeed, the fact that the "700 Club" is "television" is part of its glamor and appeal. In this respect, Robertson's relationship to the medium is very different from Swaggart's. Robertson accepts that television has become a central cultural form and social institution in modern society. He does not question television's aesthetic conventions or its production techniques. The problem is not that television has become a "new religion," but that the content of that new belief system is flawed. His goal, therefore, is to give people what they want (e.g., to give them television), but to fill it with different content.

Swaggart, on the other hand, rejects television precisely because it is so central to modern life and as such is the epitome of the "spirit of the world." Swaggart endorses television only as an amplification device—a medium of communication that is "good" only insofar as it is subordinated to evangelism. In this respect Swaggart follows his predecessor, Charles Finney, who believed a preacher should use any "appropriate means" to save souls.[40] From this perspective, the end justifies, indeed sanctifies, the means. Swaggart justifies his use of television by treating it as a means—a medium for transmitting the "good news." As he says, it is "the greatest tool of world evangelization that has ever been known."[41] This is why Swaggart never refers to his crusade as a TV program. Rather, it is a "telecast," a term that stresses that the medium is merely a means of transmission, not an independent cultural form.

Robertson, in contrast, treats television as a site of symbolic production in its own right. To create an alternative network is to already accept the logic of television. Robertson competes with secular television on its own terms (e.g., adopting its strategies of program flow, copying its formats, buying its old products, etc.). CBN and the "700 Club" are not tools or megaphones, but parallel institutions. In

Robertson's words, his program is "God's television."[42] The appeal of the "700 Club" derives from its similarity to secular broadcasting. Viewers are not required to reject television, but only to avoid unwholesome, "secular humanist" programming. In this respect, Robertson's viewers are not asked to cut themselves off from society; they retain their status as TV consumers by becoming a specialized market. The "700 Club" (and CBN and the Family Channel) are presented as one among several television alternatives, comparable to ESPN, movie channels, or the Playboy channel. Swaggart's message, on the other hand, implies that television cannot exist as an end in itself (as a source of entertainment), but must be used only to convey the salvation message. Swaggart's repeated attacks on glamorized Christian television are grounded in this belief. The emphasis on celebrity and Hollywood production values, he says, is part of the "worldly system of 'entertainment'—which is almost totally opposed to the things of God."[43] Those viewers who take his message seriously are not free to participate in television as an institution of entertainment. Unlike other Americans, they must not see themselves as a market.

Despite Swaggart's rejection of television, his program, like the "700 Club," is shaped by what Frankl calls TV "imperatives," both technical and economic. One of television's technical imperatives stems from its visual form. Early religious broadcasters, who did not worry about ratings, employed a talking heads format, because it was technically simple and cheap to produce. Indeed, talking heads were a staple of many early commercial programs. The development of television into a competitive, multimillion dollar industry brought technical innovations designed to attract larger and larger audiences. Increasingly sophisticated equipment permitted programmers to experiment with new ways to add visual appeal. As competition grew within the industry, so did pressure to create entertaining and visually stimulating programs. The stationary camera, talking heads format was nearing obsolescence. Given "pray TV's" dependence on audience support, religious programmers were forced to develop strategies that made their products competitive with secular shows.[44]

One way that television attracts and holds viewers is by creating visual stimulation with "technical events." Special effects such as zooms, cuts, voiceovers, words printed on the screen, shifts in action, changes in sound, visual juxtapositions, and so on, "create the fiction that something unusual is going on, thereby fixing attention," according to Mander.[45] Most commercial programs use 8 to 10 technical events per minute, and advertisements nearly double this technical action. Religious programming has adopted the use of technical events to build action and liven the pace of a program. Talk and interview segments of the "700 Club," for example, use approximately eight events each minute, and sometimes as few as five or six (mainly changes in camera angle and speaker). Pretaped inserts and promotions employ more of these effects—about 12 to 13 per minute, speeding up the pace and balancing the slower on-set segments.[46] In Swaggart's program, technical events are paced to correspond to the exchange between him and the congregation. The number of events increases as Swaggart approaches a peak in the sermon, and this heightens viewers' perception of an ascent toward a dramatic climax. The rate of technical events ranges from about 8, as he begins a sermon, to 12 to 14 when he has reached a dramatic peak. The ministry's special fund-raising programs rely more heavily on technical events to sustain audience interest, because producers cannot count on Swaggart's performance to supply its own dramatic appeal.[47] Through technical events, television creates an artificial "bias" toward "the more vivid, more powerful, more cathartic, more definite, 'clean' peaks of content."[48]

Effective video storytelling also depends on skillful editing. A narrative is given internal unity by weaving together visual, verbal, and musical threads. Swaggart's program is structured around two "stories": a short promotion that conveys the urgency and import of the ministry's world mission, and the service itself. The most difficult job for Swaggart's editors is to retain audience interest for 30 or 40 uninterrupted minutes. They accomplish this task by intercutting and pacing shots of Swaggart and the audience and by exploiting technical events (both those created with the original camerawork and those produced in the editing process).

The "700 Club" builds and maintains audience interest in increments. An important part of the show's appeal is its upbeat tone and rapid pace. According to Straub: "Keep it simple, keep it moving, and keep it entertaining was the threefold key to success that I used while producing the '700 Club'."[49] The live portions of the show are given dramatic interest by spontaneous "editing" (e.g., mixing camera perspectives); the pretaped segments are enriched through production techniques. As Straub says, the "creatively enhanced" taped version of a salvation testimony has "far more dramatic impact than the lived reality."[50]

How a program is framed has much to do with how we understand its story. The frame is part of the message. Viewers accept Swaggart's passionate exhortations and warnings, not just because he is an evangelist, but because televisual techniques effectively portray him as such. Similarly, the "700 Club" audience accords Robertson the authority of a professional broadcaster because it recognizes the technical conventions that legitimize this television persona.

THE STRUCTURE OF APPEAL WITHIN HISTORICAL FORMS

The structure of appeal of these two programs,indeed of any media product—resides in their form, which effectively synthesizes the collective memories of speakers and listeners. The form of Swaggart's crusade and Robertson's talk show represent separatist versus assimilative perspectives that coexist within evangelicalism. The crusade fashions a "sacred canopy" that denigrates and attempts to transcend ordinary existence in "the world." The talk show's canopy is firmly attached to the everyday world; it legitimizes preoccupation with the self and encourages political activism and material accumulation.

Swaggart's revivalism is anti-modernist, stressing traditional themes of personal piety, individual redemption, and asceticism. His dualist theology rejects this world and longs for the next. He speaks to (and is appealing to) listeners who share his belief that earthly life is a struggle and that society is doomed. Swaggart's followers share both his disdain for the problem of the self and his desire to transcend and lose the self by uniting with God. Essential to this rejection of the world is the flight away from rationalism and the mind toward passion and the sanctified body. The "infilling of the Holy Spirit" is a technique of transcendence; it transports the vessel/believer to a state beyond ordinary reality. Swaggart is a catalyst—a means to and a model of this desired state. His style, mode of address, and the setting of his speech must facilitate the journey if he is to create communion. He must construct an identity as a prophet and employ grand-style rhetoric to fuel the passions and elicit the emotional and physical responses of his listeners. By staging his communication as an old-fashioned camp meeting, he helps build a site for religious ritual—a setting for the enactment of belief. Swaggart's appeal resides in his risk—both as a performer and as an immortal soul who risks death to gain everlasting life. There are few occasions in modern life in which the stakes are so high—where our actions take on such absolute significance—and to participate in this risk is exhilirating for the audience.

Because Swaggart's theology asks people to risk earthly happiness, it tends to appeal to those who have already lost out on many of the fruits of modern society. Thus it is a rhetoric of consolation. Robertson's belief system, in contrast, is not about loss, but gain. His conversionist theology preaches that life is a blessing and that true believers may reside in the world and prosper. His cultural fundamentalist themes harken back to a world where orthodox Protestants dominated society and encourages Christians to reclaim their historical hegemony. At the same time, Robertson's worldview has accommodated modernism by embracing material accumulation and incorporating subjectivism—the modern preoccupation with the self. Robertson encourages listeners to take control of their lives and the world rather than abandon them to an enemy culture and does so in terms that are thoroughly modern. He employs the plain-style rhetoric used by teachers, politicians, experts, and television commentators. Further, his message is constituted wholly within the conventions of television. Robertson's persona is that of a congenial host, a TV father figure.

The "700 Club" makes minimal demands on viewers, and its health and wealth gospel parallels the values of consumer culture. Robertson appeals to people who feel relatively "at home" in the world; his theology does not ask viewers to give up their security or material comfort, but justifies both as their divine right. It thus employs a rhetoric of compensation, suggesting that believers will recoup their earlier losses and come out ahead in the end. In this sense, the message of the "700 Club" is safe. It does not ask people to question either the world or their existence at a structural level. Rather, the program promises to make their social position even more secure and grounds this guarantee in religious symbolism. Christians will come to rule the world, Robertson insists, because the Bible tells them so.

THE INTERPRETATION OF FORM

The journey from curious spectator to engaged interpreter of religious television leads ever deeper into the forms of the programs while simultaneously placing us squarely inside history where we confront the social life of cultural forms and the kinds of subjectivity they realize and make available.[51] The preliminary stage of textual analysis is like an "inventory" of key features of the text, such as narrative structure, prominent themes, patterns of organization, and so on.[52] The act of interpretation, however, must go beyond this compilation to establish some kind of formal relationship among those observations that gives them meaning and coherence. I have argued that one path to such coherence is through the interpretation of form—understood not as the external skeleton into which content is poured, but as integral to a text's (or utterance's) function, intention, and history. Analyzing a text's form is therefore a process of discerning the informing purpose which unites all of its components and makes them meaningful.

Form is also the bridge that connects speakers and listeners, the vehicle for arousing and fulfilling desires and creating identification in a concrete time and place. If, as Grossberg and Treichler argue, "media criticism is a domain struggling, in the spaces between competing theories, to find a way of making sense of the relations between media texts, audiences, and contexts,"[53] the interpretation of form may provide a technique of recuperation and reintegration. Beginning with the notion that the form of a text contains its history, structure, and motives gives us a way to avoid separating speaker, text, and listener into isolated moments or units of analysis. So understood, form ceases to be formalist abstraction and becomes instead the embodiment of concrete social relationships. As Davis argues, such a conception of form "enables us to synthesize all three [speaker, text, listener] in a single order of inquiry that is rooted in the text and controlled by its primacy."[54] The interpretation of form, then, "contains the possibility of unifying the entire critical enterprise."[55]

This approach necessarily locates cultural texts in history, because form itself is historically created and determined. That is, the study of form is the study of history.[56] The strategies and structure of any act of communication are a response to the historical moment in which it is situated and to the problems which that history has posed. Every text has a history which becomes intelligible only by examining its past, present, and aims for the future. Similarly, every form is motivated by a quest to establish identification between specific speakers and listeners; its significance cannot be understood without grasping the character, values, and aspirations of those historical subjects. The possibility of identification between speaker and listener issues from their shared memory of what has been, their mutual conceptions of what is, and their overlapping desires for what might be. Cultural texts are thus always involved in "the making or unmaking of an audience as community."[57] I have tried to show that the programs of Swaggart and Robertson are appeals to the making of very different communities of believers. Further, it is through the form of their communication that those appeals become concrete and effective.

Finally, I have argued that interpretive method is a relationship one takes toward the text and toward the communities it summons. I could not stand "outside" the programs and understand their appeal, because to do so would turn them into mere objects of curiosity. To comprehend the "claims about life and experience" made by these programs and "make them explicit and articulate,"[58] I had to enter their domain of meaning, let those appeals speak to me, and investigate my own responses to them. Davis calls such a stance a "hermeneutics of engagement": "[its] ruling assumption is that our involvement in our own subjectivity is not a barrier to interpretation but the circumstance that enables us to enter most deeply into a text."[59] In other words, as a historical subject, I had to actively listen to both the "voice without" in the text and the "voice within" in me, hold myself open to the possibility of identification, and envision who

I might be if I were a member of the communities invoked by the programs. This, it seems to me, is what historical imagination is about.

I am not suggesting that all other approaches to the study of evangelical television (or of any cultural product) are without value. But if we wish to comprehend the meanings embedded in specific cultural texts, an interpretive approach that finds in its form the historical link between speaker, text, and listeners seems a fruitful place to begin. It is, admittedly, an ambitious undertaking to approach a text and to try to synthesize the motives of the speaker, the listeners' patterns of experience, the themes and structure of the narrative, the strategies of appeal, the purpose of the communicative act, and the history that has given rise to all these elements. But it is precisely through such synthesis that the "web of meaning" emerges.[60] The explanatory power of the concept of form outlined here is that it enables cultural analysts to "use all that there is to use," in Burke's words, because, as Davis says, "we have found a way to use all the knowledge available to us."[61]

While the structure of appeal of these programs is embedded in their forms—as symbolic responses to the historical problems posed by capitalist modernization—they operate within a contemporary context. The concluding chapter speculates on why these two versions of evangelical belief continue to be powerfully appealing in the context of modern, secularized consumer society.

NOTES TO CHAPTER 9

1. Gregor Goethals, *The TV Ritual: Worship at the Video Altar* (Boston: Beacon Press, 1981), pp. 8-9.

2. Ibid., p. 6.

3. Quoted in Anthony Blasi, "Ritual as a Form of Religious Mentality," *Sociological Analysis* 46 (1985): pp. 60, 66, from Monica Wilson, *Religion and the Transformation of Society* (London: Cambridge University Press, 1971), p. 62, and Monica Wilson, "Nyakyusa Ritual and Symbolism," *American Anthropologist* 56 (1954): p. 240 (second quote).

4. Wilson, *Religion and the Transformation of Society*, p. 67.

5. Goethals, *TV Ritual*, p. 6.

6. Ibid., p. 2.

7. And, of course, much of the Bible originated in oral narratives.

8. For an extensive discussion of the differences between oral and written communication, see Walter J. Ong, *Orality and Literacy: The Technologizing of the Word* (London: Methuen, 1982).

9. For a fuller discussion of the relationship of sound and image in television, see John Ellis, *Visible Fictions* (London: RKP, 1982).

10. George Kennedy, *New Testament Interpretation Through Rhetorical Criticism* (Chapel Hill and London: University of North Carolina Press, 1984), pp. 21, 37. Kennedy argues that "an orally received text is characterized by a greater degree of repetition than is a text intended to be read privately." Repetition, or amplification, in rhetorical communication "is necessitated by the oral nature of the situation and by the constraints of the audience."

11. "700 CLub," February 16, 1987.

12. Kennedy, *New Testament Interpretation*, p. 25.

13. Religious rhetoric is expressed in sacred language which has the following characteristics: (a) a revelatory or evangelical character; (b) immediate and spontaneous claims about reality; (c) an imagistic and metaphorical quality that gives new meaning to ordinary experience; (d) an absolute, urgent cast to its assertions so that "whatever does not fit into them is outrageous;" and (e) the appearance of existing outside time and arising from a cosmic universal reality. Ibid., p. 6 quoted from Ernest Grassi, *Rhetoric as Philosophy: The Humanist Tradition* (University Park and London: Penn State University Press, 1980), pp. 103-104.

14. Sizer makes this point as well in *Gospel Hymns and Social Religion* (Philadelphia: Temple University Press, 1978).

15. "Jimmy Swaggart Telecast," November 16, 1986.

16. Sizer found similar dichotomies in the 19th century gospel hymns. *Gospel Hymns* pp. 125-126, 171.

17. "Jimmy Swaggart Telecast," May 24, 1987.

18. Ibid., January 18, 1987. April 26, 1987; and interview, January 19, 1988, with Gail Yargus, assistant director of "I Believe," an evangelical program produced and aired weekly in Seattle.

19. "Jimmy Swaggart Telecast," April 26, 1987.

20. Kennedy, *New Testament Interpretation*, p. 27.

21. Bruce Rosenberg, *The Art of the American Folk Preacher* (New York: Oxford University Press, 1970), Chapter 5.

22. "Jimmy Swaggart," April 12, 1987.

23. Luke 6:38: "give, and gifts will be given you. Good measure pressed down, shaken together, and running over, will be poured into your lap." The opening reference to "dried beans" in the final stanza also originates in this passage.

24. James Weldon Johnson, *God's Trombones* (New York: Penguin 1975), p. 10.

25. Ibid., p. 5.

26. Rosenberg, *American Folk Preacher*, pp. 42, 48.

27. Kenneth Burke, *Counter-Statement* (Berkeley: University o

California Press, 1968), p. 140.

28. Ibid., pp. 140-141.

29. Ibid., p. 38.

30. Indeed, this level-headed approach is what Dabney initially found attractive about the "700 Club" host: "Robertson did not come on like a preacher at all; he was no thundering sermoneer nor twittering bird smirker, but a reasonable and educated man, with a unified point of view that was especially intriguing to intellectuals." Dick Dabney, "God's Own Newtork," *Harper's*, August 1980, p. 35.

31. Kenneth Burke, *Permanence and Change: An Anatomy of Purpose* (Berkeley: University of California Press, 1969), p. 74.

32. Stuart Hall, "Encoding/Decoding," in S. Hall et al., eds., *Culture Media, Language* (London: Hutchinson, 1980), pp. 128-138. Framing is a concept used by several media analysts. Gitlin defines media frames as "persistent patterns of cognition, interpretation, and presentation, of selection, emphasis, and exclusion, by which symbol-handlers routinely organize discourse, whether verbal or visual." Todd Gitlin, *The Whole World is Watching, Mass Media in the Making and Unmaking of the New Left* (Berkeley: University of California Press, 1980), p. 7. Gaye Tuchman also uses this concept in *Making News* (New York: Free Press, 1978).

33. The placement and use of cameras is based on my observation of and participation in the Vancouver crusade, and on my observations of the program.

34. "Jimmy Swaggart Telecast," January 11, 1987.

35. Lewis Hyde, *The Gift: Imagination and the Erotic Life of Property* (New York: Vintage, 1983, c. 1979), p. 168.

36. "Jimmy Swaggart Telecast," January 11, 1987.

37. Although the cameras and monitors were certainly visible at the revival I attended, they remained peripheral to the focus of the crusade—the music, singing, preaching, and praying. I probably paid more attention to the technology than most participants and still found myself oblivious to it much of the time.

38. "Jimmy Swaggart," March 1, 1987. During the promotional and fund-raising segments, however, he speaks to viewers separately from revival participants; the fund-raising portion of the live crusade is not televised.

39. Studio audience members can never forget they are participating in television—the technology will not let them forget. I was unable to attend the "700 Club" in person, but I did participate in the studio audience for KOMO-TV's "Northwest Afternoon" in Seattle, May 1987. We were coached before and throughout the show by floor directors and told where to look and when to clap. Often the cameras obstructed our view of the performers, who only occasionally looked in our

direction and most often focused on the cameras.

40. Finney characterized the revival as "the right use of the constituted means." Razelle Frankl, *Televangelism* (Carbondale: Southern Illinois University Press, 1987), pp. 35, 36; quoted from Charles Grandison Finney, *Lectures: On Revivals of Religion*, W. McLoughlin, ed. (Cambridge, MA: The Belknap Press or Harvard University Press, 1960).

41. "Jimmy Swaggart Telecast" ("Partners in the Harvest" episode), March 15, 1987.

42. Quoted in Edwin Diamond, "God's Television," in Karl Love, ed., *Television and American Culture* (New York: W. Wilson, 1981), p. 80.

43. Swaggart, "The Spirit of the World," p. 16.

44. J. Harold Ellens, in *Models of Religious Broadcasting* (n.p.: Eerdman's 1974), refers to religious broadcasters' early debates about how to compete with commercial television.

45. Jerry Mander, *Four Arguments for the Elimination of Television* (New York: Quill, 1978), p. 301.

46. These figures do not result from methodical tests or content analyses, but from random counts as I watched the programs.

47. Again, the number of technical events is based on random counts I made while watching the show.

48. Mander, *Four Arguments*, p. 314.

49. Gerard Straub, *Salvation for Sale* (Buffalo, NY: Prometheus, 1986), p. 293.

50. Ibid., p. 170.

51. Richard Johnson, "What Is Cultural Studies Anyway?", *Social Text* (1986): p. 62.

52. Walter Davis, *The Act of Interpretation* (Chicago: University of Chicago Press, 1978), p. 9.

53. Lawrence Grossberg and Paula Treichler, "Intersections of Power: Criticism, Television, Gender," *Critical Studies in Mass Communication* 6 (1987): p. 278.

54. Davis, *Act of Interpretation*, p. 7.

55. Ibid., p. 6.

56. As Fredric Jameson points out, this is not to say that history is a "text," but that history "is inaccessible to us except in textual form." Jameson describes "ideological analysis" as the attempt to grasp cultural texts as the "rewriting or restructuration of a prior ideological or historical subtext" which must always be "(re)constructed after the fact." Jameson, "The Symbolic Inference; or, Kenneth Burke and Ideological Analysis," *Critical Inquiry* 4 (1978): p. 511. This parallels my argument about the interpretation of form as an act of historical imagi-

nation.

57. Walter Davis, *Inwardness and Existence, Subjectivity in/and Hegel, Heidegger, Marx, and Freud* (Madison: University of Wisconsin Press, 1989), p. 230.

58. James Carey, "Mass Communication Research and Cultural Studies: An American View," in James Curran et al., eds., *Mass Communication and Society* (Beverly Hills: Sage, 1979), p. 421.

59. Davis, *Inwardness and Existence*, p. 4.

60. Clifford Geertz, *The Interpretation of Cultures* (New York: Basic Books, 1973), p. 5.

61. Davis, *Act of Interpretation*, p. 6.

10

The Meaning of Evangelical Television: Desire, Consumption, and the Flight of Faith

Swaggart and Robertson may be listened to primarily by the already converted, but what they say speaks to all of us about the kind of world we inhabit and the world(s) we might imagine or hope for. Relegating religious programs and evangelicalism to the realm of the exotic is both myopic and elitist. A belief system that claims 20% of the adult population in the U.S. and programming that has reached some 15 million regular viewers a week cannot be written off as the death rattle of an outdated religious tradition. On the contrary, orthodox Protestantism has proven itself remarkably durable—adapting to social changes and historical circumstances and extending its appeal to people outside its traditional boundaries. The fact that evangelicalism has managed to dominate religious television and plant itself firmly in the political landscape also raises deeper social questions. Why has this belief system failed to wither away, as its critics predicted? What social and individual needs does it meet that cannot be satisfied by modern secular society?

In this chapter I offer some speculative answers to these questions. Like the programs I have analyzed, I too am a product of my society and its contending histories. My reading of the shows is therefore neither a purely subjective reaction, nor an objective truth that exists independently of me. Rather, it reflects the synthesis of text and

223

reader that creates new meanings by selecting from those that have already been given us by history. It may be apparent in my analysis that I am somewhat more sympathetic to Swaggart's world view than to Robertson's. That is, I am partially persuaded by Swaggart's message and rhetorical strategies. But this identification is full of what Burke calls doubt—my "voice within" and Swaggart's "voice without" form a very imperfect union. While, like Swaggart, I am critical of the dominant values of modern consumer society, his solution is highly reactionary: His answer to the failings of modernity is to reject the present and return to the past. In my view, this is no solution at all, because it presupposes some idyllic history in which tensions between morality and the social order and between public and private life did not exist. As anthropologist William Roseberry cautions, we must be careful not to imagine some "unambiguous transition from an ordered past to a disordered present," but "instead need to view a movement from a disordered past to a disordered present."[1] Because the stories told by "Jimmy Swaggart" and the "700 Club" operate under the shadow of the larger, dominant narrative provided by secular consumer culture, they must be interpreted in light of that larger cultural framework.

THE DISENCHANTMENT OF THE WORLD

I have argued that the transition from a traditional, precapitalist society to a capitalist, market-industrial society had profound social and personal consequences. This historical process transformed values, beliefs, and meanings; it altered the ways that people understood and lived their relationships to each other, to nature, and to themselves. In traditional or premodern society, human beings derived their sense of self from a more integrated network of divine explanations and sacred symbols. The self was not autonomous or individuated, but collectively defined through one's position in the social fabric. The question "Who am I?" was answered through explicit social hierarchies, based on immutable sacred foundations, that told people who they were and who they could be. The "problem of meaning"—human bafflement, suffering and evil—was solved through an elaborate metaphysical framework, thus minimizing the need for personal, idiosyncratic solutions. This relatively unified universe, where all meaning was interconnected and grounded in the sacred, was gradually replaced by a world where meaning was transitory, relative, and based in the secular realm of exchange. The intertwined development of Protestantism, modern science, and capitalism created new rationales that explained people's place in society and introduced the modern individual who stood alone before God, before nature, and before the marketplace. Protestantism rerouted belief around the institutional church and made salvation an individual rather than collective endeavor. It also made doctrine, or the Word, central to religious identity and presupposed a body of rational believers who could interpret and uphold the Word.[2] The ascendance of scientific rationalism further unraveled humanity's already loosened ties to the sacred. The Enlightenment opened people's eyes and told them that the invisible (or metaphysical) was illusion. This was a process of disintegration: culture was split from nature, subject from object, mind from body, thought from feeling. The Enlightenment insisted that everything could be known through reason.[3] This new type of knowing demanded distance from the object of knowledge, however, and distance implies disconnectedness. The human subject, who now stood apart from the "objective" world, eventually sought to master it, hence, the development of the notion that nature was a "thing" to be dominated and controlled rather than an animated field of being to which one was divinely connected.[4] Humanity thus found itself "outside" nature—no longer "at home." As the natural world lost its divinity and mystery, so too did human existence. Like nature, human beings themselves became objects of knowledge.[5] Scientific rationalism turned its microscope on human relationships (sociology), cultural practices and expression (anthropology), thought and language (analytical philosophy, linguistics, psychology), and finally on the soul (psychoanalysis). Not even the sacred escaped the cool eye of reason; witness the development of a sociology of religion and more recently, the "scientific study of religion." Smith terms this process the "disparagement of the personal" which has been

> achieved through an almost inescapable glorification of natural science, whose knowledge was of the impersonal world of things (so that knowledge of human matters was considered not knowledge unless it were scientific, 'objective,' amoral, perceiving persons in the manner of things).[6]

The historical development of capitalism, culminating in its modern manifestation in a market-industrial society, also undermined traditional values and social relationships. It was a similarly disintegrative process, splitting production from consumption.[7] In this new system, money came to be the measure of all value, both the value of things as commodities and the value of individuals as producers of labor. Through this process, say Leiss, Kline, and Jhally,

more and more elements of both the natural environment and
human qualities are drawn into the orbit of exchanged things, into
the realm of commodities [so that] fewer and fewer aspects of the
environment and ourselves remain 'outside' the domain of buying
and selling."[8]

In other words, in modern society, money or the marketplace has
taken over the function of the ultimate term that incorporates and
interprets all social and natural phenomena and binds society together into a meaningful whole.

This historical process, which we can call Enlightenment or
progress or modernization or the death of God, has produced a world
that delegitimizes metaphysical symbolic systems, replacing them
with the logic of commodity exchange. It also poses a distinctly modern "problem of meaning." If the natural world is usurped from supernatural dominion and brought under human control, if the soul is
nothing more than the ego which is open to inspection, analysis, and
modification, then the meaning of one's life calls for human rather
than divine solutions. Such are the roots of the modern self that now
has to be constructed within the fluid field of meaning created by a
market-industrial society. Cut off from traditional, institutionalized
systems of meaning, we are forced to turn elsewhere for answers to
the questions "Who am I?" and "What is the meaning of my existence?"
Modern society is characterized by subjectivism, a preoccupation
with the self, because identity is no longer fully determined by social
roles or divine ordination. As the marketplace has evolved into the
"privileged institution for the reworking and transmission of the cultural symbols that shape our lives," we increasingly turn to the realm
of consumption to fashion a sense of who we are and what our lives
signify.[9] That is, we look to the marketplace for answers to questions
about being and meaning.

It is possible to look at this as a liberating process; traditional
society offered little or no social and economic mobility, and religion
was often used to legitimize political domination and personal oppres-
sion. But this freedom has a price, as Leiss et al. note:

consumer society arises from the ashes of traditional cultures,
which are characterized by relatively fixed forms for the satisfaction of needs, and unleashes a grand experimentation with the
individual's experience of both needs and the ways to satisfy
them.[10]

As needs and the means of meeting them proliferate, we face an over-whelming array of choices about what constitutes satisfaction, happi-ness, and social connectedness. Consumer society, then, "has eroded the guidelines for the sense of satisfaction and well-being laid out in traditional cultures" while offering (particularly through advertising) "an endless series of suggestions about the possible routes to happi-ness and success."[11]

Another way to say this is that the world of goods has replaced the world of the gods as the modern source of meaning and being and that advertising produces the "icons" of this new "religion." I am arguing that advertising, the modern "discourse through and about objects," has usurped religion as the dominant modern symbol-ic system.[12] Like religion in traditional society, the marketplace and its language of advertising is a totalizing system; it provides the metaphorical foundation on which rests the meaning of individual and social existence. Consumer culture has become the source of being: I know who I am and what my existence signifies by attending to the icons of the marketplace, by partaking in the right "sacraments" in the proper context, and by faithfully matching my consumption patterns to shifts in the production and marketing of goods and lifestyles. I am a full-fledged member of my culture, a fully modernized person, through my "recognition of consumption as a legitimate sphere for individual self-realization."[13]

If, as Leiss et al. suggest, the modern individual's sense of satisfac-tion and well-being is based on "subjective, shifting estimates of where one stands in relation to others and what values are most important," then the contemporary self must be perpetually reconstituted from the complex symbolic materials of the world of consumption.[14] The self is thus as transitory, relative, and temporal as the latest market trends. Further, the acceleration of such emphemerality, as Harvey points out, is a distinct feature of "flexible accumulation" or of the "postmodern condition."[15] In such a society, transcendence is reduced to a lifestyle choice or a matter of personal taste. Frames of orienta-tion and devotion are translated into worship of the consumption ideals of celebrity and material success. Happiness is transformed into a commodity, tied to goods and evoked by advertising. Satisfaction perpetually recedes from our grasp, however, because a consumer society is predicated on an infinite increase of wants and the means to fill them. In consumer society, meaning "focuses on questions like, Who is the person I become in the process of consump-tion? Who are the other consumers like me? What does the product mean in terms of the type of person I am and how I relate to others?"[16]

The self created through the world of consumption experi-ences a continual process of constitution/dissolution—an unending

series of deaths and rebirths without redemption or salvation. As long
as the self remains "in motion" in this way, the process itself becomes
the means and end of existence. The meaning of life resides in ever-
renewed consumption. But this movement is also a flight because it
postpones and avoids the *actual* "end" of our existence—the fact of
our death. Consumer society has no solution to this existential dilem-
ma other than the logic of further consumption, that is, having more
equals being more.[17] At the heart of this response to the problem of
meaning is a paradox: The marketplace offers a self based on the infinite proliferation and satisfaction of needs to beings who are themselves finite. The tension generated by this contradiction does not disappear, but erupts in other social locations—in critiques of consumer
culture, in environmental politics, in an array of social movements, in
individual psychotherapy, and in religion.[18]

THE TEXTS: TWO EVANGELICAL STORIES

It is against this backdrop that the "dramas" of Swaggart's eschatolog-
ical separatism and Robertson's theological triumphalism must be
considered. Their narratives about being and meaning are responses—and quite different ones—to the "story" produced by modern consumer culture.

Swaggart's worldview rejects the rationale of the dominant
consumer culture and reaches back to 19th-century Protestantism for
its source of meaning. Swaggart eschews reason in favor of the emotion experienced in religious ecstasy. His theology denies human consciousness the power to master either nature or itself. Conscious
reflection, in fact, creates a chasm between the individual and the
sacred. Self-consciousness is sin because it separates people from
God. Swaggart preaches a modified version of Christian asceticism
based on self-denial and self-discipline. "Without God," Swaggart says,
"you are eaten up with yourself." Salvation occurs through the denial
of self: "You need to be melted. You need to lose your identity."[19]
Modern society, in contrast, is obsessed with individual identity—with
creating a self through the process of consumption. (What other kind
of culture produces a consumer magazine entitled *Self?*) Swaggart's
cosmology sees consumerism as an activity that anchors people to
"the world" and to temporal happiness; the route to eternal joy, on the
other hand, is through self-denial, which thwarts consumption. As
Swaggart says, the things of the world "do not satisfy"—they do not
quench people's spiritual "thirst." By stressing the temporal nature of

earthly existence, this belief system also constantly reminds followers of their own earthly finitude. It makes central the existential problem of suffering and death. As Swaggart warns listeners, "You might be in the prime of life, but you're already dying."[20] Life on earth, then, is merely a preparation period—a state to be endured and transcended in anticipation of immortality in the next world.

Swaggart's worldview is grounded in what Wilber calls "mythical religion": It stresses intense conformity needs, sees God as a "cosmic parent," relies on charismatic authority figures (e.g., preachers and evangelists who represent the "parent"), employs mythic ritual, has an in-group/out-group mentality, and lacks rational justification.[21] It is, as well, a belief system predicated on individuated and passive followers. The source of good—or the sacred—resides outside the believer. Salvation demands that followers rid themselves of "the world" or earthly desire in order to receive the sacred or the Holy Spirit. Only the preacher remains an active agent in this system. It is his role to produce a receptivity in believers and prepare them to "yield" to the infilling of the Spirit. The self must be denied, or emptied, to make room for the sacred to enter. This belief system, I suggest, robs followers of their own potential for praxis—instead they are objects of the external praxis of God, the Holy Spirit, and the preacher. According to Anthony, this version of evangelicalism is a "charismatic religion," because it relies on a "personal relationship with a spiritually realized person as the essential means of spiritual attainment."[22] The ultimate "spiritually-realized person," of course, is Christ, but the preacher also achieves this status vicariously through his privileged role which places him in proximity to Jesus. Because this belief system makes charismatic leaders into agents, and followers into objects, it creates a radical separation between believers: They are not responsible to each other as members of a community, but only to themselves and to God. They are expected to contribute to the Great Commission, but only in terms of supporting evangelism as an abstract value. Other people become abstract souls to be saved, rather than reciprocal agents of Christian charity. Nonbelievers, in particular, are objectified as alien others. In fact, this separation between the saved and the damned is necessary to legitimize the conviction that one is chosen.

Robertson's theology conserves some elements of mythical belief while accommodating and assimilating the rationalism of modernity. One "decides" to be a Christian in the same way that one chooses a career or lifestyle. This belief system appeals to people's reason and self-interest. One opts for Christ in order to be happy and successful. It is a "technical religion," in Anthony's terms, because it offers specific techniques for achieving belonging and spiritual attainment.[23] Practicing the Kingdom Principles, following the guidelines of expert advice, and joining the "700 Club" family are techniques that guarantee emotional and spiritual satisfaction. Robertson's belief system accommodates many of the values of modern consumer society and incorporates them into religious doctrine. He accepts that happiness and self-identity can be found in consumption, as long as this activity is undertaken in the right Christian spirit. Earthly satisfaction is not evil or sinful, but desirable and attainable. Developing a proper relationship with God, in fact, leads to material success and personal well-being. This cosmology encourages preoccupation with the self and offers a wealth of expert advice on how to construct a contented Christian identity. The structure of this belief system has been similarly rationalized. Less reliant on charismatic preachers, it operates through a bureaucratic hierarchy in which roles are assigned by expertise and rational authority. Effective leaders and ministers are more like managers, chief executive officers, or counselors, than prophets. Mythic rituals are modernized by turning them into easy-to-follow guidelines, techniques, and steps to success. Leaders counsel, advise, and encourage rather than exhort and castigate their followers.

Robertson's theology, then, bows to the rationale of a market-industrial society, whereby all aspects of existence are subsumed into the domain of buying and selling. In this way, being born again acquires exchange value: It purchases financial success, improved family relationships, and eternal happiness. Indeed, "700 Club" fans can buy miracles. This perspective also handles mortality quite differently than does Swaggart's cosmology. Like illness, depression, anxiety, and financial difficulties, death is easy to conquer with the right attitude and techniques. The believer has only to follow the advice and example of Christian experts and leaders and the problem of mortality evaporates. Robertson holds up his life as evidence of the tranquility to be found in opting for Christ. He suggests viewers should follow his example and "get right" with God "before it's too late," so they too will be able to say: "It's all taken care of. I don't have to worry about death and I don't have to worry about the future. That's so exciting."[24]

By accommodating the values of modern consumer society, Robertson constructs a belief system that is easy to swallow. He legitimates the consumerism and preoccupation with the self of the larger society. This version of evangelicalism has striking parallels with consumer culture. Both "sell" perfect satisfaction: one by attaching identity and happiness to goods, the other by connecting success and emotional well-being to religious beliefs and practices. The effect of this accommodation is to desacralize the traditional sacred elements of evangelical belief. The "profane" character of the "700 Club"—its mimicry of secular television and its emphasis on celebrity and success—

suggests that orthodox Protestantism may be undergoing a transformation. It may be in the process of becoming an alternative modern lifestyle that gains persuasive power through its use of religious symbolism. Indeed, I am tempted to say that this belief system is ideally suited to a modern consumer society, because it sanctifies the values that are already dominant in our culture. This is the basis of its appeal. The assimilative form of evangelicalism tells believers they can have the best of both worlds—they can be "in" the world and "of" it—and still receive God's blessing.

CONSERVATIVE EVANGELICALISM AS A FIELD OF STRUGGLE

At the beginning of the 1980s, Pat Robertson commented that Christian conservatives had "enough votes to run the country."[25] While right-wing Christianity has certainly become a prominent feature of the U.S. political scene in the last decade, it is important to place this development in a larger historical and social context. One of the most thoughtful essays on the New Christian Right provides that context and argues that the NCR is not a mass political movement at all, but the vehicle of an elite group of preachers and politicians tied to the right wing of the Republican Party.[26] Leinesch's analysis of Christian conservativsm contends that the NCR consists of two distinct groups: a small elite group of well-educated, well-to-do, mostly professional middle-class activists, and a large, changeable, mass membership of marginally educated, lower- and working-class followers.[27] The elite leaders, which include the likes of Robertson, Falwell, and James Robison, with connections to political figures such as Weyrich, Viguerie, Dan Quayle, and Senator Jesse Helms, are in the business of building a political base from which to effect their policies and platforms and to achieve power within the Republican Party. They are not interested in mobilizing a mass movement, Leinesch argues, because movements are characterized by spontaneous protest and are difficult to bring under centralized control. NCR leaders "are anxious to extend their organizational influence" but "reluctant . . . to oversee the transfer of power downward."[28] Hence, there is a need for some means for unifying the Christian Right internally and maintaining a hierarchy of authority and power. The leadership of the Christian Right provides this unity and control by organizing around broad moral issues and side-stepping points of dissension—be they theological, geographical, denominational, or economic.

The NCR, then, is not the single voice of all conservative Christians in America. Rather, as Thomas might argue, it is one of several competing factions within evangelicalism striving to "articulate a new moral order." To win legitimacy, it must seek to make its "claims, goals, methods and rhetoric" fit the experiences and desires of the people it purports to represent, and this involves avoiding possible sites of conflict and dissent.[29] In particular, the NCR elite has avoided addressing the economic interests of its actual and potential followers, because the economic priorities of most orthodox Protestants are in direct conflict with those of the elite activists. Conservative Christian activists have therefore organized around symbolic issues, "not to meet economic ends, but to override them." The NCR leadership uses "moral symbolism" to consolidate its power in local issues and campaigns and to turn potential followers away from liberal candidates and economic policies.[30]

This strategy has both internal and external weaknesses. It leaves the conservative Christian "movement" open to internal divisions and provides a point of attack from those outside who wish to counter the Christian Right at local or national levels. The history of orthodox Protestantism contains a strong aversion to and mistrust of political activism, because it erodes the boundaries between spirituality and "the world," and because it threatens to transform religion into political ideology and destroy its metaphysical claims to authority. Further, conservative evangelicalism is not monolithic. The diversity of religious beliefs and practices among evangelicals makes it difficult to create absolute consensus around specific issues. The NCR's "interest group strategy" must operate by building coalitions across differences; conservative Christian organizations (such as the Moral Majority, Religious Roundtable, Liberty Foundation, Freedom Council, Christian Coalition, Eagle Forum, etc.) must form "uneasy alliances" by employing "widely accepted but vaguely defined issues" in order to "reconcile the constant potential for conflict."[31]

As we have seen, however, conflict resides in the very heart of orthodox Protestantism (and of all Christianity): The battles between orthodoxy and liberalism, between fundamentalists and charismatics, between left and right evangelicals, and between pre- and postmillennialists, have provided the fuel for the proliferation and perpetuation of belief. Those divisions are manifested in the contest for control over the powerful Southern Baptist Convention and in debates over the meaning of the gospel epitomized in the theologies of Swaggart and Robertson.[32]

Tension exists as well within Robertson's worldview, and this has to do with his quest to reconcile the goals of cultural fundamentalism with the apocalyptic nature of premillennial theology. During his presidential campaign, Robertson tried to achieve this reconciliation by fashioning one rhetoric for hard-core Fundamentalists and

Pentecostals and another for the general population of conservative Americans. This strategy backfired, however, raising suspicions among both groups. Further, Robertson's dualist perspective, which holds that Christians must actively transform culture in accordance with God's design, comes into direct conflict with his premillennialist eschatology, which emphasizes individual salvation and passive preparation for the end of the world. These internal contradictions are evident in the "700 Club," which is a disconcerting mix of apocalyptic prophesies and political strategies, of recipes for successful living and invocations of miracles. The dual audience of the show reflects this thematic dichotomy—those who watch for the healing and miracles and those who watch for the news, advice, and social analysis. Robertson's public persona is similarly "divided." At one moment he is the Christian broadcaster overseeing the long-term success of the Family Channel and planning ways to expand his political reach via the "700 Club" and appearances as a political commentator on secular television. At the next moment he is predicting the imminence of the last days and exorting listeners to "get right with God before it's too late."

These contradictions stem from the impossible task of simultaneously transcending and conserving the insider/outsider paradox. Because religious outsiderhood has historically provided conservative evangelicals with unity and identity, it is deeply embedded in both evangelical institutions and individual consciousness. But because cultural fundamentalism is premised on the conviction that conservative Protestantism is the one belief system mandated by God, adherents must also see themselves as the true "insiders" charged with leading the world to salvation. Perpetuating the insider/outsider tension has therefore been a necessary condition for the maintenance of a distinctly evangelical worldview, because without clear markers of difference, terms of belonging lose their persuasive power. The coalition character of the NCR—while attempting to minimize internal divisions—may actually dilute its potency and effectiveness by underemphasizing the outsider stance that has supplied evangelicalism with its critical edge. In seeking to broaden its base, the Christian Right tends to incorporate an increasing number of issues into its agenda. As issues proliferate, so too do possible points of internal dissension. For example, a national school prayer amendment is objectionable to many Baptists who believe prayer is an essentially private matter; many charismatics strenuously object to voting for non-Christian politicians, even if those candidates take the proper political position; and a significant percentage of evangelicals see any involvement in politics as capitulation to "the world."[33] Robertson's presidential campaign, in fact, brought many of these tensions to the surface.

Christianity, like all the great world religions, has an exceed-

ingly complex tradition, and its history is rich with contending interpretations. Disagreements about what constitutes proper Christian
belief and practice have informed social and political struggles from
Christianity's inception. There is no historical evidence to suggest
that these internal disputes will dissolve simply because of efforts by
a group of right-wing activists. Christian conservatives are not necessarily political conservatives—a fact that could become particularly
evident if issues were framed in economic terms. Philanthropism and
pacifism are as much a part of the Christian tradition as "Christian sol-
diers" and "custodians of social morality." As Leinesch aptly puts it:
"whether their right-wing leaders like it or not, conservative Christians
worship a populist prophet, the son of a carpenter who preached to
the poor, who drove the money changers from the temple, and who
blessed the peacemakers."[34]

DESIRE AND FULFILLMENT:
TWO ROUTES TO SATISFACTION

This brings me full circle to the question of why the contending theologies and programs of Swaggart and Robertson appeal to millions of
people. What desires do they summons and promise to satisfy?

Robertson appeals to the "wealth of wants and expectations
which our society has fashioned" for all of us.[35] He endorses material
consumption and subjectivism and thus validates the hedonistic or
narcissistic qualities of modern society. The "700 Club," with its
Kingdom Principles and prosperity gospel, rejects the traditional
asceticism of orthodox Christianity. It acknowledges the emotional
and psychological strains of contemporary society and offers
Christian solutions that promise happiness, well-being, "emotional balance," and, not coincidentally, material success. In this respect,
Robertson's religious system is well adapted to the modern social situation. Through an accommodation to modernity, this version of evangelicalism has managed to achieve "a contemporaneity of cultural
expression, more or less attendant to the sensitivities and 'needs' of
modern people."[36]

The format of the "700 Club" reflects this contemporary flavor;
it is formally indistinguishable from commercial television. This type
of religious programming, like the belief system it expresses, is no
longer fully "outside" the larger society. It has become instead one
among many lifestyle and programming choices—an assessment that
is echoed by several critics of evangelical television. In Horsfield's
words: "Rather than providing a religious alternative to other television programs, [evangelical] programs appear to have become sub-

merged in the television environment to the extent that they have become an indistinguishable part of it.[37] Or, as Fore puts it: "The values implicit in most successful electronic church programs are actually the values of the secular society it pretends to reject."[38] Luke concurs:

> Televangelism . . . has gained more visibility and influence only as it has dropped the trappings of religious ritual and more closely embraced the average consumers' secular talk-show/game-show/variety-show consciousness in its productions.[39]

Robertson's worldview appeals to people by seeking to transcend the outsider tension, showing them how to be "at home" in the modern world by actively transforming society in accordance with evangelical doctrine. Followers may then feel themselves to be both "inside" and superior to the dominant culture with the aid of a theology that promises to restore orthodox Protestantism's cultural centrality.

Swaggart, on the other hand, embraces the position of embattled outsider and appeals to people on this basis. His refusal to accommodate modernity and his demand for self-denial place his theology in tension with the broader culture. This tension is what fuels his belief system and perpetually recreates the terms of belonging between Swaggart and his followers, who feel themselves to be at odds with the dominant social values and seek explanations and justifications for this exclusion in his rhetoric. They feel themselves to be both "outside" of and superior to "the world." Believers are invited to enact these feelings in the ritual form of the revivals and to thus construct a community that protects them from the pressures of the dominant culture. Further, the tension implicit in trying to exist apart from "the world" is made less painful by the promise of achieving insider status in the next world. This is particularly comforting for older people who make up the majority of Swaggart's following. Forfeiting earthly happiness for eternal joy thus becomes an acceptable exchange, especially for people who find worldly satisfaction hard to come by.

These two versions of evangelicalism co-exist uneasily in contemporary society, as the PTL dispute and Swaggart's attacks on apostasy indicate. Whether this awkward co-habitation can continue indefinitely is open to question. Robertson's version of orthodox Christianity has been gaining in popularity, as has the religious programming associated with it. Swaggart's separatism, in contrast, is a less-common voice in evangelical broadcasting, which reflects a trend in evangelicalism generally.[40] I believe that the waning of Swaggart's traditional, separatist evangelicalism has to do with built-in limits to the social basis of its appeal. Its distinctly anti-modern character

makes this worldview much harder to maintain in the face of modernization; this is related as well to the powerful inroads into consciousness that have been made by consumer culture. This belief system is
most appealing to pockets of the population who are furthest removed
from modernizing forces—older people of lower education in rural
areas of the Southern Bible Belt and midwest. The largest portion of
its adherents are middle-aged and older. As these believers age and
die, and as the rural south and midwest come increasingly into the
orbit of modernization, it may be much harder to maintain the separation demanded by this theology. Further, Swaggart's brand of religion
is heavily dependent on charismatic preachers and evangelists to
effect salvation among followers, and these beacons on the road to
redemption are themselves the product of specific historical circumstances. The country preacher is a historical phenomenon, and social
and cultural changes may make him (or her) an endangered species.
That is, Swaggart and preachers like him may no longer find the proper social context in which to reproduce their roles and themselves.
This is already apparent with Swaggart's son, Donnie, who lacks his
father's charisma and rhetorical talents.[41]

THE EVOCATION OF DESIRE

Conservative evangelicalism may have so far survived the secularizing pressures of modernization precisely because it has preserved the
raw revivalist separatism of Swaggart, while also developing a more
contemporary expression in the smooth accommodation of
Robertson.[42] If the abrasive separatist pole becomes obsolete, will the
more palatable assimilative pole be able to carry on the core beliefs of
traditional Protestant orthodoxy? Or might conservative evangelicalism eventually be forced to adopt sweeping doctrinal changes to complement the deep cultural accommodations it has already internalized? Is it plausible that this contemporary form of evangelicalism will
ultimately lose its spiritual basis and evolve into a straightforward
political movement, an alternative lifestyle choice, or, in Luke's words,
a "consumption community"?[43] These questions can only be resolved
in history. But the current appeal of these two forms of religious belief
raises important concerns about the character of our society. The fact
that these two stories about the nature of the world—about the relationship between being and meaning—continue to resonate for a substantial number of Americans suggests that there are limits to the secular consumer society's ability to make people's lives meaningful.

To talk about meaning in this existential and transcendental sense in the secularized world of the academy is to risk being dismissed as nostalgic or essentialist. As Garrett puts it, modern social science finds it difficult indeed to deal with "troublesome transcendence."[44] I am going to take that risk, however, and side with Geertz in arguing that the quest for a meaning that transcends individual existence is fundamentally human—whether we call that quest religious or not. In Geertz's words, "The drive to make sense out of experience, to give it form and order, is evidently as real and as pressing as the more familiar biological needs."[45] While traditional societies (and many people today) look to religious symbolic systems to provide solutions to the problem of meaning, modern society has fashioned its own response through the "privileged institution" of the marketplace and advertising. I do not claim this is the only function of modern advertising, but simply that it is one way to look at the symbolic character of the contemporary "discourse through and about objects." In this sense, advertising operates as a metaphysical symbol system, or, in Williams's words, as a "magic system."[46]

Magic has to do with transformations that occur outside of conscious human action; it points to divine or supernatural intervention. Advertising operates as magic by investing things with the power to transform their consumers. It thereby implies the possibility of rebirth. Advertising's magical character is exhibited in its capacity to animate consumer objects—it makes goods "come alive," as Leiss et al. say.[47] The wish for magical transformation, however, implies an original desire to be other than what one is, to be born anew. Magic thus speaks to human desire and points to an initial lack. Drawing on Hegel, Davis argues that desire itself reveals "the radical lack of being at the heart of the [human] subject" and thus "introduces a fundamental instability into our relationship with the world."[48] How, then, do the marketplace and advertising propose to satisfy desire, and what transformations of self do they promise? Magic also connotes sleight of hand or deception, and Williams uses the term this way to suggest that advertising works by appealing to our needs (or to desire) and by convincing us they can be fulfilled through the consumption of goods. But as Davis points out, while desire may motivate us in pursuit of objects, we inevitably discover that the act of consuming things does not sate, but merely reignites desire: "Attainment breeds discontent because an 'I want' arises in the midst of all fulfillments. We repeatedly experience the desire for something else, something more." Indeed, repetitious consumption "introduces a vertigo into consciousness . . . in which we become indistinguishable from the objects we pursue."[49] That is, the self becomes a mere reflection of the goods with which it surrounds itself.

It is incorrect to say that advertising induces false needs in people; the needs to which advertising appeals are genuine. The sleight of hand involves the promise that those needs can be filled exclusively in the marketplace, thereby precluding other possible sources and sites of satisfaction. These genuine human desires, according to Williams, include the need for social relatedness, for respect and recognition, for avenues of expression and engagement that affect our social and natural environments.[50] Studies of "quality of life" and analyses of indexes of satisfaction report that people's sense of well-being is most strongly grounded in interpersonal relations, or in "nonmaterial" goods, rather than in the acquisition of things. Consumer society, however, "encourages individuals to express all their wants as wants for goods and services, that is, commodities," despite the fact that commodities are "only weakly related to the things that make people happy: autonomy, self-esteem, family felicity, tension-free leisure, friendships. This is a major defect in a want-satis-fying mechanism."[51]

Consumer society deals with this defect by pulling more and more social and natural elements into the sphere of commodity exchange. The marketplace fails to make good its promise of ultimate satisfaction, however, because consumer culture depends on the constant reproduction of desire, which can then be channeled toward objects. Thus, if we were truly satisfied, we would fail to be good consumers. Desire does not originate in the modern marketplace, however; it only takes on specific social and historical characteristics there. As Ewen argues, "there are wishes and needs which are generated in spite of the marketplace, yet the marketplace purports to address them."[52] Chasing after objects fails to deliver us from the lack that motivates desire, Davis says, because for satisfaction to occur, "it must survive the moment of consumption."[53] The endless pursuit of objects is futile, because the satisfaction we seek is not quantitative but qualitative: The "defining human desire" is not about "the absence of new objects" but about "the desire for recognition." Thus, human desire is "inherently interpersonal."[54] Indeed, the human needs that Williams points to all involve some form of social connectedness to and recognition from others. The wish for identity, significance, and well-being through a relationship to others is characteristic of the human quest for being and meaning. The discourse of the marketplace beckons to this desire for meaning from behind the latest product or lifestyle. It appeals, Ewen says, by promising to deliver the "real thing." But at the same time, by appealing to deep human desires, advertising also implicity contains the message that the product "isn't the real thing after all; and what is more, people do feel the need for the actual real thing."[55]

The gospel of prosperity heightens the promise of the "real

thing" by sacralizing the language and values of consumption. Swaggart's theology, in contrast, tries to strip the magic from the marketplace by exposing its inability to supply what he sees as the true object of desire—divine communion and eternal life. Each of these symbolic universes—Robertson's, Swaggart's, and that of the marketplace—derive their persuasive power from the fact that human beings desire the "real thing" in the first place. The endurance and adaptability of these two versions of religious belief suggest that the modern symbolic system of consumption is an inadequate source of being and meaning for a significant number of people. Indeed, Williams says, the "magic system" of advertising attempts to reconcile us to the fact that "the meanings and values generally operative in society give no answers to, no means of negotiating, the problems of death, loneliness, frustration and the need for identity."[56] Evangelicalism is not alone in proposing alternatives to the dominant values and symbols of consumer society. An array of contemporary social, political, and religious groups are also in the process of fashioning interpretations about the nature of existing society and possible alternatives to it. All of these "stories" meet in the conflictual terrain of history where they constitute a field of contending definitions about what is meaningful and what is not.

THE FLIGHT OF FAITH

To take seriously the worldview of conservative evangelicalism—to "grasp hold of the meanings people build into their words and behavior and make these meanings, these claims about life and experience, explicit and articulate"—is to also raise questions about the nature of modern religiosity.[57] What kind of society makes the theologies of Swaggart and Robertson a viable cultural option? Does a society produce the forms of religion it deserves? If human beings do need frames of orientation and devotion in order to conduct their lives meaningfully, are there "sacred canopies" preferable to conservative Christianity? Are there forms of faith, or metaphysical symbolic systems, that are not reactionary flights into the past or uncritical celebrations of the present, but that create the possibility of authentic, liberatory social relationships in the future? How should the secular academy approach the study of religion if its present methods and conceptual frameworks are ill-equipped to deal with these questions and with the troublesome problem of transcendence? Or, has history already rendered transcendence an obsolete concern?
  Smith suggests that the historical rationalization of culture in

the West has replaced faith—an orientation of being toward reality—
with belief—an attitude toward propositions about reality. In the modern context, to be a believer means one has accepted the truth value
of a set of propositions; failure to accept those truth claims constitutes disbelief. Doctrine, therefore, becomes determinate in establishing the conditions for belonging. This, in turn, creates a radical separation between insiders and outsiders, between believers and nonbelievers, and makes the defense of doctrine a primary goal of religion.
Smith argues that to understand belief in this way is to already con-
cede to the rationalization and privatization of religiosity. To counter
this view of religion, he contrasts belief, which is a property of doctrine, to faith, which is a quality of the person. Rather than dividing
people along doctrinal lines, faith offers the potential for unity and
interpersonal connectedness because it is not exclusionary. Faith,
Smith says,

> is an orientation of the personality, to oneself, to one's neighbour,
> to the universe; . . . a capacity to live at a more than mundane
> level, to see, to feel, to act in terms of, a transcendent dimension . . .
> Faith is a quality of human living. At its best it has taken the form
> of serenity and courage and loyalty and service: a quiet confidence
> and joy which enable one to feel at home in the universe, and to
> find meaning in the world and in one's own life, a meaning that is
> profound and ultimate, and is stable no matter what may happen
> to oneself at the level of the immediate event.[58]

The failure of the modern market-industrial society to provide satisfying answers to the problems of being and meaning, I believe, lies in its
incompatibility with such faith. As Smith says, "The West has devised,
as one of its major specialities, the notion that faith does not really
matter." Modern society is predicated on the view that religious belief
is a private, socially inconsequential concern, and "that what human
beings have in common is the non-religious, the non-transcendent—
this is the contemporary orthodoxy."[59] The absence of faith produces
a world without meaning in this deeper sense, a society characterized
by an attitude of nihilism, or "a bleak inability to find either the world
around one, or one's own life, significant."[60] Because human beings, as
symbol-using animals, cannot endure meaninglessness for long, they
create meaning from the available cultural options. In modern society,
those options are primarily secular. Contemporary religious responses to the secularization of meaning have tended toward accommodation to, or reactionary rejection of, the surrounding dominant culture
of consumption. Neither route, it seems to me, has been particularly
successful at dealing with the flight of faith.

The theologies of Swaggart and Robertson, while premised on the defense and maintenance of belief, must operate in a social environment that has, for the most part, abolished faith. In this respect, evangelical Christianity is already a victim of the Enlightenment. Heidegger once characterized the post-Enlightenment world as suffering from a "double lack": "the No-more of the gods that have fled and the Not-yet of the god that is coming."[61] Swaggart's ethos and worldview are attached to the shadow of an already departed deity; Robertson's god is indistinguishable from a successful businessman; and modern consumer society fashions its own gods in the form of goods that "come alive." Whether there are other gods on the horizon will be determined by the resiliency of human faith, by the kinds of strategies we select to set forth new cultural options, and by the meanings we make of the meanings we are given.

NOTES TO CHAPTER 10

1. William Roseberry, *Anthropologies and Histories; Essays in Culture, History and Political Economy* (New Brunswick and London: Rutgers University Press, 1989), p. 58.

2. This argument is developed in Wilfred Cantwell Smith, *Belief and History* (Charlottesville: University of Virginia Press, 1977).

3. As Harvey argues, "The Enlightenment project . . . took it as axiomatic that there was only one possible answer to any question. From this it followed that the world could be controlled and rationally ordered if we could only picture and represent it rightly." In *Condition of Postmodernity* (London and Cambridge, MA: Basil Blackwell, 1989), p. 27.

4. William Leiss makes this argument in *The Domination of Nature* (New York: G. Braziller, 1972).

5. This critique is elaborated in Max Horkheimer and T. W. Adorno, *Dialectic of Enlightenment*, translated by John Cumming (London: Continuum, 1986, c. 1972).

6. Wilfred Cantwell Smith, *Faith and Belief* (Princeton, NJ: Princeton University Press, 1979), p. 150.

7. This is a key theme in William Leiss, Stephen Kline, and Sut Jhally, *Social Communication in Advertising: Persons, Products and Images of Well-being* (Toronto: Methuen, 1986), especially pp. 270-277.

8. Ibid., p. 273.

9. Ibid., p. 263.

10. Ibid., p. 239.

11. Ibid., pp. 340, 239.

12. Leiss et al use this phrase to describe advertising. Ibid., p. 3. See also Sut Jhally, "Advertising as Religion: The Dialectic of Technology and Magic," in Ian Angus and Sut Jhally, eds., *Cultural Politics in Contemporary America* (New York and London: Routledge, 1989), pp. 271-229.

13. Ibid., p. 238.

14. Ibid.

15. Harvey, *The Condition of Postmodernity.*

16. Ibid., p. 234.

17. This point is made beautifully in John Berger (and others), *Ways of Seeing* (London: British Broadcasting Corp.; Harmondsworth: Penguin, 1978, c. 1972).

18. For a discussion of psychoanalysis as a critique of capitalism, and of the relationship between capitalism and the formation of subjectivity, see Joel Kovel, *The Age of Desire: Reflections of a Radical Psychoanlyst* (New York: Pantheon, 1981), especially Chapter 6, "Desire and the Transhistorical;" and Walter Davis, *Inwardness and Existence: Subjectivity In/And Hegel, Heidegger, Marx and Freud* (Madison: University of Wisconsin Press, 1989).

19. "The Jimmy Swaggart Telecast," October 26, 1986; April 12, 1987.

20. "Jimmy Swaggart Telecast," April 12, 1987.

21. Ken Wilber, "The Spectrum Model," in Dick Anthony, Bruce Ecker, and Ken Wilber, eds., *Spiritual Choices: The Problems of Recognizing Authentic Paths to Spiritual Transformation* (New York: Paragon), p. 244.

22. Dick Anthony and Bruce Ecker, "The Anthony Typology: A Framework for Assessing Spiritual and Consciousness Groups," in D. Anthony, B. Ecker, and K. Wilber, *Spiritual Choices*, p. 92; see also pp. 80-81.

23. Ibid.

24. "700 Club," July 8, 1985.

25. Alan Crawford, *Thunder on the Right: The 'New Right' and the Politics of Resentment* (New York: Pantheon, 1980), p. 161.

26. Michael Leinesch, "Right-wing Religion: Christian Conservatism as a Political Movement," *Political Science Quarterly* 97 (3) (Fall 1982): pp. 403-425.

27. Ibid., p. 413.

28. Ibid., p. 415.

29. George Thomas, *Revivalism and Cultural Change* (Chicago: Chicago University Press, 1989), pp. 2, 28.

30. Ibid., p. 414.

31. Ibid., p. 419.

32. Bill Moyers examined the battle within the Southern Baptist Convention in his three-part televised series on religion, "God and Politics." The SBC in the last 10 years has increasingly come under control of the right-wing fundamentalist elements, and some Baptists are now predicting that the Convention will splinter into two factions. KCTS-TV, Channel 9, "The Battle for the Bible," December 16, 1987, Seattle.

33. Leinesch, "Right-wing Religion," pp. 420-421. This was apparent in Robertson's presidential campaign. Many political analysts doubted that his candidacy would significantly affect the Republican Party unless he were to actually win the nomination because a large number of Robertson's supporters would not vote for a non-Christian, Republican or not.

34. Ibid., p. 425.

35. Robert Merton with Marjorie Fiske and Alberta Curtis, *Mass Persuasion* (Westport, CT: Greenwood Press, 1946, p. 11.

36. James Hunter, "Subjectivization and the New Evangelical Theodicy," *Journal for the Scientific Study of Religion* 20 (1982): p. 46.

37. Peter Horsfield, *Religious Television: The American Experience* (New York: Longman, 1984), p. 35.

38. William Fore, *Television and Religion* (Minneapolis: Augsberg, 1987), p. 113.

39. Timothy W. Luke, *Screens of Power: Ideology, Domination, and Resistance in Informational Society* (Urbana and Chicago: University of Illinois Press, 1989), p. 97.

40. Ibid., p. 46; See also J. Thomas Bisset, "Religious Broadcasting: Assessing the State of the Art," *Christianity Today*, December 12, 1980, p. 31.

41. Jimmy Swaggart Ministries may also recognize Donnie's inability to follow in his father's footsteps—the ministry has chosen to air reruns of Swaggart's old crusades rather than send Donnie on the crusade trail.

42. I am indebted to William Leiss for this characterization.

43. Luke, *Screens of Power*, p. 88.

44. William R. Garrett, "Troublesome Transcendence: The Supernatural in the Scientific Study of Religion," *Sociological Analysis* 35 (3) (1974): pp. 167-180.

45. Clifford Geertz, "Ethos, World-view and the Analysis of Sacred Symbols," *Antioch Review* (December 1957): p. 436.

46. Raymond Williams, "Advertising: The Magic System," in R. Williams, *Problems in Materialism and Culture* (London: Verso, 1980), pp. 170-195.

47. Leiss et al., *Communication in Advertising*, pp. 259-263.

48. Walter Davis, *Inwardness and Existence* (Madison: University of

Wisconsin Press, 1989), p. 28.

49. Ibid., p. 27.

50. Williams, "The Magic System," pp. 185-190.

51. First quote from Leiss et al., *Communication in Advertising*, p. 252; second quote from Robert E. Lane, "Markets and the Satisfaction of Human Wants," *Journal of Economic Issues* 12 (1978): p. 815, in op. cit, p. 252.

52. Stuart Ewen, *Captains of Consciousness: Advertising and the Social Roots of the Consumer Culture* (New York: McGraw-Hill, 1970), p. 189.

53. Davis, *Inwardness and Existence*, p. 31.

54. Ibid., pp. 32, 30.

55. Ewen, Captains of Consciousenss, p. 189.

56. Williams, "The Magic System," p. 190.

57. James Carey, "Mass Communication Research and Cultural Studies: An American View," in J. Curran, M. Gurevitch, and J. Woollacott, eds., *Mass Communication and Society* (Beverly Hills, CA: Sage, 1979), p. 421.

58. Smith, *Faith and Belief*, p. 12.

59. Ibid., p. 139.

60. Ibid., p. 13.

61. Martin Heidegger, *Existence and Being* (Chicago: Henry Regnery Co., 1949; 1967, 5th ptg.), p. 289.

Bibliography

Alhstrom, Sydney. "From Puritanism to Evangelicalism: A Critical Perspective." In *The Evangelicals*, pp. 269-289. Edited by D. F. Wells and J. D. Woodbridge. Nashville: Abingdon, 1975.

Altheide, David L. and John M. Johnson. "Counting Souls: A Study of Counseling at Evangelical Crusades." *Pacific Sociological Review* 20 (July 1977): 323-348.

Altheide, David L. and Robert P. Snow. *Media Logic*. Beverly Hills: Sage, 1979.

Amin, Samir. *Eurocentrism*. New York: Monthly Review Press, 1989.

"An Unholy War in the TV Pulpits." *U.S. News and World Report*, April 6, 1987, pp. 58-65.

Andrew, Dudley. *Concepts in Film Theory*. New York and Oxford: Oxford University Press, 1984.

Anthony, Dick and Bruce Ecker. "The Anthony Typology." In *Spiritual Choices*, pp. 35-105. Edited by D. Anthony, B. Ecker and K. Wilber. New York: Paragon House, 1987.

Anthony, Dick, Bruce Ecker, and Ken Wilber. *Spiritual Choices: The Problems of Recognizing Authentic Paths to Spiritual Transformation*. New York: Paragon House, 1987.

Applebome, Peter. "Swaggart's Troubles Show Tension of Passion and Power in TV Evangelism." *New York Times*, February 28, 1988, p. A30.

Applebome, Peter. "Scandals Aside, TV Preachers Thrive." *New York Times*, October 8, 1988, p. A24.

Armstrong, Ben. *The Electric Church*. Nashville: Thomas Nelson Publishing, 1979.

Aufderheide, Pat. "The Next Voice You Hear." *Progressive*, September 29, 1985, pp. 34-37.

"Back to the Oldtime Religion." *Time*, December 26, 1977, pp. 52-58.
Barnes, Fred. "Rarin' to Go." *New Republic*, September 29, 1986, pp. 14-15.
Bellah, Robert, Richard Madsen, William Sullivan, Ann Swidler and Steven Tipton. *Habits of the Heart*. Berkeley: University of California Press, 1985.
Bennett, Tony. "Theories of Media, Theories of Society." In *Culture, Society and the Media*, pp. 30-55. Edited by Michael Gurevitch, Tony Bennett, James Curran and Janet Woollacott. London: Methuen, 1982.
Bennett, W. Lance. *News: The Politics of Illusion*. New York and London: Longman, 1983.
Berger, John, and others. *Ways of Seeing*. London: British Broadcasting Corp., Harmondsworth: Penguin, 1978, c. 1972.
Berger, Peter. *The Sacred Canopy: Elements of a Sociological Theory of Religion*. Garden City, NY: Doubleday, 1967.
Berman, Marshall. *All That is Solid Melts Into Air: The Experience of Modernity*. New York: Simon & Schuster, 1982.
Bisset, J. Thomas. "Religious Broadcasting: Assessing the State of the Art." *Christianity Today*, December 12, 1980, pp. 28-31.
Blasi, Anthony. "Ritual as a Form of Religious Mentality." *Sociological Analysis* 46 (1) (1985): 59-72.
Blumhofer, Edith. "Swaggart and the Pentecostal Ethos." *Christian Century*, April 6, 1988, pp. 333-335.
Blumler, Jay and Elihu Katz, eds. *The Uses of Mass Communication*. Beverly Hills: Sage, 1974.
Bourgault, Louise. "The 'PTL Club' and Protestant Viewers: An Ethnographic Study." *Journal of Communication* 35 (Winter 1985): 132-148.
Brake, Mike. *The Sociology of Youth Culture and Youth Subcultures*. London: Routledge and Kegan Paul, 1980.
Braverman, Harry. *Labor and Monopoly Capital: The Degradation of Work in the Twentieth Century*. New York: Monthly Review Press, 1974.
Burke, Kenneth. *Language as Symbolic Action*. Berkeley: University of California Press, 1966.
Burke, Kenneth. *Philosophy of Literary Form*. 2nd ed. Baton Rouge: Louisiana State University Press, 1967.
Burke, Kenneth. *Counter-Statement*. Berkeley: University of California Press, 1968.
Burke, Kenneth. *Permanence and Change: An Anatomy of Purpose*. Berkeley: University of California Press, 1969.
Burke, Kenneth. *Rhetoric of Motives*. Berkeley: University of California Press, 1969.
Burke, Kenneth. *Rhetoric of Religion; Studies in Logology*. Berkeley: University of California Press, 1970.
Bushman, Richard. *From Puritan to Yankee; Character and the Social Order in Connecticut, 1690-1765*. Cambridge: Harvard University Press, 1967.

Carey, James W. "Canadian Communication Theory: Extensions and Interpretations of Harold Innis." In *Studies in Canadian Communications*, pp. 27-59. Edited by G. Robinson and D. F. Theall. Montreal: McGill University Press, 1975.

Carey, James W. "Mass Communication Research and Cultural Studies: An American View." In *Mass Communication and Society*, pp. 409-425. Edited by James Curran, Michael Gurevitch and Janet Woollacott. Beverly Hills: Sage, 1979.

Carey, James W. "Culture, Geography, and Communications: The Work of H. A. Innis in an American Context." In *Culture, Communication and Dependency*, pp. 73-91. Edited by William Melody, Liora Salter and Paul Heyer. Norwood, NJ: Ablex, 1981.

Carpenter, Joel A. "Fundamentalist Institutions and the Rise of Evangelicalism." *Church History* 49 (March 1980): 62-75.

Carpenter, Joel A. "From Fundamentalism to the New Evangelical Coalition." In *Evangelicalism and Modern America*, pp. 3-16. Edited by George Marsden. Grand Rapids: Eerdmans, 1984.

Carter, Paul A. "The Fundamentalist Defense of Faith." In *Change and Continuity in Twentieth-Century America: The 1920s*, pp. 179-214. Edited by J. Braemen, R. Bremner and D. Brody. Columbus: Ohio State University Press, 1968.

Cathcart, Robert. "Defining Social Movements by their Rhetorical Form." *Central States Speech Journal* 31 (Winter 1980): 266-273.

Chapple, Steve. "Whole Lotta Savin' Going On." *Mother Jones*, July/August 1985, pp. 37-45, 86.

Chodorow, Nancy. *The Reproduction of Mothering: Psychoanalysis and the Sociology of Gender.* Berkeley: University of California Press, 1978.

Clark, David W. and Paul H. Virts. "Religious Television Audience: A New Development in Measuring Audience Size." Paper presented at the Center for the Scientific Study of Religion. Savannah, Georgia, October 25, 1985.

Clark, Kenneth R. "'Christian News' a CBN Objective." *Chicago Tribune*, July 26, 1985, Sect. 5, p. 3.

Clark, Kenneth R. "The $70 Miracle Named CBN." *Chicago Tribune*, July 26, 1985, Sect. 5, pp. 1, 3.

Clendinen, Dudley. "'Christian New Right's' Rush to Power." *New York Times*, August 18, 1980, p. B7.

Clendinen, Dudley. "Pat Robertson Looks to South and Evangelicals as Key to 1988." *New York Times*, June 24, 1986, p. 8.

Clendinen, Dudley. "Robertson's Camp Hopes to Capture Vast TV Evangelical Vote in Nation." *New York Times*, September 30, 1986, p. B4.

Clendinen, Dudley. "Challenging Humanism in Answer to God's Call." *New York Times*, October 17, 1986, p. 8.

Clymer, Adam. "Religious-oriented Right-wing Group Plans Drive." *New York Times*, April 12, 1981, p. 13.

Clymer, Adam. "Survey Finds Many Skeptics Among Evangelical

Viewers." *New York Times*, March 31, 1987, pp. 1, 14.

Conason, Joe. "The Religious Right's Quiet Revival." *Nation*, April 27, 1992, pp. 541, 553-556, 558-559.

Conway, Flo and Jim Siegelman. *Holy Terror: The Fundamentalist War on America's Freedoms in Religion, Politics and Our Private Lives.* Garden City, NJ: Doubleday, 1982.

Crawford, Alan. *Thunder on the Right: The "New Right" and the Politics of Resentment.* New York: Pantheon, 1980.

Crowley, David and Paul Heyer. *Communication and History: Technology, Culture, Society.* New York: Longman, 1991.

Dabney, Dick. "God's Own Network." *Harper's*, August 1980, pp. 33- 52.

Davis, Walter. *The Act of Interpretation.* Chicago: University of Chicago Press, 1978.

Davis, Walter. *Inwardness and Existence: Subjectivity In/And Hegel, Heidegger, Marx and Freud.* Madison: University of Wisconsin Press, 1989.

DeMar, Gary and Peter Leihart. *The Reduction of Theology: Dave Hunt's Theology of Cultural Surrender.* Ft. Worth: Dominion Press, 1988.

Diamond, Edwin. "God's Television." *In Television and American Culture*, pp. 78-87. Edited by Karl Love. New York: W. Wilson, 1981.

Diamond, Sara. "Preacher Pat for Prez?" *Mother Jones*, January 1986, p. 8.

Diamond, Sara. "Pat on the Head." *Nation*, February 13, 1988, pp. 207-208.

Duncan, Hugh Dalziel. *Communication and Social Order.* New York: Bedminster Press, 1962.

Dunne, Mike. "Swaggart to Oversee Troubled Empire Upon Return to Pulpit." *Baton Rouge Morning Advocate*, May 22, 1988, pp. 7-8.

Dunne, Mike. "Swaggart TV Rating Nose-Dive." *Baton Rouge Morning Advocate*, June 28, 1988, p. 1.

Eagleton, Terry. *Literary Theory.* Minneapolis: University of Minnesota Press, 1983.

Ehrenreich, Barbara, Elizabeth Hess, and Gloria Jacobs. "Unbuckling the Bible Belt." *Mother Jones*, July/August 1986, pp. 46-51, 78.

Eisenstein, Elizabeth. *The Printing Press as an Agent of Change: Communications and Cultural Transformations in Early-Modern Europe.* 2 vols. Cambridge: Cambridge University Press, 1979.

Eisenstein, Elizabeth. "The Emergence of Print Culture in the West." *Journal of Communication* 30 (Winter 1980): 99-106.

Ellens, J. Harold. *Models of Religious Broadcasting.* Grand Rapids, MI: Eerdmans, 1974.

Ellis, John. *Visible Fictions.* London: RKP, 1982.

"Evangelists Fear Controversies Will Damage the Cause." *Seattle Times*, March 25, 1987, p. A3.

Ewen, Stuart. *Captains of Consciousness: Advertising and the Social Roots of Consumer Culture.* New York: McGraw-Hill, 1976.

Farah, Joseph. "TV's Assault on Families is No Joke." *Focus on the Family*, November 1990, pp. 9-11.

Finch, Susan. "Swaggart Ministries Going Off the Air." *(New Orleans)*

Times-Picayune, October 26, 1991, pp. A1, 9.

Fiske, John. "British Cultural Studies and Television." In *Channels of Discourse*, pp. 254-289. Edited by Robert C. Allen. Chapel Hill and London: University of North Carolina Press, 1987.

FitzGerald, Frances. *Cities on a Hill: A Journey through Contemporary American Cultures*. New York: Simon and Schuster, 1986.

Fitzpatrick, Tim. "Money Keeps Pouring in to Televangelists, Expert Says." *Salt Lake Tribune*, October 28, 1989, p. 11.

Fore, William. "Religion and Television: Report on the Research." *Christian Century*, July 18-25, 1984, pp. 710-713.

Fore, William F. *Television and Religion: The Shaping of Faith, Values, and Culture*. Minneapolis: Augsburg, 1987.

Frame, Randy. "Surviving the Slump." *Christianity Today*, February 3, 1989, pp. 32-34.

Frankl, Razelle. *Televangelism: The Marketing of Popular Religion*. Carbondale: Southern Illinois University Press, 1987.

Fromm, Erich. *Man for Himself*. Greenwich, CT: Fawcett, 1947.

Garrett, William R. "Troublesome Transcendence: The Supernatural in the Scientific Study of Religion." *Sociological Analysis* 35 (3) (1974): 167-180.

Garrison, Greg. "After the Fall: Swaggart Preaches to Dwindling Flock." *Birmingham News*, May 7, 1989, pp. 9-11.

Geertz, Clifford. "Ethos, World-view and the Analysis of Sacred Symbols." *Antioch Review* (December 1957): 421-437.

Geertz, Clifford. "Ritual and Social Change: A Javanese Example." In *Reader in Comparative Religion: An Anthropological Approach*, 2nd. ed., pp. 547-559. Edited by William A. Lessa and Evon Z. Vogt. New York: Harper and Row, 1965.

Geertz, Clifford. "Deep Play: Notes on the Balinese Cockfight." In *Myth, Symbol and Culture*, pp. 1-37. Edited by C. Geertz. New York: W. W. Norton, 1971.

Geertz, Clifford. *The Interpretation of Cultures*. New York: Basic Books, 1973.

Geertz, Clifford. "Religion as a Cultural System." In *Reader in Comparative Religion*, 4th ed., pp. 78-89. Edited by William A. Lessa and Evon Z. Vogt. New York: Harper and Row, 1979.

Gerbner, George with Kathleen Connolly. "Television as New Religion." *New Catholic World*, March/April 1978, pp. 52-56.

Gerbner, George, Larry Gross, Stuart Hoover, M. Morgan, Nancy Signorielli, H. Cotugno, and Robert. Wuthnow. *Religion and Television, A Research Report by the Annenberg School of Communications, University of Pennsylvania and the Gallup Organization, Inc.* Philadelphia: Annenberg School of Communications, University of Pennsylvania, April 1984.

Gerlach, Luther P. and Virginia H. Hine. "Five Factors Crucial to the Growth and Spread of a Modern Religious Movement." *Journal for the Scientific Study of Religion* 7 (1) (1968): 23-40.

Gerlach, Luther and Virginia Hine. *People, Power, Change: Movements of Social Transformation*. Indianapolis: Bobbs Merrill, 1970.

Gitlin, Todd. "Prime Time Ideology: The Hegemonic Process in Television Entertainment." *Social Problems* 26 (February 1979): 251-266.

Gitlin, Todd. *The Whole World is Watching: Mass Media in the Making and Unmaking of the New Left*. Berkeley: University of California Press, 1980.

Gitlin, Todd. "Television's Screens: Hegemony in Transition." In *Cultural and Economic Reproduction in Education*, pp. 202-246. Edited by Michael Apple. London: Routledge and Kegan Paul, 1982.

Gitlin, Todd. *Inside Prime Time*. New York: Pantheon, 1983, 1985.

"God and Money." *Newsweek*, April 6, 1987, pp. 16-22.

Goethals, Gregor. *The TV Ritual: Worship at the Video Altar*. Boston: Beacon Press, 1981.

Goethals, Gregor. "Religious Communication and Popular Piety." *Journal of Communication* 35 (Winter 1985): 149-156.

Goethals, Gregor. *The Electronic Golden Calf: Images, Religion, and the Making of Meaning*. Cambridge, MA: Cowley Publications, 1990.

Graham, Lamar. "700 Club." *Norfolk Virginian-Pilot*, August 2, 1988, pp. 9-11.

Grassi, Ernest. *Rhetoric as Philosophy: The Humanist Tradition*. University Park and London: Penn State University Press, 1980, pp. 103-104.

Griffin, Leland. "A Dramatistic Theory of the Rhetoric of Social Movements." In *Critical Responses to Kenneth Burke*, pp. 456-478. Edited by William Reuckart. Minneapolis: University of Minnesota Press, 1969.

Grossberg, Lawrence. "The Circulation of Cultural Studies." *Critical Studies in Mass Communication*, 6 (1989): 413-420.

Grossberg, Lawrence and Paula Treichler. "Intersections of Power: Criticism, Television, Gender." *Communication*, 9 (1987): 273-287.

Guth, James, L. "The Politics of the 'Evangelical Right': An Interpretive Essay," paper presented to the American Political Science Association Annual Meeting, September 1981, p. 1.

Hadden, Jeffrey K. "Getting to the Bottom of the Audience Size Debate." *Christianity Today*, February 22, 1980, pp. 88, 116, 122-126.

Hadden, Jeffrey K. "Soul-Saving Via Video." *Christian Century*, May 28, 1980, pp. 609-613.

Hadden, Jeffrey K. and Charles E. Swann. *Prime Time Preachers: The Rising Power of Televangelism*. Reading, MA: Addison Wesley, 1981.

Hadden, Jeffrey K. "The Great Audience Size Debate." *Religious Broadcasting*, January 1986, pp. 20-22.

Hahn, Dan F. and Ruth M. Gonchar. "Studying Social Movements: A Rhetorical Methodology." *The Speech Teacher* 20 (1971): 44-52.

Hall, Stuart. "Cultural Studies: Two Paradigms." *Media, Culture and Society*, 2 (1980): 57-72.

Hall, Stuart. "Encoding/Decoding." In *Culture, Media, Language*, pp. 128-138. Edited by Stuart Hall, Dorothy Hobson, Andrew Lowe and Paul Willis. London: Hutchinson, 1980.

Hall, Stuart. "Recent Developments in Theories of Language and Ideology: A Critical Note." In *Culture, Media, Language*, pp. 157-162. Edited by Stuart Hall, Dorothy Hobson, Andrew Lowe and Paul Willis. London: Hutchinson, 1980.

Hall, Stuart and Tony Jefferson. *Resistance Through Rituals*. London: Hutchinson, 1978.

Halsell, Grace. *Prophecy and Politics: Militant Evangelists on the Road to Nuclear War*. Westport, CT: Lawrence Hill, 1986.

Harrell, David. *Pat Robinson: A Personal, Political and Religious Portrait*. New York: Harper & Row, 1988.

Harvey, David. *The Condition of Postmodernity*. London and Cambridge: Basil Blackwell, 1990.

"Heart To Heart" (with Sheila Walsh). The Family Channel, Channel 28, Minneapolis, Minnesota.

Hebdige, Dick. *Subculture: The Meaning of Style*. London: Methuen, 1979.

Heidegger, Martin. *Existence and Being*. 5th ptg. Chicago: Henry Regnery Co., 1967; c. 1947.

Heiler, Freidrich. *Prayer: A Study in the History and Psychology of Religion*. Translated by Samuel M. Comb. London: Oxford University Press, 1932.

Heinz, Donald. "The Struggle to Redefine America." In *The New Christian Right*, pp. 133-148. Edited by Robert Liebman and Robert Wuthnow. New York: Aldine, 1983.

Heschel, Abraham. *Who Is Man?* Stanford: Stanford University Press, 1968.

Hill, Christopher. *Reformation to Industrial Revolution, 1530-1780*. 6th ptg. New York: Penguin, 1978.

Hill, George H. and Lenwood Davis. *Religious Broadcasting, 1920- 1983: A Selectively Annotated Bibliography*. New York: Garland, 1984.

Hill, Samuel S. and Dennis E Owen. *The New Religious Political Right in America*. Nashville: Abingdon, 1982.

Hoover, Stewart M. "Television Myths and Ritual: The Role of Substantive Meaning and Spatiality." Philadelphia, March 6, 1987. (Mimeographed).

Hoover, Stewart. *Mass Media Religion: The Social Sources of the Electronic Church*. Newbury Park, CA: Sage, 1988.

Horkheimer, Max and Theodor W Adorno. *Dialectic of Enlightenment*. Translated by John Cumming. New York: Continuum, 1986; c. 1972.

Horsfield, Peter. *Religious Television: The American Experience*. New York: Longman, 1984.

Horsfield, Peter. "Evangelicalism by Mail: Letters from the Broadcasters." *Journal of Communication* 35 (1985): 89-97.

Horton, Donald and R. Richard Wohl. "Mass Communication and Para-

Social Interaction: Observations on Intimacy at a Distance." In *Drama in Life: The Uses of Communication in Society*, pp. 212-228. Edited by James E. Combs and Michael W. Mansfield. New York: Hastings House, 1976.

Hunt, David. *The Seduction of Christianity*. Eugene, OR: Harvest House, 1985.

Hunter, James D. "Subjectivization and the New Evangelical Theodicy." *Journal for the Scientific Study of Religion* 20 (1) (1982): 39-47.

Hunter, James Davison. *American Evangelicalism: Conservative Religion and the Quandary of Modernity*. New Brunswick: Rutgers University Press, 1983.

Huntington, Deborah and Ruth Kaplan. "Whose God is Behind the Altar? Corporate Ties to Evangelicals." *Contemporary Marxism* 4 (Winter 1981-82): 62-94.

Hyde, Lewis. *The Gift: Imagination and the Erotic Life of Property*. New York: Vintage, 1983; c. 1979.

Illouz, Eva. "Reason Within Passion: Love in Women's Magazines." *Critical Studies in Mass Communication* 8 (1991): 231-248.

Innis, Harold A. *Empire and Communication*. Oxford: Clarendon, 1950.

Innis, Harold A. *The Bias of Communication*. Toronto: University of Toronto Press, 1964.

Jameson, Fredric. *The Prison-House of Language: A Critical Account of Structuralism and Russian Formalism*. Princeton: Princeton University Press, 1972.

Jameson, Fredric. "Criticism in History." In *Weapons of Criticism, Marxism in America and the Literary Tradition*, pp. 31-50. Edited by N. Rudich. Palo Alto: Ramparts Press, 1976.

Jameson, Fredric. "The Symbolic Inference; or, Kenneth Burke and Ideological Analysis." *Critical Inquiry*, 4 (1978): 507-523.

Jhally, Sut. "Advertising as Religion: The Dialectic of Technology and Magic." In *Cultural Politics in Contemporary America*, pp. 217-229. Edited by Ian Angus and Sut Jhally. New York and London: Routledge, 1989.

Johnson, James Weldon. *God's Trombones*. New York: Penguin, 1985.

Johnson, Richard. "What Is Cultural Studies Anyway?" *Social Text*, 16 (1986): 38-80.

Jorstad, Erling. "The Church in the World: The New Christian Right." *Theology Today* 38 (1981): 193-200.

Kelley, Dean M. *Why Conservative Churches are Growing*. New York: Harper and Row, 1972.

Kelley, Dean M. "Why Conservative Churches are Still Growing." *Journal for the Scientific Study of Religion* 17 (2) (1978): 165-172,

Kennedy, George. *New Testament Interpretation Through Rhetorical Criticism*. Chapel Hill and London: University of North Carolina Press, 1984.

Kickham, Larry. "Holy Spirit or Holy Spook?" *Covert Action Information Bulletin* 27 (Spring 1987): 15-17.

Kovel, Joel. *The Age of Desire: Reflections of a Radical Psychoanlyst.* New York: Pantheon, 1981.

Lane, Robert E. "Markets and the Satisfaction of Human Wants," *Journal of Economic Issues* 12(1978), p. 815.

Lears, T. Jackson. "From Salvation to Self-Realization: Advertising and the Therapeutic Roots of the Consumer Culture, 1880-1930." In *The Culture of Consumption: Critical Essays in American History, 1880-1980,* pp. 3-38. Edited by R. W. Fox and T. J. Lears. New York: Pantheon, 1983.

Lechner, Frank J. "Fundamentalism and Sociological Revitalization in America: A Sociological Interpretation." *Sociological Analysis* 46 (3) (1985): 243-260.

Leinesch, Michael. "Right-wing Religion: Christian Conservatism as a Political Movement." *Political Science Quarterly* 97 (3) (Fall 1982): 403-425.

Leiss, William. *The Domination of Nature.* New York: G. Braziller, 1972.

Leiss, William, Stephen Kline, and Sut Jhally. *Social Communication in Advertising: Persons, Products and Images of Well-being.* Toronto: Methuen, 1986.

LeSage, Julia. "Why Christian Television is Good TV." *The Independent,* May, 1987, pp. 14-20.

Liebman, Robert C. and Robert Wuthnow, eds. *The New Christian Right: Mobilization and Legitimation.* Hawthorne, NY: Aldine, 1983.

Linder, Robert D. "The Resurgence of Evangelical Concern." In *The Evangelicals,* pp. 189-210. Edited by D. F. Wells and J. D. Woodbridge. Nashville: Abingdon, 1975.

Lipsitz, George. "'This Ain't No Sideshow': Historians and Media Studies. *Critical Studies in Mass Communication,* 5 (1988): 147-161.

Lord, Lewis J. "An Unholy War in the TV Pulpits." *U.S. News and World Report,* April 6, 1987, pp. 58-65.

Luke, Timothy W. *Screens of Power: Ideology, Domination, and Resistance in Informational Society.* Urbana and Chicago: University of Illinois Press, 1989.

Maltby, Butch. Former Vice President for Institutional Advancement, Regent University. November 30, 1990.

Mander, Jerry. *Four Arguments for the Elimination of Television.* New York: Quill, 1978.

Mann, James. "A Global Surge of Old-time Religion." *U.S. News and World Report,* April 27, 1981, pp. 38-40.

Marsden, George. "The Gospel of Wealth, the Social Gospel, and the Salvation of Souls in Nineteenth Century America." *Fides et Historia* (Spring 1973): 10-21.

Marsden, George. "From Fundamentalism to Evangelicalism: A Historical Analysis." In *The Evangelicals,* pp. 122-143. Edited by D. F. Wells and J. D. Woodbridge. Nashville: Abingdon, 1975.

Marsden, George. "Fundamentalism as an American Phenomenon, A Comparison with English Evangelicalism." *Church History* 46

(June 1977): 215-232.

Marsden, George. *Fundamentalism and American Culture: The Shaping of Twentieth Century Evangelicalism: 1870-1925.* New York: Oxford University Press, 1980.

Marsden, George, ed. *Evangelicalism in Modern America.* Grand Rapids: Eerdmans, 1984.

Martin, William. "The Birth of a Media Myth." *Atlantic Monthly,* June 1981, pp. 9-16.

Martin, William. "Waiting for the End." *Atlantic Monthly,* June 1982, pp. 31-37.

Marty, Martin A. "Tensions Within Contemporary Evangelicalism." In *The Evangelicals,* pp. 170-188. Edited by D.F. Wells and J.D. Woodbridge. Nashville: Abingdon, 1975.

Marx, Karl and Friedrich Engels. *Basic Writings in Politics and Philosophy.* Edited by Lewis Feuer. Garden City, NY: Anchor Books, 1959.

Masterman, Len. *Teaching the Media.* London: Comedia, 1985.

Mayer, Allan J. "A Tide of Born-Again Politics." *Newsweek,* September 15, 1980, pp. 28-36.

Mayfield, Marjorie. "For CBN, the Worst May Be Over." *Norfolk Virginian-Pilot,* March 5, 1989, pp. 7-8.

Mayron, Michelle. "O, Brother." *Spin,* December 1986, pp. 58-66.

McCombs, Maxwell. "The Agenda-Setting Function of the Mass Media." *Public Opinion Quarterly* 36 (1972): 176-187.

McLoughlin, William G., Jr. *Modern Revivalism: Charles Grandison Finney to Billy Graham.* New York: Ronald Press, 1959.

McLoughlin, William G., Jr. *Revivals, Awakenings and Reform: An Essay in Religious and Social Change in America, 1607-1977.* Chicago: University of Chicago Press, 1978.

McLuhan, Marshall, *The Gutenberg Galaxy.* Toronto: University of Toronto Press, 1962.

Merton, Robert with Marjorie Fiske, and Alberta Curtis. *Mass Persuasion: The Social Psychology of a War Bond Drive.* Westport, CT: Greenwood Press, 1946.

Moore, R. Laurence. "Insiders and Outsiders in American Historical Narrative and American History." *American Historical Review,* 87 (1982): 390-412.

Moore, R. Laurence. *Religious Outsiders and the Making of Americans.* New York: Oxford University Press, 1986.

Morgan, John H. "The Concept of 'Meaning' in Religion and Culture: Toward a Dialogue Between Theology and Anthropology." In *Understanding Religion and Culture: Anthropological and Theological Perspectives,* pp. 88-140. Edited by John H. Morgan. Washington, D.C.: University Press of America, 1979.

Morley, David. *The Nationwide Audience: Structure and Decoding.* London: British Film Institute, 1980.

Nash, Gary. *The Urban Crucible: Social Change, Political Consciousness, and the Origins of the American Revolution.* Cambridge: Harvard University Press, 1979.

Nickerson, Colin. "Great Reawakening in New England, Fundamentalist Religion Grows." *Boston Globe*, July 26, 1981, p. 2.

Niebuhr, Gustav. "TV Evangelists Rebound From Viewer Erosion." *Atlanta Journal*, May 1, 1989, pp. 6-8.

Niebuhr, H. Richard. *Christ and Culture.* New York: Harper & Row, 1951.

Nord, David Paul. "The Evangelical Origins of the Mass Media: 1810-1835." *Journalism Monographs* 1978 (entire issue).

O'Leary, Stephen and Michael McFarland. "The Political Use of Mythic Discourse: Prophetic Interpretation in Pat Robertson's Presidential Campaign." *Quarterly Journal of Speech*, 75 (1989): 433-452.

Ong, Walter J. "Communications Media and the State of Theology." *Cross Currents* 19 (1969): 462-480.

Ong, Walter J. *Orality and Literacy: The Technologizing of the Word.* London: Methuen, 1982.

Ostling, Richard N. "Evangelical Publishing and Broadcasting." In *Evangelicalism in Modern America,* pp. 46-55. Edited by G. Marsden. Grand Rapids: Eerdmans, 1984.

Ostling, Richard. "Jerry Falwell's Crusade." *Time*, September 2, 1985, pp. 48-57.

Ostling, Richard. "Power, Glory and Politics." *Time*, February 12, 1986, pp. 62-69.

Ostling, Richard. "Offering the Hope of Heaven." *Time*, March 16, 1987, p. 69.

Ostling, Richard. "TV's Unholy Row." *Time*, April 6, 1987, pp. 60-67.

Owens, Virginia Stem. *The Total Image: or, Selling Jesus in the Modern Age.* Grand Rapids, MI: W.B. Eerdmans, 1980.

Parker, Everett C. "Old-time Religion on TV—Bane or Blessing?" *Television Quarterly* (Fall 1980): 71-79.

Parker, Everett C., David W. Barry, and Dallas W. Smythe. *The Television-Radio Audience and Religion.* New York: Harper & Brothers, 1955.

Pattison, E. Mansell. "Ideological Support for the Marginal Middle Class: Faith Healing and Glossolalia." In *Religious Movements in Contemporary America,* pp. 418-455. Edited by Irving I. Zaretsky and Mark P. Leone. Princeton: Princeton University Press, 1974.

Payne, David. *Coping With Failure: The Therapeutic Uses of Rhetoric.* Columbia: University of South Carolina Press, 1989.

Piccirillo, M. S. "On the Authenticity of Televisual Experience: A Critical Exploration of Para-Social Closure." *Critical Studies in Mass Communication* 3 (1986): 337-355.

Pierard, Richard. *The Unequal Yoke: Evangelical Christianity and Political Conservatism.* Philadelphia and New York: J. B. Lippincott, 1970.

Pierard, Richard. "The New Religious Right in American Politics." In

Evangelicalism in Modern America, pp. 161-174. Edited by G. Marsden. Grand Rapids: Eerdmans, 1984.

Postman, Neil. *The Disappearance of Childhood*. New York: Dell, 1982.

Postman, Neil. *Amusing Ourselves to Death: Public Discourse in the Age of Show Business*. New York: Viking, 1985.

"Praise the Lord." KTBW-TV, Channel 20, Tacoma, Washington (Trinity Broadcasting Network).

"Pray TV." *Canada and the World*, May 1982, pp. 4-5.

Quebedeaux, Richard. *The Young Evangelicals*. New York: Harper & Row, 1974.

Range, Peter Ross. "Thunder from the Right." *New York Times Magazine*, February 8, 1981, pp. 23-54.

Rapping, Elayne. *The Looking-Glass World of Non-fiction TV*. Boston: South End Press, 1987.

Reid, Ronald. "Apocalypticism and Typology: Rhetorical Dimensions of a Symbolic Reality." *Quarterly Journal of Speech* 69 (August 1983): 229-248.

Reinhold, Robert. "Pentecostals' Split Exposed by Bakker Affair." *New York Times*, March 3, 1987, p. 1.

Ribuffo, Leo. "Liberals and That Old-time Religion." *Nation*, November 29, 1980, pp. 570-573.

Riesman, David with Reuel Denny, and Nathan Glazer. *The Lonely Crowd: A Study of the Changing American Character*. New Haven: Yale University Press, 1950.

Robertson, Pat with Jamie Buckingham. *Shout It from the Housetops*. Plainfield, NJ: Logos International, 1972.

Roseberry, William. *Anthropologies and Histories; Essays in Culture, History, and Political Economy*. New Brunswick and London: Rutgers University Press, 1989.

Rosenberg, Bruce. *The Art of the American Folk Preacher*. New York: Oxford University Press, 1970.

"Ruling that Bans Textbooks Draws Sharp Criticism." *Seattle Times*, March 8, 1987, p. A3.

Sandeen, Ernest. "Fundamentalism and American Identity." *Annals of the American Academy of Political and Social Science* 387 (January 1970): 56-65.

Sartre, Jean-Paul. *Search for a Method*. Translated by Hazel E. Barnes. New York: Alfred A. Knopf, 1963; reprint ed., New York: Vintage, 1968.

Schultze, Quentin. "Vindicating the Electronic Church? An Assessment of the Annenberg-Gallup Study." *Critical Studies in Mass Communication* 2 (1985): 283-290.

Schultze, Quentin. "The Mythos of the Electronic Church." *Critical Studies in Mass Communication* 4 (1987): 245-261.

Schultze, Quentin. "Balance or Bias? Must TV Distort the Gospel?" *Christianity Today*, March 18, 1988, pp. 28-32.

Schultze, Quentin. "Researching Televangelism." *Critical Studies in*

Mass Communication 5 (1988): 271-275.

Schultze, Quentin, ed. *American Evangelicals and the Mass Media.* Grand Rapids, MI: Academie Books, 1990.

Schultze, Quentin. *Televangelism and American Culture.* Grand Rapids, MI: Baker Book House, 1991.

Simmel, Georg. *On Individuality and Social Forms: Selected Writings.* Edited and with an introduction by Donald N. Levine. Chicago: Chicago, 1971.

Simons, Herbert W. "Requirements, Problems and Strategies: A Theory of Persuasion for Social Movements." *Quarterly Journal of Speech* 56 (February 1970): 1-11.

Sizer, Sandra. *Gospel Hymns and Social Religion: The Rhetoric of Nineteenth Century Revivalism.* Philadelphia: Temple University Press, 1978.

Smith, Dennis A. "The Gospel According to the United States: Evangelical Broadcasting in Central America." In *American Evangelicals and the Mass Media,* pp. 289-305. Edited by Quentin Schultze. Grand Rapids, MI: Academie Books, 1990.

Smith, Ralph R. and Russell R. Windes. "The Rhetoric of Mobilization: Implications for the Study of Movements." *Southern Speech Communication Journal* 42 (Fall 1976): 1-19.

Smith, Wilfred Cantwell. *Belief and History.* Charlottesville: University of Virginia Press, 1977.

Smith, Wilfred Cantwell. *Faith and Belief.* Princeton: Princeton University Press, 1979.

"Some Evangelists on TV Make Finances Known." *Washington Post,* November 29, 1987, p. A14.

Stacey, William and Anson Shupe. "Correlates of Support for the Electronic Church." *Journal for the Scientific Study of Religion* 21 (4) (1982): 291-303.

Stoll, David. *Is Latin America Turning Protestant? The Politics of Evangelical Growth.* Berkeley: University of California Press, 1990.

Straub, Gerard. *Salvation for Sale: An Insider's View of Pat Robertson's Ministry.* Buffalo: Prometheus, 1986.

"Swaggart's One-edged Sword." *Newsweek,* January 9, 1984, p. 65.

Swaggart, Jimmy. "The Spirit of the World." *The Evangelist,* September 1987, pp. 16-21.

Swaggart, Jimmy with Robert Paul Lamb. *To Cross a River.* n.p.: Logos International, 1977.

Sweet, Leonard I. "The 1960s: The Crisis of Liberal Christianity and the Public Emergence of Evangelicalism." In *Evangelicalism in Modern America,* pp. 29-45. Edited by G. Marsden. Grand Rapids: Eerdmans, 1984.

Sweet, Leonard I., ed. *The Evangelical Tradition in Contemporary America.* Mercer, GA: Mercer University Press, 1984.

Synan, Vinson. *The Holiness-Pentecostal Movement in the United States.* Grand Rapids: Eerdmans, 1971.

"Teachings in the Word" (with Jimmy Swaggart). KCPQ-TV, Channel 13, Seattle/Tacoma, Washington.

"Television Preacher Turns into an Important Player in GOP Presidential Race." *Seattle Times*, June 10, 1986, p. A3.

"The 700 Club." KCPQ-TV, Channel 13, Seattle/Tacoma, Washington; and The Family Channel, Channel 28, Minneapolis, Minnesota.

"The Battle for the Bible." Part 2 of "God and Politics." KCTS-TV, Channel 9, Seattle, Washington, December 16, 198

"The Christianity Today-Gallup Poll: An Overview." *Christianity Today*, December 21, 1979, pp. 12-19.

"The Jimmy Swaggart Telecast." KCPQ-TV, Channel 13, Seattle/Tacoma, Washington; and Trinity Broadcasting Network, Channel 1, Minneapolis, Minnesota.

"The Religious Personality of the Populace." *Christianity Today*, December 21, 1979, pp. 15-17.

Thomas, George. *Revivalism and Cultural Change: Christianity, Nation-Building, and the Market in the Nineteenth Century United States.* Chicago: University of Chicago Press, 1989.

Thomas, Sari. "The Route to Redemption: Religion and Social Class." *Journal of Communication* 35 (Winter 1985): 111-131.

Tosches, Nick. "Pentecostals in Heat." *Village Voice*, May 12, 1987, pp. 75, 82-84.

Tuchman, Gaye. *Making News*. New York: Free Press, 1978.

Turner, Graeme. *British Cultural Studies*. Boston: Unwin Hyman, 1990.

Tuveson, Ernest L. *Redeemer Nation: The Idea of America's Millennial Role*. Chicago: University of Chicago Press, 1968.

Wacker, Grant. "The Search for Norman Rockwell: Popular Evangelicalism in Contemporary America." In *The Evangelical Tradition in America*, pp. 288-315. Edited by L. I. Sweet. Mercer, GA: Mercer University Press, 1984.

Wacker, Grant. "Uneasy in Zion: Evangelicals in Postmodern Society." In *Evangelicalism in Modern America*, pp. 17-28. Edited by G. Marsden. Grand Rapids: Eerdmans, 1984.

Wander, Philip and Stephen Jenkins. "Rhetoric, Society and the Critical Response." *Quarterly Journal of Speech* 58 (December 1972): 441-450.

Warner, R. Stephen. "Theoretical Barriers to the Understanding of Evangelical Christianity." *Sociological Analysis* 40 (1979): 1-9.

"We Poll the Pollster." *Christianity Today*, December 21, 1979, pp. 10-11.

Weber, Max. *The Sociology of Religion*. Boston: Beacon Press, 1964.

Whitson, Robley E. *The Coming Convergence in World Religion*. New York: Newman Press, 1971.

Wilber, Ken. "The Spectrum Model." In *Spiritual Choices*, pp. 237- 264. Edited by D. Anthony, B. Ecker and K. Wilber. New York: Paragon House, 1987.

Wilentz, Sean. *Chants Democratic: New York City and the Rise of the American Working Class, 1788-1850*. New York: Oxford University Press, 1984.

Williams, George H. and Rodney L. Petersen. "Evangelicals: Society, the State, the Nation." In *The Evangelicals*, pp. 203-231. Edited by D. F. Wells and J. D. Woodbridge. Nashville: Abingdon, 1975.

Williams, Raymond. *Television: Technology and Cultural Form*. New York: Schocken Books, 1975.

Williams, Raymond. *Marxism and Literature*. Oxford: Oxford University Press, 1977.

Williams, Raymond. "Advertising: The Magic System." In *Problems in Materialism and Culture*, pp. 170-195. London: Verso, 1980.

Willis, Paul. *Profane Culture*. London: Routledge and Kegan Paul, 1978.

Wilson, John F. *Public Religion in American Culture*. Philadelphia: Temple University Press, 1979.

Wilson, Monica. "Nyakyusa Ritual and Symbolism," *American Anthropologist* 56, 1954, p. 240.

Winston, Brian. "How Are Media Born?" In *Questioning the Media*, pp. 55-72. Edited by J. Downing, A. Mohammadi and A. Sreberny-Mohammadi. Newbury Park, CA: Sage, 1990.

Witham, Larry. "Churches Promote Religious Network for Cable TV." *Washington Times*, March 16, 1990, pp. 10-11.

Witt, April. "Robertson Likely to Rejoin CBN." *Norfolk Virginian-Pilot*, May 11, 1988, pp. 10-11.

Wood, Daniel. "Family Channel Focuses on the Inoffensive." *Christian Science Monitor*, February 9, 1990, p. 10.

Wood, Philip. "From Existentialism to Postmodermisn, and the Coming of the Postindustrial Age." Seattle, 1987. (Mimeographed).

Woodward, Kenneth L. "Born Again!" *Newsweek*, October 25, 1976, pp. 68-78.

Woodward, Kenneth L. "Arguing Armageddon." *Newsweek, November* 5, 1984, p. 91.

Wuthnow, Robert. "The Political Rebirth of American Evangelicals." In *The New Christian Right*, pp. 167-185. Edited by R. Liebman and R. Wuthnow. New York: Aldine, 1983.

Author Index

Subject Index